Student Manual

Understanding Generalist Practice

FIFTH EDITION

Karen K. Kirst-Ashman
University of Wisconsin, Whitewater

Grafton H. Hull
University of Utah

Prepared by

Vicki Vogel
University of Wisconsin, Whitewater

BROOKS/COLE
CENGAGE Learning

Australia • Brazil • Japan • Korea • Mexico • Singapore • Spain • United Kingdom • United States

ISBN-13: 978-0-495-50878-6
ISBN-10: 0-495-50878-0

Brooks/Cole
10 Davis Drive
Belmont, CA 94002-3098
USA

Cengage Learning is a leading provider of customized learning solutions with office locations around the globe, including Singapore, the United Kingdom, Australia, Mexico, Brazil, and Japan. Locate your local office at: **international.cengage.com/region**

Cengage Learning products are represented in Canada by Nelson Education, Ltd.

For your course and learning solutions, visit **academic.cengage.com**

Purchase any of our products at your local college store or at our preferred online store **www.ichapters.com**

Printed in the United States of America
1 2 3 4 5 6 7 11 10 09 08 07

Student Manual Contents

Chapter 1
Introducing Generalist Practice: The Generalist Intervention Model

I. **Introducing Generalist Practice**

    A.   Three Dimensions of Definition

        1.   Multiple level interventions

        2.   Knowledge base carefully chosen from a range of theories

        3.   Focus on private issues and social justice concerns

II. **The Uniqueness of Social Work**

    A.   Purpose of Social Work

        1.   Enhance the problem solving and coping capacities of people

        2.   Link people with systems that provide them with resources, services, and opportunities

        3.   Promote the effective and humane operation of these systems

        4.   Contribute to the development and improvement of social policy

    B.   *Figure 1.1: Social Work and Other Helping Professions*

    C.   Common Core of Helping Professions: Interviewing and Counseling Skills

    D.   Five Dimensions of Social Work

        1.   Focus attention on any problem or cluster of problems

        2.   Focus on targeting the environment for change

        3.   Advocate for client

        4.   Emphasis and adherence to core of professional values

        5.   Practice in a *partnership* with clients

III. **Defining Generalist Practice**

    A.   The Application of an Eclectic Knowledge Base, Professional Values, and a Wide Range of Skills to Target Systems of Any Size, for Change Within the Context of Four Primary Processes

1. Emphasis on client empowerment

2. Work effectively within an organizational structure under supervision

3. Assume wide range of professional roles

4. Apply critical thinking skills to the planned change process

B. *Highlight 1.1: An Outline of Concepts Involved in the Definition of Generalist Practice*

C. *Figure 1.2: The Definition of Generalist Practice: A Pictorial View*

D. Defining Generalist Practice: An Eclectic Knowledge Base

1. An Eclectic Knowledge Base: Fields of practice

2. An Eclectic Knowledge Base: Systems theory

a. Focus on the interactions of various systems in the environment

1) Individuals

2) Groups

3) Families

4) Organizations

b. Concepts of systems model

1) System—A set of elements that forms an orderly, interrelated, and functional whole

2) Dynamic—Constant movement because problems and issues are forever changing

3) Interact—Systems constantly interact with each other

4) Input—Energy, information, or communication flow received from other systems

5) Output—Energy, information, or communication flow emitted from a system

6) Homeostasis—Tendency of a system to maintain a stable, constant state of equilibrium or balance

7) Equifinality—Many different means to the same end

c.   Conceptualizing workers and clients as systems

        1)   Client system—Individual, family, group, organization, or community that will benefit from generalist social work intervention

        2)   Change agent system—Individual who initiates the planned change process

        3)   Action system—People who agree and are committed to work together to attain proposed change

3.   An Eclectic Knowledge Base: The Ecological perspective

a.   Concept of social environment is grounded in ecological perspective

b.   Ecological concepts

        1)   Social environment—Conditions, circumstances, and human interactions that encompass human beings

        2)   Person-in-environment—People constantly interact with various systems around them

        3)   Transactions —Communication and interaction with others in their environment

        4)   Energy—Natural power of active involvement among people and their environments

        5)   Interface—Exact point at which the interaction between an individual and the environment takes place

        6)   Adaptation—Capacity to adjust to surrounding environmental conditions

        7)   Coping—Human adaptation and struggle to overcome problems

        8)   Interdependence—Mutual reliance of each person on each other person

c.   Similarities between systems theory and ecological perspective

        1)   Emphasize systems and focus on the dynamic interaction among levels of system

        2)   Some terms and concepts are the same

        3)   Each provides framework to view the world

        4)   Both emphasize external interactions instead of internal functioning

d.   *Highlight 1.2: Summary of Some of the Major Concepts in Systems Theory and the Ecological Perspective*

e.   Differences between system theory and the ecological perspective

     1)   Ecological approach refers to living, dynamic interactions and emphasis on active participation—Systems theory is broader, can refer to inanimate, mechanical operation and functioning of a human family

     2)   Ecological perspectives theories focus on transactions between individual and the environment at the point where the individual and environment meet—Systems theory addresses boundaries of subsystems within a system and maintenance of homeostasis or equilibrium within a system. The ecological model is more limited in scope and application than systems theory

f.   Which perspective is best?

4.   An Eclectic Knowledge Base: Curriculum Content Areas

a.   Social work values and ethics

     1)   Values—Involve what you do and do not consider important (what is good and desirable)

     2)   Ethics—Involve principles that specify what is good and what is bad and clarify what should and should not be done (what is right and correct)

     3)   National Association of Social Workers' *Code of Ethics*

          a)   Social workers' ethical responsibilities to clients

          b)   Social workers' ethical responsibilities to colleagues

          c)   Social workers' ethical responsibilities in practice settings

          d)   Social workers' ethical responsibilities as professionals

          e)   Social workers' ethical responsibilities to the social work profession

          f)   Social workers' ethical responsibilities to the broader society

     4)   *Highlight 1.3: Ethical Dilemmas*

     5)   *Critical Thinking Question 1.1*

b. Diversity

   1) Diversity—The vast range of differences among people, including those related to race, ethnicity, cultural background, place of origin, age, physical and mental ability, spirituality, values, sexual orientation, and gender

   2) Discrimination—The act of treating people differently based on the fact that they belong to some group rather than on their own merit

   3) Oppression—Putting extreme limitations and constraints on the members of some identified group

   4) Stereotypes—Fixed mental images of members belonging to a group based on assumed attributes that portray an overly simplified opinion about that group

c. Cultural competency—The set of knowledge and skills that a social worker must develop to be effective with multicultural clients

   1) Development of an awareness of personal values, assumptions, and biases

   2) Establishment of a positive orientation toward multiculturalism, an appreciation of other cultures, and a nurturance of attitudes that respect differences

   3) Understanding of how their own cultural heritage and belief system differs from and may influence interaction with clients who have a different cultural background

   4) Recognition of the existence of stereotypes, discrimination, and oppression of various diverse groups

   5) Commitment to learning about clients' cultures

   6) Acquisition of effective skills for working with people from other cultures

d. Curriculum content area: Populations-at-risk and promotion of social and economic justice

   1) Populations-at-risk—Certain populations or groups of people who, based on some identified characteristics, are at greater risk of social and economic deprivation than the general mainstream of society

   2) Social justice—The idea that in a perfect world all citizens would have identical rights, protection, opportunities, obligations, and social benefits regardless of their backgrounds and membership in diverse groups

   3) Economic justice—Concerns the distribution of resources in a fair and equitable manner

e. Curriculum content area: Human behavior and the social environment

   1) Micro events

   2) Mezzo events

   3) Macro events

   4) *Critical Thinking Question 1.2*

f. Curriculum content area: Social welfare policy and services

   1) Rules that tell us which actions among a multitude of actions we may and may not take

   2) Some policies are unfair or oppressive to clients

g. Curriculum content area: Social work practice

   1) The *doing* of social work

   2) Social workers' skills are eclectic

h. Curriculum content area: Research

   1) Reasons for importance

      a) Help social workers be more effective in their practice and get better and clearer results

      b) Helps build a foundation for planning effective interventions

   2) Three dimensions of basic research skills

      a) Evaluate effectively the work they do with clients on all levels

      b) Evaluate macro system effectiveness

      c) Ability to understand, analyze, and critically evaluate social work literature and research

i. Curriculum content area: Field education

   1) The culmination of the social work education

   2) Provides the opportunity for students to apply their classroom learning in supervised agency settings

E.   Defining Generalist Practice: Emphasis on Client

1.   Empowerment—The process of increasing personal, interpersonal, or political power so that individuals can take action to improve their life situations

2.   Social work historically has focused on dysfunction, pathology, and individual inadequacies

3.   Strengths perspective—An orientation focusing on client resources, capabilities, knowledge, abilities, motivations, experience, intelligence, and other positive qualities that can be put to use to solve problems and pursue positive changes

4.   Principles of the strengths perspective

a.   Every individual, group, family, and community has strengths

b.   Trauma and abuse, illness, and struggle may be injurious but they may also be sources of challenge and opportunity

c.   Assume that you do not know the upper limits of the capacity to grow and change and take individual, group, and community aspirations seriously

d.   We best serve clients by collaborating with them

e.   Every environment is full of resources

5.   Resiliency: Seeking strength amid adversity

a.   Resiliency—The ability of an individual, family, group, community, or organization to recover from adversity and resume functioning even when suffering serious trouble, confusion, or hardship

b.   Risk factors

c.   Protective factors

F.   Defining Generalist Practice: Application to a Wide Range of Skills to Target Systems of Any Size

1.   Micro skills for generalist practice—Skills used for working with individuals

2.   Mezzo skills for generalist practice—Skills used to work with small groups

3.   Macro skills for generalist practice—Building upon the mastery of both micro and mezzo skills, macro skills are those used to work with large systems including communities and organizations

G.   *Highlight 1.4: The Macro Level Approach*

H. Defining Generalist Practice: Working in an Organizational Structure

    1. Organizational structure—The formal and informal manner in which tasks and responsibilities, lines of authority, channels of communication, and dimensions of power are established and coordinated within an organization

    2. You are most likely to work within an organizational structure

I. Defining Generalist Practice: A Wide Range of Roles

    1. Counselor—Provides guidance to clients and assists them in a planned change or problem solving process

    2. Educator—Gives information and teaches skills to other systems

    3. Broker—Links client systems to needed resources

    4. Case manager—Coordinates, on behalf of a specific client, needed services provided by agencies, organizations, or facilities

    5. Mobilizer—Identifies and convenes community people and resources to identify unmet community needs and effect changes in community

    6. Mediator—Resolves arguments or disagreements among micro, mezzo, or macro systems in conflict

    7. Facilitator—Guides a group experience

    8. Advocate—Speaks out on behalf of clients to promote fair treatment or gain needed resources

J. Defining Generalist Practice: Critical Thinking Skills

    1. Critical thinking—(1) The careful scrutiny of what is stated as true or what appears to be true and the resulting expression of an opinion or conclusion based on that scrutiny, and (2) the creative formulation of an opinion or conclusion when presented with a question, problem, or issue

    2. Triple A approach

        a. **A**sk questions

        b. **A**ssess the established facts and issues involved

        c. **A**ssert a concluding opinion

    3. "Facts" may not be true

    4. The widespread application of critical thinking

5. *Highlight 1.5: Pitfalls to Critical Thinking*

    a. Outward appearance of science

    b. Absence of skeptical peer review

    c. Reliance on personal experience and testimonials

    d. Wishful thinking

    e. The "ancient wisdom" fallacy

    f. The popularity fallacy

6. *Critical Thinking Question 1.3*

K. Defining Generalist Practice: Planned Change

    1. Planned change—The development and implementation of a strategy for improving or altering some specified condition, pattern of behavior, or set of circumstances that affects social functioning

    2. Problem solving—Same as planned change; however, has a negative connotation

IV. The Generalist Intervention Model (GIM)

A. Three Features:

    1. Workers acquire an eclectic knowledge base, wide range of skills to target any size system, and a professional values base

    2. Core seven-step planned change process that emphasizes the assessment of client strengths

    3. Generalist approach—virtually any problem may be analyzed and addressed from multiple levels of intervention

B. *Figure 1.3: Planned Change Steps in the Generalist Intervention Model (GIM)*

C. *Figure 1.4: Initiating Micro, Mezzo, or Macro Change During Assessment*

D. Planned Change Steps in the GIM

    1. Step 1: Engagement

        a. Orient yourself to problem

        b. Establish communication and relationship with others addressing problem

c.   Alleviate initial client anxiety

d.   Warmth—Involves enhancing the positive feelings of one person toward another by promoting a sense of comfort and well-being in that other person

e.   Empathy—Involves not only being in tune with how a client feels but also conveying to that client that you understand how the client feels

f.   Genuineness—Means that you continue to be yourself, despite the fact that you are working to accomplish goals in your professional role

2.   Step 2: Assessment

a.   *Figure 1.5: Assessment in the Generalist Intervention Model (GIM)*

b.   Identify your client

c.   Assess the client-in-situation and identify issues

     1)   Micro aspects

     2)   Micro/mezzo aspects: Families

     3)   Mezzo aspects

     4)   Macro aspects

     5)   Aspects of diversity

         a)   Ageism—Refers to discrimination based on predisposed notions about older people, regardless of their individual qualities and capabilities

         b)   Sexism—Refers to predisposed notions about a person based on that person's gender

d.   Assessment and planning

3.   Step 3: Planning

a.   *Figure 1.6: Planning in the Generalist Intervention Model (GIM)*

b.   Eight sub-steps:

     1)   Work with the client

     2)   Prioritize problems

     3)   Translate problems into needs

            4)   Evaluate levels of intervention

            5)   Establish goals

            6)   Specify objectives

            7)   Specify action steps

            8)   Formalize a contract

    4.   Step 4: Implementation

        a.   Involves the actual *doing* of the plan

        b.   *Figure 1.7: Implementation in the Generalist Intervention Model (GIM)*

    5.   Step 5: Evaluation

        a.   Critical for accountability

        b.   *Figure 1.8: Evaluation in the Generalist Intervention Model (GIM)*

    6.   Step 6: Termination

    7.   Step 7: Follow-Up

V.   Other Practical Generalist Skills: A Perspective on the Rest of the Text

Experiential Exercises and Simulations

Seven exercises are provided for this chapter. Exercise 1 describes a simple activity to "break the ice" and help people feel more comfortable in class. In addition to serving as another ice breaker, Exercise 2 encourages students to think about their future roles in social work practice. Exercise 3 introduces students to a variety of concepts involved in generalist practice. Exercises 4 and 5 respectively explore systems and ecological concepts. Exercise 6 explores the macro approach to generalist practice versus the micro and mezzo approaches. Finally, Exercise 7 introduces students to the concepts of social work values and ethical dilemmas in practice.

Exercise 1.1: Breaking the Ice

A.   Brief description:
       You will be asked to share some personal information about yourself with the class to begin to "break the ice" in the group.

B.   Objectives:
       You will be able to:
       1.   Reveal some personal information about yourself to others in the class.
       2.   Begin to demonstrate your communication skills.

C.   Procedure:
          1.   In order to introduce yourself and share some information with others in the class, take a
                    sheet of paper and write down the following information:
                    a.   Your name.
                    b.   One adjective that describes what you like best about yourself.
                    c.   One adjective that describes what you like least about yourself.
                    d.   Your hometown or area in the city where you live.
                    e.   How you feel having to talk about yourself right now.
          2.   One person in the class should volunteer to begin. In turn, share what you've written
                    with the rest of the class.

Exercise 1.2: Where Are You Going in Social Work?

A.   Brief description:
          You will be asked to respond to a number of questions regarding personal and professional goals.
B.   Objectives:
          You will be able to:
          1.   Clarify your interest in the field of social work.
          2.   Identify some of your specific areas of interest and need.
          3.   Tell your instructor something about yourself, especially your specific areas of interest
                    and need.
C.   Procedure:
          1.   Take a sheet of paper, put your name on it, and answer the following questions (label
                    each answer with the appropriate letter):
                    a.   In which areas of helping are you specifically interested (for example, adoptions,
                              mental health, work with the older adults, alcohol and other drug abuse)? List all
                              that you can think of. If you aren't sure or don't know as yet, say so. That's OK.
                    b.   Ideally, what would you like to learn from this course? Please be as specific as
                              possible. What skills do you think you really need to learn?
                    c.   What are your reasons for going into social work?
                    d.   What practice situations do you think you might run into that scare you?
                    e.   What strengths do you feel you bring to the field?
                    f.   What weaknesses do you feel you have that might affect your work in the field?
          2.   Break into small groups of four to six persons. Pick *two* of your answers and share them
                    with the others in your small group.
          3.   Hand your papers in to your instructor.

Exercise 1.3: What Do Social Workers Do?

A.   Brief description:
          You will be given a series of vignettes that illustrate problems commonly encountered by social
          workers in social service agencies. Small groups then brainstorm some of the possible
          intervention strategies generalist social workers might consider to solve the problems involved.
B.   Objectives:
          You will be able to:
          1.   Discuss basic types of social worker interventions at micro, mezzo, and macro levels.
          2.   Recognize the complexity of many of the problems encountered in generalist social work
                    practice.
          3.   Recognize the importance of interpersonal skills.
          4.   Identify some practice areas in which you could benefit from skill development.

C. Procedure:
1. Read chapter 1 and/or listen to your instructor's lecture concerning chapter 1 prior to beginning the exercise.
2. Divide into small groups of four to six persons. Below are three vignettes. Read each one and discuss possible answers to the questions following each scenario. Select one member in each group to jot down the ideas your group proposes. This is in preparation for sharing these ideas later in a discussion involving the entire class.

Vignette #1

A fifteen-year-old can hardly make it through the morning until he can meet with his dealer and get some crack. He thinks briefly how it didn't used to be this bad, how he didn't used to "need" it this much. But he doesn't want to think about that for very long. It's too uncomfortable. He rationalizes that life is short and he wants to make the most of it. Besides, all of his friends use drugs, too. He's no different.

Questions for small group discussion:
a. How might a social worker approach this young man regarding his drug use?
b. What questions might you as a social worker ask?
c. How might you encourage this young man to open up to you about his problems?
d. What if the young man won't say anything?
e. What if the young man expresses hostility or anger at you?
f. What types of resources might be available to help him at the micro and mezzo levels?
g. What types of programs and services at the macro level might be available?
h. What types of programs and services might be developed at the macro level?

Vignette #2

Forlorn, homeless people are starving in the streets. Public funding for a community mental health program has been drastically cut back. That program had provided a halfway house where people could stay, receive counseling, and have their medication monitored. Years ago, the long-term, inpatient mental institution had been shut down. It was much too expensive. Now with the cutbacks, the community program can barely exist. People with serious mental and emotional problems have been turned away and are roaming the streets with nowhere to go.

Questions for small group discussion:
a. What services do you feel these people need at the micro, mezzo, and macro levels?
b. How might you as a generalist social work practitioner go about advocating for these people? What types of social service agencies and organizations could you target for such advocacy?
c. What programs could be developed?
d. What are some ideas for possible funding sources?

Vignette #3

A family of four who have lived on their family farm for five generations is dispossessed. They had several bad years of crop failures and were unable to pay back the loans they so desperately needed to survive at the time. They are living in their '93 Chevy van now. They can't find any housing they could possibly afford even while working full-time, minimum-wage jobs.

Questions for small group discussion:

    a.   What services do you feel these people need at the micro, mezzo, and macro levels?

    b.   How might you as a generalist social work practitioner go about advocating for these people?

    c.   What types of social service agencies and organizations could you target for such advocacy?

    d.   What programs could be developed?

    e.   What are some ideas for possible funding sources?

3.   The small groups should then come back together to discuss their ideas. The instructor will lead the discussion. Each group's selected representative should summarize the group's findings.

4.   The instructor will then lead the entire class in a discussion addressing the following questions:

    a.   In summary, what types of micro, mezzo, and macro interventions did the groups discuss?

    b.   What was your reaction to the complexity of the problems?

    c.   Did this experience help you to see social work intervention in new ways? If so, in what new ways?

    d.   Where did you "get stuck"? What problems seemed exceptionally difficult to solve?

    e.   What skill areas do you feel you need to develop?

Exercise 1.4: Understanding Systems [1]

A.   Brief description:

You will be given a description of a family and its members followed by a series of situations occurring within the family. Discussion focuses on the direct application of systems concepts to this family and its situations.

B.   Objectives:

You will be able to:

1.   Examine the meanings of various systems theory concepts.

2.   Apply these concepts to a series of concrete family life situations.

C.   Procedure:

1.   After reviewing the systems theory concepts presented in the text, arrange yourselves in a circle. This allows for maximum observation of the role-play activity.

2.   The instructor will describe members of a family system and other people involved with the system. (As the text describes, families are systems which lie somewhere between micro and mezzo systems.) The family you'll discuss are the Abbots.[2] The basic family system is pictured below. Rectangles indicate males; round-cornered rectangles indicate females. Double-pointing arrows indicate that the couple is married. Children are depicted by a vertical line descending from the arrow to their names. Dotted lines

---

[1] The description, objectives, and much of the procedure and commentary for this exercise are taken from "Exercise 1: The Family System" in K. Kirst-Ashman and C. Zastrow, *Student Manual of Classroom Exercises and Study Guide for Understanding Human Behavior and the Social Environment* (Chicago: Nelson-Hall, 1990).

[2] Thanks are extended here to Ruth Kirst who provided help regarding character development.

indicate relationships between people who are not married. The ages of characters follow their names. The specific characters are as follows:

➢ **John Abbot** and **Jill Abbot** are married. They have two children, **Ashley** and **Jack**.
➢ Ashley is married to **Victor Newman**. They have no children.
➢ Jack is married to **Nikki**. Jack and Nikki have a daughter named **Victoria**.
➢ Victoria is in love with **Ryan**, her boyfriend.
➢ **Nina**, a friend of Ryan's, really enters the picture a little later in the exercise.

THE ABBOT FAMILY

3.   The instructor will ask for volunteers to play each of the characters. Each role-player's first name should be written on an eight-by-five-inch note card and placed in front of him or her so that class observers can remember who is playing what character. The family members are to sit together inside the class circle.

4.   Your instructor will present the role players with a series of situations. The situations are not sequential; each stands alone. For each situation, each member involved will be asked to respond as if he or she really was that family member. Players can add any additional details they wish about the family members they play.

5.   The instructor will separately present each of the following situations to the role players:

> **Situation #1**
> Jack finds out that Victor and Nikki are in love with each other. Jack is mad and moves out.

> **Situation #2**
> Victor dies of AIDS. How he contracted HIV is unknown, although Ashley suspects drug use with tainted needles. The entire family is horrified and fearful.

> **Situation #3**
> Victor is involved in the upper levels of management in DideeDry, John's paper diaper company. John owns 40 percent of the stock and is president of the company. John has a stroke and loses the use of his right side. Victor vies for control of the company. He goes to the board of directors and proposes that he take over the presidency. The board is seriously considering his request. The company needs a capable president. John is furious at Victor, as he wants to relinquish neither his control nor the presidency. John feels it will simply take some time for him to recover. Jill feels such wishful thinking is totally unrealistic.

> **Situation #4**
> Jill finds out that John had an incestuous relationship with Ashley in her early teens.

> **Situation #5**
> Victoria doubts Ryan's faithfulness and gets an HIV test. She eagerly awaits the results and tells only her mother, Nikki, about her worst fears. Much to Victoria's dismay, Nikki is so worried that she tells the rest of the family about it.

> **Situation #6**
> Ryan breaks up with Victoria. Two months later, Victoria discovers she's pregnant with Ryan's baby. Victoria runs into Ryan and Nina together. Nina announces that she and Ryan are engaged.

6. Each role player involved in the situation should share his or her feelings and describe how the situation might affect the family.

7. After receiving feedback from the individual role players, observers and role players should discuss the situation using systems theory concepts. Relate each systems theory term to the dynamics that might be occurring in the family. For example, any of the situations might upset the family's *homeostasis*. Other examples include the types of *input* and *output* involved, and the formation of various *subsystems*.

Exercise 1.5: Comparing Systems and Ecological Concepts

A. Brief description:
    You will be given a description of a family and its members followed by a series of situations occurring within the family. Discussion focuses on the direct application of ecological concepts to this family and its situations. (This exercise is identical to Exercise 4 above except that ecological concepts are substituted for systems theory concepts.)

B.   Objectives:
        You will be able to:
        1.   Examine the meanings of various ecological concepts.
        2.   Apply these concepts to a series of concrete family life situations.
C.   Procedure:
        1.   After reviewing the ecological concepts presented in the text, arrange yourselves in a circle. This allows for maximum observation of the role-play activity.
        2.   Follow steps 2 through 6 presented above in Exercise 4, but replace ecological concepts with those of systems theory.

Exercise 1.6: Change the System, Not the Person

A.   Brief description:
        You will be given three vignettes and asked to propose potential solutions based on macro system (versus micro or mezzo system) changes.
B.   Objectives:
        You will be able to:
        1.   Assess problematic situations within a macro system context.
        2.   Propose potential macro level intervention solutions.
C.   Procedure:
        1.   Divide up into groups of four to six persons.
        2.   Read the following three vignettes. Take approximately eight to ten minutes to discuss each vignette. For this exercise, do not change or move the individual. Think in terms of how the problem might be solved through macro level changes—what major organizations or community groups can do to effect change. For each vignette, focus on the following questions:
                a.   What policies might be changed?
                b.   What community services might be developed?
                c.   What might your strategies be to achieve these changes and services?
        (Remember, do not change the individual. Focus only on macro system change.)

> **Vignette #1**
> You are a public social services worker in a rural county. Your job includes doing everything from helping older adults obtain their social security payments to investigating alleged child abuse. Within the past six months, six farm families in the county have gone bankrupt. Government farm subsidies that used to be available have been withdrawn. It's been a bad past two years for crops. Now the banks are threatening to foreclose on the farm mortgages. Thus, the six families will literally be put out in the cold with no money and no place to go.
> What do you do?

Vignette #2

You are a social worker for Burp County Social Services. It's a rural county with a few towns of ten thousand people but none larger. Your job as intake worker is to do family assessments when people call up with problems (anything from domestic violence to coping with serious illnesses). Your next task is to make referrals to the appropriate services.

You have been hearing about a number of sexual assaults in the area. Women are expressing fear for their safety. People who have been assaulted don't know where to turn. The nearest large cities are over eighty miles away. You have always been interested in women's issues and advocacy for women.

Now what do you do?

Vignette #3

You have a seventy-year-old client named Harriet living in an old, near-inner-city neighborhood in a large city. Since her husband died seven years ago, she's been living alone. She has no children. She is still in good health and likes to be independent.

The problem is that her house has been condemned for new highway construction. The plans are to tear it down within six months. There is no public housing available for older adults within five miles of where she lives. She would like to stay in the area because she's got a lot of older adult friends there.

Now what? (Remember, don't move Harriet.)

Exercise 1.7: Resolving Ethical Dilemmas

A.   Brief description:

The ethical dilemma presented involves making tough decisions about the distribution of limited resources. You will be asked to make decisions regarding who is to receive and who is not to receive urgently needed resources.

B.   Objectives:

You will be able to:

1.   Recognize the fact that ethical dilemmas exist which have no perfect solution.
2.   Identify your personal values with respect to the situations presented.
3.   Recognize the importance of ethical decision making in social work practice.

C.   Procedure:

1.   Make decisions on an individual basis regarding the following situation:

> You have $30,000 to spend. You must choose where it will be spent. Below are ten situations. Each situation requires spending the full amount of $30,000 in order to do any good. Dividing the money up would be useless. It would help no one.

Which of the following persons should have the $30,000 made available to help them?

a.   A premature infant (born three months early) who must be maintained in an incubator and receive medical treatment.

b.   A fifty-two-year-old man who needs a heart transplant in order to survive.

c.   A fifty-two-year-old man who needs a heart transplant in order to survive and who also happens to be your father.

d.   A five-year-old child with AIDS.

e.   You, who have graduated but have been out of work for six months.

f. A divorced single mother with three children, a tenth-grade education, and nothing but the clothes on her back.

g. A person with a cognitive disability who needs to live in a group home.

h. A fourteen-year-old runaway who is addicted to cocaine and alcohol, has been prostituting herself to survive, and needs the money to enter a drug treatment program.

i. Rehabilitation for a convicted child sexual abuser who himself was sexually abused as a child.

j. A dispossessed urban family consisting of a couple in their late 20s and their three small children.

2. As an individual, decide how you would choose to spend the limited resources.

3. Subsequently, participate in a discussion involving the entire class. Your instructor can help you address the following questions and issues:

a. Who should receive priority in receiving needed funds?

b. What criteria should be used to make such decisions?

c. What personal values did you employ in making your decision?

d. What issues and considerations made decision making difficult?

e. To what extent is such a decision-making situation similar to or different from situations and decisions you have encountered in real life?

f. What could help you make such decisions more easily?

Chapter 2
Micro Practice Skills: Working with Individuals

I.   **Introduction**

II.   **Micro Skills and the Generalist Intervention Model (GIM)**

      A.   Engagement—Establish an initial relationship with an individual or group of individuals

      B.   Assessment—Must talk and relate to other individuals effectively to solicit enough information about the issue or problem involved to initiate positive change

      C.   Planning—Involves working integrally with client to establish plan of action

      D.   Implementation—Working with others in environment to achieve goals

      E.   Evaluation—Communicate with client and others to validate accomplishments

      F.   Follow-Up—Solicit information regarding how planned change goals have been maintained

III.   **Interviewing: A Key Micro Skill**

IV.   **Beginning the Worker/Client Relationship**

V.   **Verbal and Nonverbal Behavior**

      A.   Eye Contact

            1.   Important when establishing rapport with clients

            2.   Be aware of cultural differences where direct eye contact is considered disrespectful, insincere, or rude

      B.   Attentive Listing

             1.   Listening focuses on comprehending the meaning of what is said

                   a.   Three aspects of communication

                        1)   Intent

                        2)   Impact

                        3)   Environmental barriers

             2.   *Figure 2.1: Barriers to Attentive Listening*

      C.   Facial Expressions

D.   Body Positioning

      1.   Tense/relaxed

      2.   Formal/informal

      3.   *Critical Thinking Question 2.1*

      4.   The use of personal space

            a.   The European-North American expectation for appropriate distancing during interviews is usually a few inches to a few feet beyond arm's length

            b.   The English prefer even greater distances than do European-North Americans

            c.   Many Latin people often prefer half the distance as European-North Americans

            d.   People from the Middle East may talk practically eyeball to eyeball

      5.   Office space positioning

            a.   Sitting behind desk implies greater formality

            b.   Being able to talk to a client without a desk between can convey greater informality and warmth

VI.   Warmth, Empathy, and Genuineness

A.   Warmth—Conveying a feeling of interest, concern, well-being, and affection to another individual

      1.   Verbal

      2.   Nonverbal

B.   Empathy—Involves not only being in tune with how a client feels, but also conveying to that client that you understand how he or she feels

C.   *Highlight 2.1: Practicing Empathic Responses*

D.   *Critical Thinking Question 2.2*

E.   Genuineness—The honest, natural, and open expression of yourself

F.   *Critical Thinking Question 2.3*

VII.   **Client Self-Determination and Empowerment**

    A.   Self-Determination—Each individual's right to make his or her own decisions

    B.   Empowerment—The process of increasing personal, interpersonal, or political power so that individuals can take action to improve their life situations

VIII.   **Starting the Interview**

    A.   The Interview Setting

    B.   How to Dress for the Interview and for the Job

    C.   Thinking Ahead about an Interview with a Client

        1.   Gather specific information that will be needed

        2.   Time frame should be clearly specified

        3.   Purpose of interview

    D.   Initial Introductions—Be knowledgeable about cultural differences

    E.   Alleviating Client's Anxiety—"Start where the client is"

    F.   Portraying Confidence and Competence

    G.   *Highlight 2.2: Using Direct and Indirect Questions*

    H.   Beginning Statement of Purpose and Role

        1.   Clearly explain the interview's purpose to the client

        2.   Explain the worker's role to the client

        3.   Encourage client feedback on the purpose

        4.   Convey to the client the usefulness of the interview

IX.   **Conducting the Interview**

    A.   *Highlight 2.3: Enhancing Cultural Competence: Ethnographic Interviewing*

        1.   Ethnographic interviewing—focuses on learning about a client's cultural world including values, behavioral expectations, and language

        2.   Three sequential concepts

            a.   Global questions—initial, general inquiries posed to solicit information about culturally relevant aspects of the client's life b.　　Cover terms—words that cover a realm of concepts, ideas, and relationships within a cultural context and have significant and special meaning to members of the cultural group

　　　　c.　　Descriptors—words solicited to explain cover words

B.　　Verbal Responses to the Client

　　1.　　Simple encouragement

　　2.　　Rephrasing

　　3.　　Reflective responding

　　4.　　Clarification

　　5.　　Interpretation

　　6.　　Providing information

　　7.　　*Highlight 2.4: Critical Thinking: Telling a Client What to Do*

　　8.　　Empowerment:　Emphasizing clients' strengths

　　　　a.　　Reinforces a client's sense of self-respect and self-value

　　　　b.　　Provides rays of hope even in "tunnels of darkness"

　　　　c.　　Helps identify ways to solve problems by relying on the specified strengths

　　　　d.　　*Highlight 2.5: Stressing Client Strengths*

　　　　　　1)　　Five types of questions to explore client strengths

　　　　　　　　a)　　Survival questions

　　　　　　　　b)　　Support questions

　　　　　　　　c)　　Exception questions

　　　　　　　　d)　　Possibility questions

　　　　　　　　e)　　Esteem questions

　　　　　　2)　　Three basic areas in which to emphasize a client's strengths

　　　　　　　　a)　　Client behaviors and accomplishments

　　　　　　　　b)　　Personal qualities

　　　　　　　　c)　　Client's resources

9. Self-disclosure—A worker's divulgence to a client of personal thoughts, information, feelings, values, or experiences

    a. Four major types of self-disclosure

        1) Information about your professional role

        2) Your feelings and impressions about the client and the client's behavior by giving feedback

        3) Feedback about your perceptions concerning your ongoing interaction and relationship with the client

        4) Relating aspects about your own life or problems in some way to the client's feelings or situation

    b. Guidelines for self-disclosure

        1) Make certain that the self-disclosure is really for the client's benefit and not for your own

        2) Make the self-disclosure relevant to the client, which involves demonstrating both genuineness and timeliness

        3) Self-disclosures should be short and simple

    c. *Figure 2.2: Personal versus Professional Relationships*

10. Summarization—Restating the main points of an interview or a portion of an interview in a brief and concise manner

11. Eliciting information

    a. Open-ended questions— Questions that seek out the client's thoughts, ideas, and explanations for answers

    b. Closed-ended questions— Questions that seek simple "yes" or "no" answers

12. The use of *why*—can be threatening to clients because it is "intrusive"

13. Overlap of techniques

14. Interviewing, specific techniques, and the planned change process

X.   Critical Thinking: Challenges in Interviewing

A.   Dealing with Diversity: Cross-Cultural Awareness in Interviewing

1.   Dimensions of cross-cultural awareness

   a.   Learning about people from other cultures is an ongoing, continuous process

   1)   Cultural knowledge involves understanding people's values, actions, preferences, and expressions

   2)   Individualization—The social work value maintaining that every person is unique with unique characteristics, distinguished from those generally characterizing a cultural, ethnic, or racial group

   b.   National origin and the extent to which clients are assimilated into the mainstream culture

   1)   Acculturation—The process wherein the ethnic values, behaviors, and rituals clients hold from their traditional culture change over time and integrate with the values, behaviors, and rituals of the majority or host culture

   2)   Assimilation—The process of being incorporated into and becoming part of the majority culture

   3)   Full assimilation—The end product of those who have completely removed all aspects of their traditional culture and replaced them with those of the host culture

   c.   Attention to the stereotypes, prejudices, discrimination, and oppression negatively affecting people from various ethnic and racial groups

   1)   Stereotype—a fixed mental picture of members of some specified group based on some attribute or attributes that portray an overly simplified opinion about that group without considering and appreciating individual differences

   2)   Prejudice—An opinion or prejudgment about an individual, group, or issue that is not based on fact and is usually negative

   3)   Discrimination—Unequal treatment of people based on prejudgment because they belong to some category, such as one involving race, ethnicity, gender, or religion

   4)   Oppression—The longer-term result of putting extreme limitations upon or discriminating against some designated group

   d.   Importance of self-awareness of one's own ethnic and cultural background, and how it may affect a worker's ability to practice

2. *Highlight 2.6: Dealing with Diversity: Spirituality as a Source of Strength and Empowerment*

    a.   Religion—Involves people's spiritual beliefs concerning the origin, character, and reason for being, usually based on the existence of some higher power or powers. Religion implies membership in a spiritual organization with customs, traditions, and structure

    b.   Spirituality—The individual search for meaning, purpose, and values that typically rises above everyday physical limitations and connects one to something greater than oneself. Spirituality may involve religion, or it may reflect a personal, internalized view of existence

    c.   Do not impose personal beliefs on clients

    d.   How to approach spiritual issues with clients

        1)   Be alert to the client's point of view and level of awareness of his or her spirituality

        2)   Identify the role of spirituality in the client's life

        3)   Assess spiritual issues and spiritual components of the client's major concerns or difficulties

        4)   Provide opportunities for discussion by picking up on subtle openings and initiating inquiries

        5)   Be open to exploring spiritual modalities

    e.   Faith-based social services

        1)   Faith-permeated organizations—Have explicitly religious mission statements, were founded by religious groups or for religious purposes, are affiliated with external religious agencies, are explicitly religious in their selection of staff and board members, and refuse funding likely to compromise organizational religious mission or identity

        2)   Faith-centered organizations—Similar to faith-permeated organizations, but are less adamant about the need for all staff members to share organizational beliefs and less likely to have policies refusing funding that could undermine religious mission or identity

        3)   Faith-affiliated organizations—Have explicit or implicit religious mission statements, were founded by religious groups or for religious reasons, often are affiliated with external religious agencies, expect some degree of shared faith commitments among staff and board members, and often seek financial and volunteer support from religious communities

4)   Faith-background organizations—May implicitly refer to religious values in their mission statement, have weaker connections to religious institutions, hold few, if any, expectations regarding the faith commitments of board and staff members, and vary in their pursuit of support from religious communities

5)   Faith-secular partnership organizations—Varies according to the characteristics of the faith partners

6)   Secular organizations—Have no religious content or affiliations with external religious organizations

f.   *Critical Thinking Question 2.4*

B.   Silence in the Interview

1.   Client-initiated silence

a.   Gain time to organize thoughts

b.   Attempt to pressure worker to give some response or solution to a problem

c.   Resistance to or rejection of the worker's authority

2.   Negative worker-initiated silence

3.   Focusing on the client instead of yourself

4.   Therapeutic worker-initiated silence

a.   Pacing the interview—Involves using small periods of silence to allow time to think about and assimilate what is occurring

b.   Silent focusing—Enables the client to focus in on and think more intensively about an issue without having to rush right into something else. This is a bit longer than those used to pace interviews and is only allowed to occur after some significant revelation has surfaced

c.   Responding to defenses—Occurs when a client has an emotional outburst directed toward the worker

d.   Silent caring—Conveys your caring and understanding after a period of intense emotion during an interview

C.   Confronting Clients

    1.   Confrontation—The direct expression of one's view of the conflict and one's feelings about it and at the same time an invitation to the opposition to do the same

    2.   Framing discrepancies in confrontation

        a.   Four types of discrepancies

            1)   Incongruities in verbal statements

            2)   Between what one says and what one does

            3)   Between statements and nonverbal behavior

            4)   Between two or more people or the situation

    3.   Four components of confrontations

        a.   Worker should communicate that she cares about the client and is interested in the client's well-being

        b.   Worker should clearly express the client's stated goal within the problem-solving process

        c.   Worker should illustrate exactly what the discrepancy is

        d.   Worker should indicate the realistic results of the discrepancy

    4.   *Figure 2.3: Framing a Discrepancy during a Confrontation*

        a.   Communicate caring

        b.   Express the client's goal

        c.   Describe discrepancy

        d.   Indicate realistic results

    5.   Suggestions for using confrontation

        a.   Consider whether the relationship with the client is strong enough to withstand the confrontation

        b.   Be aware of client's emotional state

        c.   Never confront a client to vent your own anger or frustration

        d.   Use confrontations carefully and only when they will likely be effective

e.   Continue to demonstrate respect for client throughout the confrontation

f.   Remain empathic throughout the confrontation

g.   Use "I" statements during the confrontation

h.   Make certain your feedback is very clear and behaviorally oriented

i.   Have patience and allow the client some time to change

D.   Involuntary Clients

     1.   Suggestions to help with involuntary clients

         a.   Acknowledge to yourself that the client is involuntary

         b.   Try to put yourself in your client's shoes

         c.   Label negative feelings and help client express them

         d.   Clarify your role for the client

         e.   Know the limits of your authority and power over the client

         f.   Give them as many choices as possible, including minor options

         g.   Figure out what you can do for the client that he wants

         h.   Use pro-social modeling and positive reinforcement in order to encourage and promote client pro-social values and behaviors

                 1)   Modeling—The learning of behavior by observing another individual engaging in that behavior

                 2)   Positive reinforcement—A positive procedure or consequence that increases the frequency of the behavior immediately preceding it

                 3)   Pro-social—Refers to values and actions which, instead of being criminal, support and care for others

                 4)   The most powerful reward or reinforcer available to the worker is praise

         i.   Allow client time to gain trust in you and in the intervention process

         j.   Accept the fact that the client has the right to choose whether or not to cooperate

2.   *Highlight 2.7: Handling Hostility*

    a.   Do not get angry or defensive

    b.   Focus on the client's hostile *behavior* instead of labeling the client a hostile *person*

    c.   Allow the client briefly to voice his or her anger

    d.   Emphasize the client's personal strengths

    e.   Know the facts regarding the client's situation

    f.   Focus on the present and future

    g.   Look at the various alternatives open to the client and their consequences

    h.   Do not moralize

    i.   Summarize what has occurred during the interview and what recommendations have been made

    j.   Establish short-term, initial goals with a hostile client

E.   Suspicion of Untruth

    1.   Evaluate the situation logically

    2.   Examine the client's pattern of prior behavior

    3.   Consider not confronting the client if this is the first time the possibility of lying has come up

    4.   Evaluate the costs of believing or not believing your client

F.   *Figure 2.4: Social Work Roles with Micro Systems*

    1.   Broker—Involves linking clients with needed resources

    2.   Enabler—Involves providing support, encouragement, and suggestions to a client system so that the client may proceed more easily and successfully in completing tasks or solving problems

    3.   Mediator—Works to help conflicting parties settle disputes and agree on compromises

    4.   Educator—Conveys information to a client

    5.   Evaluator—Determines effectiveness of their own practice

6. Case manager/coordinator—Involves seeking out resources, planning how they might be delivered, organizing service provision, and monitoring progress

7. Advocate—Champions the rights of others with the goal of empowering their clients

XI. **Terminating the Interview**

A. Mention how much time is left (e.g., five or fifteen minutes)

B. Tell the client how you feel as the interview is coming to a close

C. Ask clients to summarize what they have learned and accomplished

D. Encourage clients to share their own feelings about the intervention process

EXPERIENTIAL EXERCISES AND SIMULATIONS

Nine exercises are included for this chapter. Since micro practice skills form the basis for mezzo and macro practice, these skills are especially important to master. The exercises follow chapter 2's content very closely. They are designed to apply many of the specific skills discussed.

Exercise 1 concerns increasing awareness of nonverbal behavior. Exercise 2 addresses enhancing listening ability. Exercise 3 provides opportunities to practice empathic responses. Exercise 4 features self-exploration with the intent of more clearly defining one's own genuineness. Exercise 5 involves asking direct and indirect questions. Exercise 6 allows you to practice a wide range of responses.

The final exercises deal with difficult situations frequently encountered in practice. Exercises 7, 8, and 9 address, respectively, uncomfortable silence, hostility, and suspicion of untruth within the context of practice interviews.

Exercise 2.1: Noting Nonverbal Behavior

A. Brief description:
    Students break up into pairs. Taking turns, each describes for the other some minor problem she or he is experiencing while the other observes nonverbal behavior.
B. Objectives:
    You will be able to:
    1. Identify various aspects of nonverbal behavior.
    2. Articulate and provide feedback about such behavior.
C. Procedure:
    1. Review the material on nonverbal behavior in the text.
    2. Think of and write down a brief summary of some minor problem currently being experienced. Since you will be asked to share it, it should be something that is not too personal. For example, it might be how someone you live with doesn't pick up his or her dirty socks or insists that you do the dishes immediately after eating. It can be any small thing that annoys you.
    3. Break up into pairs. In the event that there is an odd number in class, form one group of three.
    4. Members in each pair take turns being the talker and the observer. The talker should briefly explain to the observer the problem he or she previously wrote down. This should take approximately five minutes. The observer may ask questions of the talker for clarification. However, the talker should do the majority of the talking.

5.   While the talker is talking, the observer should write down brief notes concerning the talker's nonverbal behavior in the following three areas (for each area, a number of questions are raised to indicate some specific aspects of behavior the observer can note):

Eye Contact
- To what extent does the talker look you in the eye while explaining his or her problem?
- Does the talker appear to be comfortable in making eye contact with you, or does he or she frequently look away in a nervous gesture?
- Might there be some cultural differences between you and the talker that would affect the extent to which eye contact is appropriate?

Facial Expressions
- How would you describe the talker's facial expressions as she or he describes the problem?
- What specific facial movements indicate concern, humor, anger, embarrassment, or other emotions
- What specific facial movements seem to emphasize the points that the talker appears to feel are the most significant?

Body Positioning
- What specific aspects of the talker's body positioning indicate that she or he is tense or relaxed or somewhere in between?
- What specific aspects of the talker's body positioning indicate either a formal or informal style in presenting information?
- How tense/relaxed and formal/informal do you feel yourself as you sit there observing the talker?
- What zone of personal space exists between you and the talker?
- To what extent is this zone comfortable or uncomfortable to you under these conditions?

---

6.   After approximately five minutes of listening to the talker, the observer should take a few minutes to note whatever information she or he can remember about the talker's nonverbal behavior but didn't have a chance to record earlier. These notes can be rough and brief as they will only be used by the observer to give the talker feedback.

7.   The observer should now provide feedback to the talker concerning his or her nonverbal behavior. The observer should use the notes recorded during the activity's process. This should take about five minutes.

8.   Each pair should now reverse the roles of talker and observer. They should follow procedural steps 4 through 7, except that their roles are reversed. (In the event that there is one group of three, one of the three will be an observer twice instead of assuming a talking role.)

9.   After all feedback concerning nonverbal behavior has been given, the entire class should discuss the experience together. The instructor will focus on the following questions, among others:

    a.   What types of nonverbal behaviors in the four areas did you notice?

    b.   What aspects of nonverbal behavior, if any, did this exercise help to sensitize you to?

    c.   How did participating in this exercise feel?

    d.   What did you learn from this exercise?

A.   Brief description:

The class will break up into pairs. Each person takes turns speaking about an issue or listening to what the other says. They then compare the *intent* of the talker with the communication's *impact* upon the listener.

B.   Objectives:

You will be able to:

1.   Examine your ability to listen accurately.

2.   Compare the intent of a sender's messages with the impact upon yourself as listener.

C.   Procedure:

1.   Take a moment to focus on some problem you have or some issue about which you have exceptionally strong feelings (for instance, a political issue or a religious stance). It's important that you select a topic about which you have strong feelings and opinions.

2.   Divide into pairs.

3.   Take turns at being talker and listener. The first talker (Talker #1) should spend three minutes describing the problem or issue "off the top of his or her head." The listener (Listener #1) should remain completely silent. No written notes should be taken. It's important to rely on memory alone when it's time to give feedback.

4.   Your instructor will alert you when the three minutes are up. At that point, talkers should remain silent while listeners relate to talkers what they heard talkers say. The instructor will allot three minutes for this.

5.   At the end of this three-minute period, the talker and listener should answer the following questions. Do so silently without letting each other know what you're writing.

Questions for the Talker:

a.   To what extent did you feel the listener heard the major *intent* of what you were trying to say? (Circle a number.)

Didn't listen to me at all	Listened to me moderately well	Listened to me extremely well
1 2 3 4	5 6 7 8	9 10

b.   To what extent do you feel that the listener heard what you had to say *with accurate detail*? (Circle a number.)

Little or no accurate detail	Moderately accurate detail	Extremely accurate detail
1 2 3 4	5 6 7 8	9 10

c.   *What percentage of all that you said* did the listener relate back to you? _____ %

d.   What were the *major errors and inaccuracies* evident in the listener's feedback?

_____

_____

Questions for the Listener:

a. To what extent did you feel you heard the major *intent* of what the talker was trying to say? (Circle a number.)

Not at all				Moderately well				Extremely well	
1	2	3	4	5	6	7	8	9	10

b. To what extent do you feel that you heard what the talker had to say *with accurate detail*? (Circle a number.)

Little or no accurate detail				Moderately accurate detail				Extremely accurate detail	
1	2	3	4	5	6	7	8	9	10

c. *What percentage of all that the talker said* did you relate back to him or her? _____ %

d. What specific topics and areas did you *not understand or remember* very well?

_____

_____

_____

_____

6. Now exchange roles and repeat steps 3 through 5. Because your roles are reversed, it's appropriate for you to complete the alternate talker/listener questionnaire. Once again, do so silently without showing each other what you've written.

7. In each pair, you can now share with each other your results. Remember that the Talker Questionnaire for one should be contrasted with the Listener Questionnaire for the other. Between the two of you, take five to ten minutes to discuss the following questions and issues:

a. To what extent did you agree in each experience that the talker's intent (that is, what the talker intended to say) coincided with the listener's impact (that is, what the listener heard)?

b. To what extent did you agree in each experience on the amount of detail that the listener actually heard?

c. For each experience, how did your percentages compare regarding how much of what the talker said was related back by the listener?

d. For each experience, compare and contrast the talker's perception of the listener's feedback with the listener's inability to understand or remember what the talker said.

8. The instructor will recall the pairs for a general class discussion. Address the following questions:

a. What differences did you find between what talkers said and what listeners heard?

b. What types of information were omitted in the listeners' feedback?

c. What thoughts and ideas did you gain from this exercise about communication and attentive listening?

A.   Brief description:
     You will be asked to demonstrate empathic responses to a variety of case vignettes.

B.   Objectives:
     You will be able to:
     1.   Identify various ways you can verbally demonstrate empathy.
     2.   Apply empathic phrases to simulated case situations.

C.   Procedure:
     1.   Review the section on warmth and empathy discussed in the text.
     2.   The instructor will read the series of case situations illustrated below, and will then ask for a volunteer to respond with an empathic response.
     3.   The following are some examples of leading phrases that you can use to begin an empathic statement:

     - My impression is that . . .
     - It appears to me that . . .
     - Is what you're saying that . . . ?
     - Do I understand you correctly that . . . ?
     - I'm hearing you say that . . .
     - Do you mean that . . . ?
     - Do you feel that . . . ?
     - I feel that you . . .
     - I'm getting the message that . . .
     - You seem to be . . .
     - When you say that, I think you . . .
     - You look as if you . . .
     - You sound so _____. Can we talk more about it?
     - You look _____. What's been happening?

     4.   Your instructor will read and ask you to respond to the five case vignettes cited below. After each case, the class can discuss the following two questions:

     a.   What various responses are possible in this case situation?
     b.   How do various responses compare and contrast in terms of their effectiveness?

Vignette #1
     You are a social worker in foster care. You're making a home visit to one of the foster homes on your caseload. The purpose is to talk with both foster parents and determine how things are going with their nine-year-old foster child, Katie. The couple has three children of their own, all of whom are in college. In the past the foster couple has expressed some interest in adopting Katie. When you get to the home, only the mother is present. After polite initial greetings, the foster mother states, "Katie certainly doesn't like to read very much like the rest of us. I think she gets bored when she's not doing something active. Many times I just don't know what to do with her."
     You *empathically* respond . . .   (Remember that you *do not* have to solve the problem right now. You only need to let your client know that you understand how she feels.)

Vignette #2

You are a social worker in a health care facility for the elderly. Helen is a resident who has been living there for approximately two years. All rooms have two residents, which has consistently been a problem for Helen. Her current roommate is Hilda, a quiet woman who rarely interacts with any of the other residents. Helen is very possessive of her things and wants no one else to touch them. Additionally, Helen does not like to share the bathroom, which is also used by the two residents in the next room. Helen, a strong, outspoken woman even at age ninety-seven, approaches you and states, "Hilda keeps using my bathroom and pushes my things around. I want her out of there right now! You do something right now!"

You *empathically* respond . . .

Vignette # 3

You are a school social worker. Romy, age sixteen, was in the men's bathroom when several other students were caught using drugs. Romy insists it was the others who were guilty and he was innocent. He said he just happened to be in the restroom at the same time. The teacher who found them couldn't distinguish who was guilty and who was not, so put them all on "penalty." That means detentions after school and exclusion from any sports for two weeks. Romy is furious. He comes up to you and states, "It's not fair! It's just not fair! I'm innocent and I'm getting punished anyway. I should've used the drugs if I'm going to get the punishment."

You *empathically* respond . . .

Vignette # 4

You are a social worker at a diagnostic and treatment center for children who have multiple disabilities. Your primary function is to work with parents, helping them to cope with the pressures they are under and connecting them with resources they need. A mother of a five-year-old boy with severe cerebral palsy[1] talks with you on a weekly basis. Her son has serious difficulties. He has very little muscular control. He can't walk by himself or talk, although his speech, occupational, and physical therapists feel he has normal intelligence. The mother's husband is of a religion that denies the existence of disease and of physical impairment. Thus, he denies that his son has a disability. The burden of caregiving rests solely upon the mother. She loves her son dearly and generally does what she can for him enthusiastically. She enters your office one day, says hello, and sits down. She immediately puts her hand to her eyes and breaks down in tears.

You *empathically* respond . . .

---

[1] *Cerebral palsy* is a condition of the brain that results from damage before or during birth. Symptoms include difficulties in speech and mobility.

Exercise 2.4: What Is Your Own Brand of Genuineness?

A.   Brief description:
Students are asked to respond to a questionnaire about their individual personality traits.

B.   Objectives:
You will be able to:
1.   Identify some of your own individual personality traits.
2.   Explore how these traits might affect your relationships in social work practice.

C.   Procedure:
1.   Complete the following *Who Are You?* questionnaire as honestly as possible. You do not need to share your answers unless you choose to. Take approximately ten to fifteen minutes to complete the questionnaire.

Who Are You?
(A Self-Exploratory Questionnaire)

1)   Complete the following four *who are you* statements. They can be adjectives, nouns, or longer statements. If you had to summarize who you are, what would you say?

I am _____

I am _____

I am _____

I am _____

2)   What adjectives would you use to describe yourself? Circle all that apply. They are in no particular order or priority. They are just meant to stimulate your thinking about yourself.

Happy   Sad   Honest   Dishonest   Sensitive   Insensitive   Trustworthy
Untrustworthy   Caring   Uncaring   Outgoing Shy   Withdrawn   Friendly
Unfriendly   Religious   Not very religious   Nervous   Calm   Formal
Informal   Aggressive   Assertive   Timid   Confident Careful   Careless
Not very confident   Capable   Incapable Independent   Dependent
Affectionate   Cool   Wary   Bold   Cheerful   Witty   Unassuming
Thorough   Easy-going   Determined   Clever   Responsive   Strong-minded   Weak-willed (at least sometimes)   Leisurely   Industrious
Controlled Spontaneous Serious   Funny   Tough   Pleasant   Daring
Eager   Efficient   Not so efficient   Artistic   Tactful   Intolerant
Vulnerable   Likable   Smart   Understanding   Impatient   Patient
Imaginative   Wordy   Concise   Open-minded   Funny   Organized
Somewhat disorganized   Conscientious   Late   Emotional Unemotional
Open   Creative   Curious   Sincere   Precise   A little haphazard
Cooperative   Ethical   Brave   Mature Eager   Spunky

3)   Cite your four greatest strengths. They can involve anything from personal qualities to talents to accomplishments. They don't have to be in any particular order or priority.

Strength A _____

Strength B _____

Strength C _____

Strength D _____

---

4)   Cite your four greatest weaknesses. These don't have to be in any order or priority either.

Weakness A _____

Weakness B _____

Weakness C _____

Weakness D _____

5)   How do you think your personal strengths will help you to work with clients in social work practice?

_____

_____

_____

_____

6)   What weaknesses, if any, do you think you need to work on to improve your ability to work with clients in social work practice?

_____

_____

_____

_____

_____

2.   After you've had time to complete the questionnaire, your instructor will lead a class discussion by asking you the following questions:

a.   In general, what types of personal qualities do you think are helpful when working with clients in social work practice?

b.   What personal strengths do you have that you think will be useful in the field?

Exercise 2.5: Asking Direct and Indirect Questions

A.   Brief description:

You will be asked to phrase both direct and indirect questions in response to a variety of situations.

B.   Objectives:

You will be able to:

1.   Recognize the difference between direct and indirect questions.

2.   Respond with such questions to simulated case situations.

C.   Procedure:

1.   Review the material in the text on using direct and indirect questions. Generally, direct questions are those that clearly ask for information. They usually can be identified because they end in a question mark. Indirect questions, on the other hand, ask questions more subtly. They imply a leading question, usually hidden in some direct statement.

2.   In a class discussion, the instructor will ask for volunteers to respond to various needs for information. First you will be asked how you might phrase a direct question in order to get the information you need. Then, you will be asked how to do so using an indirect question. After each answer, the class will discuss the question's strengths and weaknesses.

3. Consider the needs for information presented below. How might you phrase (1) a *direct* question, and how might you phrase (2) an *indirect* question to obtain the information? Supply these two questions for each of the following situations.

   a. What a single fifteen-year-old who is six months pregnant plans to do about her baby.

   b. What a single, eighty-nine-year-old woman, still living in her own home but experiencing rapidly failing health, plans to do about her future.

   c. How a recently divorced single mother plans to care for her three small children when she returns to work.

   d. What a twenty-three-year-old man just out of prison and on probation (he had been convicted on several burglary charges) plans to do to support himself.

   e. How much a thirty-five-year-old man convicted of drunk driving drinks.

   f. What the financial resources are of a couple in their thirties applying to adopt a baby.

   g. How a twelve-year-old girl with a cognitive disability (who has been designated as "mildly retarded") feels about her new special education teacher.

   h. How many friends a shy, eight-year-old boy has in his neighborhood.

   i. The amount of stress a fifty-three-year-old female executive is experiencing in her high-level administrative position.

   j. How well a couple in their twenties who claim they're experiencing marital difficulties are able to communicate with each other.

4. Now, discuss the following questions:

   a. How difficult was it to think up the questions, especially the indirect ones?

   b. How would you describe indirect questions, using your own words?

   c. What are the strengths and weaknesses of using direct and indirect questions?

   d. In what ways are indirect questions able to get at the needed information?

   e. What did you learn from participating in this exercise?

Exercise 2.6: How to Respond to Clients

A. Brief description:
   You will be asked to respond to a variety of simulated client statements using a range of response types.

B. Objectives:
   You will be able to:
   1. Identify a variety of response types.
   2. Recognize and explain differences among the types of responses.
   3. Propose a variety of responses to simulated client situations.

C. Procedure:
   1. Review information in the text concerning interviews, especially focusing on verbal responses to clients. Make certain you understand how each type of response is defined and how they differ.
   2. Break down into small groups of four to six persons.
   3. Below are a number of statements typically made by clients. For each statement, work with your other group members to propose and write down examples of the different types of responses possible. Here is an example:

Example of client statement: "I'm so disgusted with my life!"
Possible responses:
Simple encouragement: "Mm-mm, please go on."
Rephrasing: "You're fed up with what's happening."
Reflective responding: "It seems that you are upset."
Clarification: "Do you mean that you don't like what's happening in your personal relationships?"
Interpretation: "Perhaps things are overwhelming you so that you feel trapped."
Providing information: "I can refer you to someone who can talk to you about your problems and, hopefully, help you resolve them."
Emphasizing clients' strengths: "It's good that you're getting in touch with your feelings and have chosen to share them with me. That's usually the first step in working problems out."
Self-disclosure: "Sometimes, I feel pretty disgusted, too."
Summarization (granted, it is pretty hard to summarize one measly line, so feel free to make up a summary): "So far we've discussed a number of your problems, including finances and relationships. You've also indicated how disgusted you are at this point."
Eliciting information—Closed question: "Have you just started to feel this way?"
Eliciting information—Open-ended question: "What are your reasons for being so disgusted?"

Client Statement #1: "I'm really worried about my mother."
Possible Responses:
Simple encouragement: _____
_____
_____

Rephrasing: _____
_____
_____

Reflective responding: _____
_____
_____

Clarification: _____
_____
_____

Interpretation: _____
_____
_____

Providing information: _____
_____
_____

Emphasizing clients' strengths: _____
_____
_____

Self-disclosure: _____
_____
_____

Summarization: _____
_____
_____

Eliciting information—closed question: _____
_____
_____

Eliciting information—open-ended question: _____
_____
_____

Client Statement #2: "Hell's bells! I've got so much work to do that I don't know where
          to start."
Possible responses:
Simple encouragement: _____
_____
_____

Rephrasing: _____
_____
_____

Reflective responding: _____
_____
_____

Clarification: _____
_____
_____

Interpretation: _____
_____
_____

Providing information: _____
_____
_____

Emphasizing clients' strengths: _____
_____
_____

Self-disclosure: _____
_____
_____

Summarization: _____
_____
_____

Eliciting information—closed question: _____
_____
_____

Eliciting information—open-ended question: _____
_____
_____

Client Statement #3: "My dad beat me up last night."
Possible responses:
Simple encouragement: _____
_____
_____

Rephrasing: _____
_____

Reflective responding: _____
_____

Clarification: _____
_____

Interpretation: _____
_____

Providing information: _____
_____

Emphasizing clients' strengths: _____
_____

Self-disclosure: _____
_____

Summarization: _____
_____

Eliciting information—closed question: _____
_____

Eliciting information—open-ended question: _____
_____

Client Statement #4: "My little girl Grizelda is three-and-a-half, and hasn't started to walk yet."
Possible responses:
Simple encouragement: _____
_____

Rephrasing: _____
_____

Reflective responding: _____
_____

Clarification: _____
_____

Interpretation: _____
_____

Providing information: _____

Emphasizing clients' strengths: _____

_____

Self-disclosure: _____

_____

Summarization: _____

_____

Eliciting information—closed question: _____

_____

Eliciting information—open-ended question: _____

_____

_____

Client Statement #5: "I just don't have enough money to pay the rent. What should I
      do?"
Possible responses:
Simple encouragement: _____

_____

Rephrasing: _____

_____

Reflective responding: _____

_____

Clarification: _____

_____

Interpretation: _____

_____

Providing information: _____

_____

Emphasizing clients' strengths: _____

_____

Self-disclosure: _____

_____

Summarization: _____

_____

_____

Eliciting information—closed question: _____

_____

_____

> Eliciting information—open-ended question: _____
> _____
> _____

4. After about thirty minutes, your instructor will ask the small groups to join together in a class discussion. Address the following questions:
   a. Which types of response statements did you feel were the most difficult to develop?
   b. Which types of response statements were the easiest to think up?
   c. For each client statement, which types of response statements seem to fit best? For what reasons?
   d. To what extent did you feel that there was overlap among response types? Please specify exactly where you felt there was such overlap.

Exercise 2.7: Nobody's Saying Anything

A. Brief description:
A class volunteer role-plays a client situation where silence is emphasized. The rest of the class assumes the social work role and verbally responds to the silent "client."

B. Objectives:
You will be able to:
1. Identify ways of responding to a client who is being silent.
2. Assess your own reactions to uncomfortable situations when a client is silent.
3. Demonstrate responses that are appropriate and potentially effective in such a situation.

C. Procedure:
1. Review the material on interviewing, especially that on silence in the interview and on doing the interview which is discussed in the text. It is also helpful to review related material on breast cancer, on HIV/AIDS, and on dealing with grief prior to undertaking the respective role play.[2]
2. After reading one of the following three client scenarios, the instructor will ask for a volunteer to play the role before the class. The volunteer will sit in the front of the class and respond as if she or he was the client.

   To avoid placing full responsibility for the social work role on any one individual, the worker role will be assumed on a general basis by the remainder of the class. Volunteers may jump in with responses they feel are appropriate. In the event that more than one person responds at the same time, the instructor will monitor the progression of turns.

---

[2] The supplementary material for Role-Plays A and B is taken from C. Zastrow and K. Kirst-Ashman, *Understanding Human Behavior and the Social Environment* (Chicago: Nelson-Hall, 4th ed., 1997). The supplementary material for Role C is taken from chapter 7 of the text which addresses dealing with grief.

Role-Play A: Silence and Breast Cancer

Client Role: Verbenia is devastated. She feels that her life has just begun—and now that it might be cut cruelly short. Verbenia knows she is worried and upset, but really doesn't want to talk about it. She views herself as a private person who doesn't feel comfortable sharing personal information, especially with strangers. Talking about her own breast, for heaven's sakes, is even worse.

Worker Role: You are a hospital social worker. Verbenia has been referred to you after her physician noted the presence of a breast lump during her annual exam. The procedure at this particular hospital's health clinic is to refer patients who are anxious about diagnoses to social workers for information and counseling.

Role-Play B: Silence and AIDS

Client Role: Hank has just learned that he is HIV positive. He had visited a confidential testing site two weeks ago and just got his results today. He has had numerous female sexual partners and figures that is how he contracted HIV. He's in such shock he can hardly talk.

Worker Role: You work at a crisis intervention unit. People with problems come in off of the street for help. Hank just walked into the unit and was referred to you.

Role-Play C: Silence and Dealing with Grief

Client Role: Lois is interested in becoming a foster parent. She cannot have children herself and would love to contribute to other children's welfare if she can't to her own. The problem is that her father died a month ago. She was very close to him and can't seem to concentrate on anything else but her grief.

Worker Role: You are a placement worker for a state foster care unit. You are conducting an initial interview with Lois, a potential foster parent. The purpose of the interview is to find out some basic information about the person's life including marital status and relationships, family history, current work situation and history, personal interests, and emotional stability. Lois mentions that her father just died. She appears to be very upset about it. You feel it is an important aspect to investigate concerning her ability to function as a stable foster parent.

3.   The client for the chosen role play should take her or his place at the front of the class. Class members should then take turns asking questions. This can proceed for fifteen to twenty minutes.

4.   The instructor will intervene and begin a class discussion focusing on the following questions:

a.   Which techniques and responses demonstrated by class members appeared to be the most effective?

b.   Which techniques and responses didn't seem to work? What do you think were the reasons they didn't work?

c.   What did "social workers" find most difficult about this role play?

d.   What feelings and reactions did the client experience while doing the role play?

e.   How helpful was the information about breast cancer?

f.   What did you learn from this role play?

Exercise 2.8: Working with Difficult Clients

A. Brief description:
    The class is divided into threes, and participants play a difficult client, a worker, and an observer.

B. Objectives:
    You will be able to:
    1. Demonstrate responses to difficult clients.
    2. Assess the appropriateness and effectiveness of such responses.

C. Procedure:
    1. Review the material in the text on confronting clients and involuntary clients.
    2. Break up into groups of three. Each group member should take one of the three roles: client, worker, or observer.
    3. The instructor will read the client role. Afterwards, the client and worker should participate in the role play, continuing the scene for about 10 minutes. Meanwhile, the observer should take notes about his or her impressions of what's going on. The worker role is school social worker.

> **Client Role**
> The client is a fourteen-year-old male named Horace. Horace has been referred to the school social worker because of frequent truancy and another student's accusation that Horace stole his expensive new jacket. Unconfirmed rumors have also been going around parts of the student body that Horace often brings a concealed 9 mm semiautomatic handgun to school. Horace has been seen in the company of a gang called the Toros Machos which has been growing in popularity among the school's students.
> Horace is angry and annoyed that he's been called in to see the school "shrink" (as he calls the school social worker). He is not planning on cooperating unless he feels he has to. He comes in to see the school social worker.

    4. The instructor will tell you to stop the role play after about ten minutes. Take another ten minutes to discuss the following questions:
        a. What techniques used by the worker were effective? For what reasons?
        b. What techniques used by the worker appeared ineffective? For what reasons?
        c. What suggestions do you have for improvement?
        d. What have you learned from this role play that you think you'll be able to apply to practice?
    5. After approximately ten minutes, your instructor will call you back to participate in a large group discussion. Summarize what you concluded in your small groups.

Exercise 2.9: The Truth or Not the Truth? That Is the Question

A. Brief description:
    Students role play client and worker, and the worker suspects the client is lying.

B. Objectives:
    You will be able to:
    1. Demonstrate responses to a client suspected of not telling the truth.
    2. Assess the appropriateness and effectiveness of such responses.

C.	Procedure:
   1.	Review the material on suspicion of untruth presented in the text.
   2.	Divide up into pairs. In each pair, decide who will play the client and worker first. The worker role is the client's probation officer. The client role is described below:

Client Role

Molly Coddle, twenty-three, is on parole. She was convicted of armed robbery, and spent the past two years in a state prison. She has a history of not showing up for appointments with her other prior parole and probation officers. One of the conditions of her parole is that she meet with her parole officer every week at a specified time. If she misses her appointment even once without an adequate excuse, she is to return to prison for six months. She missed last week's appointment.

Molly maintains that she called to say she couldn't make it and left a message. Due to a glitch in the system, voice mail was not working. Therefore, Molly says that she called the main desk, but doesn't know who answered the phone. The parole officer received no message. However, the secretary who usually answers the phone was sick last week. The agency got some temporary help that is now virtually impossible to track down in order to determine whether a message was left or not.

The parole officer is pulled between believing Molly's story and not believing her. Believing the story might better maintain the worker/client relationship. However, getting a reputation with other clients for being "easy" would be a disaster.

   3.	Participate in the role play for approximately 10 minutes. The worker should concentrate on two tasks:
   a.	Label what is true and what does not appear to be true.
   b.	Decide what to do about the situation.
   The client may creatively develop excuses. For instance, the client can elaborate on anything including flat tires, oversleeping, hemorrhoids acting up, helping a friend get an abortion, etc. The client should use both (hypothetically) factual and untrue statements to the probation officer.
   4.	After about ten minutes, the instructor will tell you to reverse roles for another ten minutes. Start from the beginning. The new client can develop his or her own set of excuses. The worker should concentrate on the same two tasks described above.
   5.	At the end of the second role play, the instructor will bring the class back to participate in a large class discussion. The following questions will be addressed:
   a.	As worker, did you or did you not believe the client's excuses? What were your reasons?
   b.	As worker, what techniques did you use to establish the truth? To what extent did these techniques work? What problems did you encounter?
   c.	As client, what techniques did you feel the worker used which were exceptionally effective?
   d.	As client, what techniques do you think would have proved more effective?
   e.	What was the final decision about what to do in the role plays?
   f.	As worker, how difficult was it to come to a decision?
   g.	As client, do you feel the worker was fair or not?
   h.	To what extent do you think this role play resembles possible real-life worker-client situations?
   i.	What did you learn from this role play that you think you'll be able to apply to real practice situations?

Chapter 3
Mezzo Practice Skills: Working with Groups

I.   **Introduction**

II. **Benefits of Groups**

    A.   Mutual Assistance

    B.   Connections

    C.   Testing

    D.   Goal Achievement

    E.   Decision making

    F.   *Critical Thinking Question 3.1*

III. **Types of Groups**

    A.   Task Groups—Groups exist to achieve a specific set of objectives or tasks

        1.   Board of directors—An administrative group charged with responsibility for setting the policy governing agency programs

        2.   Task forces—Groups established for a special purpose and usually disbanded after completion of their task

        3.   Committees and commissions—Groups responsible for dealing with specific tasks or matters

            a.   Committees—Usually work in a particular area

                1)   Standing committee—Exists on a continuous basis

                2)   Ad hoc committee—Set up for one purpose and expected to cease operation after completing its task

            b.   Commissions—Usually ongoing in nature and responsible for a particular task

        4.   Legislative bodies—Include city councils, county boards of supervisors, state legislatures, and the U.S. Congress

            a.   Composed of elected representatives

            b.   Responsible for establishing laws and appropriating funds

  c. Social workers may need to testify before them or serve as members of their commissions

  d. Very important for social workers to be familiar with how they operate

 5. Staff meetings—Meetings composed of agency staff members who assemble periodically for some identified purpose

 6. Multidisciplinary teams (M teams)—Groups of professionals from various disciplines that meet to discuss specific clients with whom team members are working

 7. Case conferences and staffings—Agency or organizational meetings in which all professionals involved in a particular case (client) discuss such things as the client's identified problems, goals, and intervention plans

 8. Social action groups

  a. Social action—Efforts undertaken by individuals and groups to bring about solutions to social and economic problems

  b. Participatory Action Research (PAR)—Based on the belief that it is important to work directly with those who are affected by a situation and involve them in the process of gathering data, analyzing the results, and translate the findings to decision makers

  c. *Highlight 3.1: A Participatory Action Research Group*

  d. *Highlight 3.2: Social Action Within a University*

B. Treatment groups—Any groups where the primary focus is on members' emotional and social needs

 1. Growth groups—Groups designed to encourage and support the growth of the individual group member

 2. Therapy groups—Help clients who have an identified goal of changing some aspect of their behavior

 3. Educational groups—Include a variety of groups designed to provide members with information about themselves or others

 4. Socialization groups—Assist participants in acquiring skills necessary to become socialized into the community

 5. Support groups (self-help groups)—Groups of people sharing certain characteristics who get together to provide one another with emotional sustenance, encourage new coping mechanisms, and allow a strengths-based sharing of issues, concerns, and problems

IV.   **Worker Roles in Groups**

    A.   Broker—Helps clients obtain needed resources by connecting them with community agencies

    B.   Mediator—Helps group members resolve conflicts or other dissension

    C.   Educator—Provides group participants with new information, structures presentations, and uses modeling to help members learn new skills

    D.   Facilitator—Guides, eases, or expedites the way for others

V.   **Basic Group Dynamics**

    A.   Group Development

        1.   Four stages of development

            a.   Stage 1

                1)   A strong reliance on the leader

                2)   Often focused on trust issues as members learn whether they can trust others in the group

            b.   Stage 2

                1)   Group members begin to assert themselves more

                2)   Some level of conflict is common

                3)   Power and control issues become more frequent

                4)   Leader should encourage open discussion of conflict

            c.   Stage 3

                1)   Group productivity increases and there is greater attention to achieving its goal

                2)   This is the working phase

                3)   Trust is developed

                4)   Worker's role will be more of consultant or advisor than director

            d.   Stage 4

                1)   Separation stage where the group has reached its goals and members begin to separate emotionally from the group

                2)   There are often feelings of loss and maybe some anger

2. *Highlight 3.3: Stages in Teen Group Therapy*

   a. Stage 1 in a Teen Group: Reliance on the Leader

   b. Stage 2 in a Teen Group: Addressing Conflict

   c. Stage 3 in a Teen Group: Working

   d. Stage 4 in a Teen Group: Separation

3. Open-ended groups—Members enter and leave the group at different times

4. Closed groups—Members join and leave the group together

5. Formed groups—Members have been brought together by an outside agency, organization, or individual

6. Natural groups—Members have come together through bonds of friendship or kinship

B. Group Culture, Norms, and Power

   1. Culture—Traditions, customs, and values/beliefs shared by group members

   2. Norms—Unwritten expectations about how individuals will act in certain situations

   3. Power—Issues always exist within groups. There is usually a period in which the group or individual members of the group vie with the leader for power

C. Group Size and Composition

   1. Education groups usually have from four to fifteen members

   2. Discussion groups usually have from five to eight

   3. Personal growth groups, support groups, and therapy groups ideally have from five to eight members; there can be as few as three and as many as twelve

   4. Worker must decide the degree of heterogeneity and homogeneity appropriate for a given group

   5. Age and gender factors also should be a consideration

D. Duration

E. Decision Making in Groups

   1. *Highlight 3.4: Approaches to Decision Making*

2.   Decision making by consensus

    a.   All members support and accept the decision even if they were not initially so inclined

    b.   Requires atmosphere of openness

3.   Decision making by compromise

    a.   Reach a solution that most, if not all, members can support

    b.   May not please anyone entirely but is viewed as the best that can be done

4.   Decision making by majority

    a.   Most deliberative bodies use this

    b.   Over one-half support an idea

5.   Rule by an individual—Allowing one individual to make choices that affect the entire group

6.   Persuasion by a recognized expert—A group may accede to the recommendations of the "expert"

7.   Averaging of individual opinions

8.   Persuasion by a minority

9.   Nominal group technique—Intent is to help group members arrive at a consensus with respect to a pending decision

    a.   Stage 1: Members receive a problem statement and list their ideas about the problem without consulting other members

    b.   Stage 2: Leader asks each member to provide one idea and continues until done, writing them on the board or flip chart

    c.   Stage 3: Leader makes sure all members understand each idea

    d.   Stage 4: Each member is asked to prioritize to decrease the overall list by one-half or three-quarters

    e.   Stage 5: Leader places mark by each idea

    f.   Stage 6: Members rank the new list

    g.   Technique can produce a larger number of alternatives than most approaches

10. Brainstorming—A group technique used to encourage members to produce a variety of ideas about a specific topic

    a. No attempt is made to rate or evaluate the ideas

    b. Works best when the goal is generation of multiple alternatives

11. Parliamentary procedure

    a. *Robert's Rules of Order*—Was devised over 100 years ago and remains the most common set of guidelines in use today

    b. Filibuster—Endlessly speaking to prevent a group from conducting its business

    c. Motions—Proposed actions that a group is asked to support

        1) Primary motions—Bring business to the group for consideration

            a) Main motions

            b) Incidental motions, e.g., adjournment, repealing an action already taken

        2) Secondary motions—Used to act upon the primary motion, to amend, refer, or defer action on a motion. Also used to limit debate, reconsider a motion, or bring up for discussion an item that had been previously tabled, and to challenge improper actions or request information

            a) Point of information—Request information

            b) Point of order—Improper actions

        3) "I call the question"

            a) Motion not debatable

            b) Halts discussion if supported by two-thirds of those present

    d. Vote is recorded

        1) Chair may vote to break a tie or to create a tie

        2) If a tie occurs, the motion does not pass

    e. Amendments

        1) Voted first before main motion (with amendments) is voted on

f.   Quorum—Minimum number of group members that must be present to conduct business

g.   Agenda—An ordered list of the topics to be covered in the meeting

h.   Minutes—Official record of group action

F.   Critical Thinking and Groups

    1.   Groupthink—When groups have the illusion of agreement but have really failed to carefully consider their decisions, and simply go along with the rest of the group

    2.   *Critical Thinking Question 3.2*

G.   Group Functions and Roles

    1.   Task functions—Help to keep a group on task and working toward agreed-upon ends

    2.   Maintenance functions—Ensure that the needs of group members receive attention

    3.   Task roles

        a.   Information seeker—In addition to seeking information, a member may solicit the opinions of group members to help determine how people perceive some topic

        b.   Opinion seeker—Often wants the opinions before stating his or her own position

        c.   Elaborator—Expands on ideas proposed to the group and helps to ensure that a complete explanation is provided for all ideas

        d.   Instructor—Often clarifies and reminds the other members about previous decisions they have made

        e.   Evaluator—Makes judgments about the wisdom or appropriateness of any particular idea or course of action

        f.   Energizer—Shows excitement and enthusiasm for projects; by force of their interest, they bring other members along

        g.   Recorder—Keeps a log or record of decisions reached or actions taken. These unelected secretaries help the group stay on task, and serve as the unofficial historians in a group

        h.   Procedural technician—Helps the group follow their own agreed-upon ways of making decisions

4. Maintenance roles—More concerned with improving, enhancing, or increasing group functioning

    a.   Harmonizer

    b.   Compromiser

    c.   Encourager

    d.   Follower

    e.   Tension reliever

    f.   Listener

5. Nonfunctional roles—Meet only their own needs and do not further the progress of the group

    a.   Aggressor—Attacks others and, by putting them down, attempts to raise themselves

    b.   Blocker—No matter what the proposal, he or she will always have a reason why it will not succeed

    c.   Recognition seeker—Will engage in a variety of behaviors, all of which are designed to focus the group's attention on themselves

    d.   Dominator—Talks incessantly or seeks help from the group for his or her own problems

    e.   Help seeker—Has personal needs that are not being met

    f.   Confessor—Often embarrasses the group by inappropriately disclosing personal behavior

    g.   Scapegoat—Draws upon themselves the wrath of other members and serves as someone to blame when things are not going well

    h.   Defensive members—Do not accept blame for anything and deny responsibility for their actions

    i.   Deviant members—Engage in behavior they know the group will oppose or find annoying

    j.   Quiet members—Simply do not participate and make getting to know them impossible for anyone

    k.   Internal leader—May vie for leadership of the group and attempt to wrestle control from the designated leader

6. *Figure 3.1: A Variety of Group Roles*

VI. **Micro Skills in Groups**

    A.   Therapeutic or growth-oriented groups are likely to use these skills

    B.   Task groups typically have less emphasis on such matters as self-disclosure

VII. **Groups and the Generalist Intervention Model (GIM)**

    A.   Engagement

    B.   Assessment

    C.   Planning

    D.   Implementation

    E.   Evaluation

    F.   Termination

    G.   Follow-Up

    H.   *Critical Thinking Question 3.3*

VIII. **Task and Treatment-Group Skills**

    A.   Conflict Resolution

        1.   Recognizing conflict

            a.   Ideas suggested by one side may be routinely rejected by the other

            b.   *Highlight 3.5: The Family Treatment Program: Recognizing Conflict*

        2.   Assessing conflict

            a.   Usually requires talking directly to the parties involved

            b.   *Highlight 3.6: That Is Not What I Said: Assessing Conflict*

        3.   Choosing a strategy and intervening

            a.   *Highlight 3.7: Square Peg in a Round Hole: Choosing a Strategy*

            b.   Win-lose and win-win situations

B.   Modeling and coaching

    1.   Modeling—Teaching new skills, showing clients alternative methods for resolving problems, and helping clients develop a repertoire of responses to problematic situations

        a.   Conditions that enhance the likelihood that a model's behavior will be copied

            1)   Asking the observer to pay special attention to the model's behavior

            2)   Describing for the observer why the modeled behavior is important

            3)   Having observers role play the modeled behavior to ensure that they understood and can perform it

            4)   Using praise both for the observer and for others who perform the appropriate behavior

            5)   Giving observers immediate corrective feedback when they attempt a new behavior

    2.   Coaching—A skill that includes giving the client specific information as well as corrective feedback

    3.   *Highlight 3.8: Teaching Disciplinary Techniques: Modeling and Coaching*

C.   Team building—The process of creating a group of individuals with the expertise, dedication, and characteristics needed to achieve a specific purpose

D.   Confrontation

    1.   The worker engages in a nonblaming type of confrontation by pointing out the discrepancy and how it affects the worker by using an "I" statement

    2.   The worker in a group asks the entire group to take responsibility for problem solving

    3.   One should have both empathy and respect for the sensitivities of the person being confronted

E.   Consultation

    1.   Case consultation—Focus is on a specific client or situation

    2.   Program consultation—Focus is on agency policies and practices instead of a specific client

F.   Coordination

G.   Using structure

    1.   Structure—The use of planned, systematic, time limited interventions and program activities

    2.   Agendas help structure time

    3.   The worker is largely responsible for enforcing time constraints and models this for the members

EXPERIENTIAL EXERCISES AND SIMULATIONS

There are four exercises in this chapter, each designed to illustrate a concept or technique. The first exercise concerns brainstorming, a method of gathering ideas for making decisions in groups. Exercise 2 is an ice breaker typical of those which can be used to help members of a group become better acquainted at their first meeting. The third exercise is an activity in which you must make a group decision using the consensus model of decision making. Exercise 4 involves parliamentary procedure. It provides a role play which illustrates many of the motions and actions which occur in larger groups using *Robert's Rules of Order*.

Exercise 3.1: Brainstorming

A.   Brief description:
You will be using the brainstorming procedure described in chapter 3 to generate ideas on a specific topic. Group members will be given instructions to follow. One member of the group will be responsible for leading the group in the exercise. Several groups will be operating simultaneously.

B.   Objectives:
You will be able to:
    1.   Use brainstorming to help a group develop multiple ideas on a topic.
    2.   Recognize and follow the steps in the brainstorming process.

C.   Procedure:
    1.   You will be asked to play roles in the following vignette:

> **Vignette**
> You are members of the "Respect Diversity" task force on your campus. The task force is responding to a series of physical and verbal attacks directed at gay and lesbian students. Your responsibility is to provide the college president with a list of ideas on how the school can encourage respect for diversity on your campus. She has said that the school has a substantial budget to pursue this project and wants your group to give her all the help you can.

    2.   The instructor will assign one person to act as the group leader. That person will be responsible for ensuring that the group follows proper procedures. For example, this person will be responsible for ensuring that members do not stop to evaluate each idea and that all who wish to participate have an opportunity. Members should raise their hands before participating. The leader should encourage all contributions and clarify any ideas that are not clear. Additionally, the leader will write down the ideas generated by the group.

3. Remember that the goal is to generate as many ideas as possible. No attempt is made to rate or evaluate the ideas. Members should be free to present ideas they thought of after hearing other members' contributions.
4. The group leader begins by asking who wants to provide the first idea. She then writes the first idea on the board or flip chart provided by the instructor.
5. The group continues this process until all ideas have been collected.
6. After the brainstorming has ended, the entire class can discuss the following questions and issues:
   a. What are the positive aspects of using such a brainstorming technique?
   b. What are the negative aspects?
   c. What specifically would the task group present to the college president?
   d. Summarize the specific steps used in this brainstorming process.
   e. What other situations can you envision where brainstorming might be harmful?

Exercise 3.2: An Ice Breaker

A. Brief description:
Many groups begin with some sort of an ice breaker for helping members get to know one another better. The one described below is a nonthreatening activity which focuses on potential career choices.

B. Objectives:
You will be able to:
   1. Learn about the interests of other members of your group.
   2. Become familiar with one ice breaker which can be used with groups of various ages.
   3. Become better acquainted with other group members.

C. Procedure:
   1. Consider the fact that many people pursue a number of careers in their lives that are different from the one for which they were trained. Take a few minutes to jot down two careers other than social work in which you have some interest. Assume that you might be able to switch to any one of them at a later point in your life.
   2. Next to each career write down the characteristic you find most attractive about this career.
   3. Next, list a disadvantage or problem with that career.
   4. Take turns going around the class in round-robin fashion, with each person describing her or his three choices together with the advantages and disadvantages of each. Other group members should be free to ask the person further questions about one or more of the careers they have selected.

Exercise 3.3: A Consensus Activity

A. Brief description:
You will have the opportunity to practice decision making by consensus. You will recall that the consensus model is used in groups to reach decisions with which all members are reasonably comfortable.

B. Objectives:
You will be able to:
   1. Use a consensus model to reach decisions important to the group.
   2. Understand why reaching consensus often takes longer than other decision-making approaches such as majority rule.

C. Procedure:
    1.   Divide the class into groups of four to five.
    2.   You will be asked to participate in the following role play:

Role Play

    The social work program at your school must develop a retention policy that identifies the factors that would result in a student being counseled out of social work. The program is required to do this by its accreditation body, but faculty members want to have student input into the decision. As the student members of the program's advisory board, you have been asked to formulate at least five actions or behaviors which would warrant dismissal from social work.

    Your fellow students have decided this is such an important activity that you must reach consensus on the five actions or behaviors. That is to say, you may not vote or otherwise decide based on majority opinion. Your input must reflect substantial agreement of all members.

---

    3.   Try to follow these guidelines in order to reach consensus:
          a.   To make decisions by consensus requires an atmosphere of openness where all members have an opportunity to be heard and to influence the ultimate outcome.
          b.   Each member should be able to present ideas without being criticized.
          c.   Opposing views should be solicited and creative solutions encouraged.
          d.   The emphasis is on finding the best solution instead of on getting one's way.
    4.   Select one member as both leader and recorder to help get the process underway. You might consider having each member contribute two ideas to the project, then rank-order each of the suggestions after discussing the merits and demerits of each.
    5.   Report your results back to the larger group.
    6.   The entire class can then pursue the following questions:
          a.   How did your experience with consensus decision making compare with past decision-making activities in which you have been involved?
          b.   What are some barriers to using a consensus model of decision making?
          c.   What are the advantages to this method of making decisions?

Exercise 3.4: Parliamentary Procedure

A. Brief description:
    This exercise is designed to familiarize you with the terminology and procedure used in groups operating under *Robert's Rules of Order*. The example given is of a social work student organization. Various roles are identified. Those playing the roles read the appropriate portions of the transcript.
B. Objectives:
    You will be able to:
    1.   Recognize and use appropriate motions to conduct the business of an organization.
    2.   Understand what steps are needed to bring a matter up for discussion and vote by any group.
C. Procedure:
    1.   The instructor will assign specific roles to individual students (there are a total of eleven roles, plus those of members-at-large). Members-at-large will vote on all issues before the group.

2. The roles are: president, vice president, treasurer, secretary, chair of the activities committee, chair of the faculty relations committee, chair of the social action committee, and members 1, 2, 3, and 4.
3. Each person playing a role will read his or her script from the transcript of the meeting. It is important to stay alert and recognize your part.
4. Feel free at any point to ask the instructor about the purpose or meaning of any particular motion.
5. At the end of the role play, the class can discuss the following questions:
   a. Why is there such a seemingly rigid set of steps to be followed in parliamentary procedure (such as making a motion, seconding it, debating, and voting on it)?
   b. What steps in this process appear most confusing to you?
   c. Why does *Robert's Rules of Order* prevent a person who voted with the losing side from asking to have the matter reconsidered later?

Parliamentary Procedure Role Play
The Social Work Student Organization

President: The meeting of the Social Work Student Organization is called to order. The minutes of the April 1st meeting have been distributed. Is there a motion for approval?

Vice President: I move approval of the minutes of the April 1st meeting.

President: Is there a second?

Chair of Social Action Committee: I second the motion.

President: Is there any discussion?

Chair of Faculty Relations Committee: I think my motion last time was to ask the faculty to provide three spots on the advisory board for student representatives, not four as the minutes show.

Secretary: I think she's right. That appears to be a typo. It should have been three, not four.

President: Are there any more changes? If not, I'll ask for a vote to approve the minutes. All in favor of approving the minutes with the change noted, please say Aye.

All: Aye.

President: All opposed, please say no. The motion passes.

President: May we have the Treasurer's report, please.

Treasurer: My report has also been distributed. It shows a balance of $240.04 after our car smash fund-raiser. We only had one bill and that was dry cleaning to get the oil out of Professor Mower's sports coat from the car smash. He's such a good sport, he didn't even complain about the rest of his clothes. Are there any questions about the Treasurer's report?

President: A motion to accept the Treasurer's report is in order.

Member 1: I move to accept the Treasurer's report.

Member 2: I second the motion.

President: All in favor of the motion, please say Aye.

All: Aye.

President: All opposed?

President: The motion passes unanimously.

President: Does the Activity Committee have a report?

Chair of Activities Committee: Thank you. Yes, we do. The committee has organized the second Urban Plunge trip for the 29th of the month. We will be visiting Metropolis and spending the weekend in a homeless shelter. We will be leaving campus Friday at noon, working in the shelter Saturday and Sunday, and returning to campus Monday morning. We have room for two more people in the van. The cost is $25 plus a share of the gas. This looks like a good opportunity to learn more about the homeless first hand, and to talk to social workers from other agencies. Any questions?

Secretary: I'd like to move that our organization pay for the gas costs since we are sponsoring this activity.

President: It has been moved that SWSO pay for the gas for this trip. Is there a second?

Member 1: I second the motion.

President: Any discussion

Treasurer: I'd like to amend the motion to set a limit of $50 on the gas costs.

President: Is there a second? I don't hear a second so the amendment dies. Is there any further discussion on the original motion? Hearing none, all in favor of the motion, please say Aye.

All but Treasurer: Aye.

President: All opposed, say no.

Treasurer: No.

President: The motion carries. The Activities Committee will let the Treasurer know what the gas costs and he will reimburse you.

President: I believe the Social Action Committee has a report.

Chair of Social Action Committee: Yes, we do. We are in the final stages of planning for our social action day. At present, we have a speaker from the Gay and Lesbian Organization speaking on the latest campus problems faced by their members; another speaker from the Action Coalition, who will talk about how student organizations can join together to bring about social change; and a representative from the Chippewa Tribe, who will speak on tribal rights and history.

We have also planned a letter-writing to get the local paper and media to focus their attention on the *Cinco de Mayo* Chicano festival. We're working with the Chicano Student Organization on this project. Are there any questions?

President: Thanks for your report.

President: Is there any other old business?

Vice President: I move we disband the Social Action Committee. They're getting too radical for me.

President: You're out of order, Orrin, we already discussed and voted on that matter last time.

Vice President: I move to reconsider our previous decision. *Chair of Activities Committee:* Point of order.

President: What is your point of order?

Chair of Activities Committee: Orrin voted with the losing side on that previous vote. He is not permitted to move for reconsideration. Only a person who voted on the winning side can make such a motion.

President: You are correct. Again, Orrin, your motion is out of order. Is there any new business?

Member 2: I move that we hold an end-of-year party, like last year.

Member 1: I second the motion.

President: It's been moved and seconded to have an end-of-year party. Is there discussion?

Member 3: Given the time of day, I move we refer this motion to the Activities Committee and ask them to report by our next meeting.

Member 4: I second the motion.

President: All in favor of referring the party idea to the Activities Committee say Aye.

All: Aye.

President: All opposed, say no.

President: The Ayes have it. This matter is referred to the Activities Committee. If there is no other business to come before us, I declare the meeting adjourned.

Chapter 4
Macro Practice Skills: Working with Organizations and Communities

I. **Introduction**

II. **Defining Macro Practice**

    A.   Designed to improve or modify some aspect of society

    B.   Concerned with developing new resources when what clients need is unavailable

    C.   Helping clients get their due rights

    D.   Targets the system to determine where and how changes need to be made

    E.   Requires the use of advocacy

    F.   Occurs frequently in an organizational context

III. **The Organizational Context of Social Work Practice**

    A.   *Highlight 4.1: When the Agency You Work For Is Part of the Problem*

    B.   Professional-Organizational Conflicts

    C.   Limitations and Risk Assessment

    D.   *Critical Thinking Question 4.1*

IV. **Theoretical Base for Organizational and Community Change**

    A.   Organizational Theory—Concerned with how organizations function, what improves or impairs the ability of an organization to accomplish its mission, and what motivates people to work toward organizational goals

        1.   Early theorists believed that bureaucratic organizations were considered to be one of the most efficient and effective mechanisms for producing goods, delivering services, and making decisions

        2.   Subsequent studies of organizations left little doubt that bureaucracies had their own problems

            a.   Rigidity frustrated both employees and customers/clients

            b.   Specialization often led to narrowness of interests and stifled the ability of employees to be creative

          c.   Reward structures often resulted in employees being promoted beyond their level of competence (the Peter Principle)

          d.   Social relationships among employees often circumvented or limited the effectiveness of organizational policies

    3.   A variety of theories have been developed about how best to achieve organizational goals

B.   Community Theory—Two primary components: the nature of communities and social work practice within communities

    1.   Community—A combination of social units and systems that perform the major social functions important to the locality

    2.   Social functions of communities

          a.   Production, distribution, and consumption of goods and services

          b.   Socialization—The process by which knowledge, values, beliefs, and behaviors are taught to members of the community

          c.   Social control—The community's efforts to make sure members live within the norms of the community

          d.   Social participation—The involvement of community members in various activities designed to enhance a sense of belonging

          e.   Mutual support—Involves caring for the sick, helping the poor or homeless, and providing a variety of health and human services

    3.   *Highlight 4.2: Community Organization: The Traditional Focus on the Community in Macro Practice*

          a.   Community organization—Historically has been the term used to refer to macro practice in social work

          b.   Community—A group of individuals or families that share certain values, services, institutions, interests, or geographical proximity

          c.   Concepts inherent in Barker's and the Warrens' definitions of community

               1)   Both concern a group of people related in terms of locality

               2)   The people also have some interests or functions in common

        3)   Because of their common locality, functions, and/or interests, people in the community interact together on some level, or at least have the potential to interact

        4)   Can be organized so that its citizens can participate together and solve their mutual problems or improve their overall quality of life

    d.   Three methods of community organization in which, historically, social workers have been engaged

        1)   Social action—Can be used to remedy imbalances of power and to advocate on behalf of communities of people

        2)   Social planning—A technical process of problem solving regarding substantive social problems (the emphasis is to call in experts or consultants to work with designated community leaders)

        3)   Locality development—Community change pursued through broad participation of a wide spectrum of people at the local community level

  4.   Social work practice in the community—Includes social reform, social action, cause advocacy, case advocacy

C.   Social Reform—The development and improvement of social conditions, by actively pursuing a legislative agenda designed to improve client services and meet large-scale problems with large-scale programs

D.   Social Action—Compared to social reform which focuses on doing good *for* the client, social action more often values doing good *with* the client

  1.   Advocacy around specific populations and issues such as the homeless and food and hunger

  2.   Working in local and national elections to elect sympathetic representatives and to support new programs designed to combat large-scale problems

  3.   Networking with other groups pursuing a similar agenda

E.   Cause Advocacy—Advocate on behalf of an issue of overriding importance to a *group* of clients; also called class advocacy

F.   Case Advocacy—Advocate on behalf of a single case

V. Micro Skills for Organizational and Community Change

A.   Warmth, empathy, and genuineness are important in organizational and community change

B.   *Highlight 4.3: Social Workers Can Help Improve Delivery of Services*

VI.   Mezzo Skills for Organizational and Community Change

    A.   *Highlight 4.4: Saving a Community: A Task Group at Work*

    B.   Conflict Resolution

    C.   Developing Win-Win Outcomes

    D.   Team Building

    E.   Public Speaking

    F.   Consultation

    G.   Coordination

VII.   Macro Skills for Organizational and Community Change

    A.   Evaluating Outcomes

        1.   Practice evaluation—Focus on the effectiveness or results of what individual social workers do. It may take the form of single subject designs, task achievement scaling, client satisfaction surveys, or goal attainment scaling (also called goal accomplishment)

        2.   Program evaluation—Focus on the effectiveness and results of entire programs. It might include needs assessments, process analysis, outcome analysis, and cost-effectiveness analysis

    B.   Fund-Raising

        1.   Individual donors

        2.   Corporate donors

        3.   Foundations

        4.   Membership dues

        5.   Benefits

    C.   Budgeting

        1.   Line-item budgets—Statement of expenditures for a designated period of time, usually one year, where each cost item is noted on a separate line

            a.   Depicts how money will be spent but tells little about services the agency offers

            b.   Many social agencies use this method

2.   Program budgets—List expenditures broken down according to programs the agency provides (also known as functional budgets)

        a.   Uses same structure as line-item and also identifies functions; therefore; allowing the cost of each program to be identified

        b.   A disadvantage is that it relies on estimates of certain items

3.   *Table 4.1: Comparison of Line-Item and Program Budgets*

4.   Incremental budgets—Agency's budget from last year is used as a starting point for this year's budget

5.   *Critical Thinking Question 4.2*

D.   Negotiating—A process in which at least two individuals participate in a face-to-face interaction in order to reach a mutually acceptable decision (sometimes called bargaining)

        1.   Guidelines for effective negotiation

            a.   Separate the problem from the people involved

            b.   Direct attention to the mutual interests of both parties and not to the positions they are taking

            c.   Devise new options that benefit both sides

            d.   Save the most difficult issues for last; however, all issues need to be placed on the table at the beginning of the brainstorming session

            e.   If needed, you can have a third party suggest a compromise or agree to use some objective criteria to decide an issue

E.   Mediating—Both parties meet with a third party who serves as an impartial referee or peacemaker to resolve disputes between opposing parties

        1.   Mediation has grown as an approach used by social workers spurred by state legislation that permits alternative ways of resolving disputes

        2.   Social workers may be involved in mediating between clients and such institutions as schools, social agencies, and government agencies

F.   Influencing Decision Makers

        1.   Petitioning—Collecting signatures on a document asking an organization or person to act in a particular manner

            a.   Petition signatures are somewhat easy to obtain and, therefore, not as effective as other methods

            b.   *Highlight 4.5: Petitioning Works*

2.   Working with the media

    a.   Reach out to media

    b.   Build contacts within the media

    c.   Be certain you are authorized to speak for an organization or agency

    d.   Provide easy access for media representatives to contact you

    e.   Learn necessary timelines for all media

    f.   Do not play favorites

    g.   If media makes a mistake, consider your reactions with care

    h.   Thank the media representatives for their efforts and express satisfaction with the results

    i.   If message doesn't get reported, thank the reporters for their effort and indicate willingness to work with them again

3.   Media Releases

    a.   Use the five W's: Who, What, When, Where, and Why

    b.   First paragraph should include crucial information

    c.   Follow up with a phone call

    d.   *Figure 4.1: Using the Media: An Example of a News Release*

4.   Educating

5.   Persuading

6.   Confrontation—The act of challenging another, usually in a face-to-face meeting

    a.   Action system—The people and resources in the community with which the social worker deals to achieve desired changes

    b.   Target system—The individual, group, or community to be changed or influenced to achieve the social work goals

    c.   Two most difficult forms of confrontation are legal action and public embarrassment

    d.   Approach most likely to raise potential ethical concerns for social workers

e.   *Highlight 4.6: Embarrassing a Landlord*

f.   *Critical Thinking Question 4.3*

7.   Collaborating—Procedure in which two or more persons work together to serve a given client

   a.   Collaborative strategies

      1)   Supply facts about the actual problem

      2)   Offer options for resolving the problem

      3)   Ask permission to try a solution on a trial basis

      4)   Request permission to set up a committee to consider the problem and possible alternatives

      5)   Request increased opportunities for target and action (or client) systems to get together and share interests

      6)   Appeal to the values, ethics, or scruples of the target system

      7)   Convince the target system through rational debate and discussion

      8)   Identify adverse outcomes that arise from continuation of the present situation

   b.   Collaborative strategies should be attempted before using adversarial approaches to problem solving

8.   Letter writing

   a.   Can be effective in certain situations

   b.   *Highlight 4.7: Letter Writing Strategies*

G.   Needs Assessment—Both a product and a process that includes a systematic gathering of data designed to identify the extent and nature of a social problem or condition, the resources available to deal with the problem, and potential obstacles and solutions to an intervention

   1.   Key informant approach—Asks especially knowledgeable individuals about the needs of a given community

   2.   Community forum approach—Assumes that the general public also has knowledge of a community's needs

   3.   Rates-under-treatment approach—Counts the people who seek and receive a given service to estimate the actual need in a community

4.   Social indicators approach—Uses information in existing public records, such as the census, to estimate the actual need for a service

5.   Field study—Relies on gathering actual data in the community through interviews and observation

H.   Planning

    1.   Program Evaluation and Review Technique (PERT)

        a.   Four steps that must be undertaken in PERT

            1)   Identify major tasks to be accomplished

            2)   Place tasks in sequential order

            3)   Determine probable time needed for completion of each step

            4)   Identify those responsible for completing each task

        b.   *Figure 4.2: A Sample Program Evaluation and Review Technique (PERT) Chart*

I.   Working with Coalitions

    1.   Coalition—A collection of different groups or organizations designed to work toward a common goal

    2.   The types of groups that form a coalition may be similar or diverse

    3.   Coalitions may be ongoing or developed to respond to a specific problem

    4.   Keeping every coalition member informed of what is happening is important

VIII.   Worker Roles in Organizational and Community Change

A.   Initiator—The person or persons who call attention to an issue

B.   Negotiator—Represents organization with other groups

C.   Advocate—Speaks out and acts on behalf of client

D.   Spokesperson—Authorized to speak on behalf of others

E.   Organizer—Coordinates individuals or groups to pursue some designated function(s)

F.   Mediator—Neutral person who resolves disagreement among various systems in conflict

G.   Consultant—Provides advice, suggestions, or ideas for another person, group, or organization

IX.   **Generalist Intervention Model (GIM) in Macro Practice**

   A.   Engagement

   B.   Assessment

   C.   Planning

   D.   Implementation

   E.   Evaluation

EXPERIENTIAL EXERCISES AND SIMULATIONS

The three exercises for this chapter are designed to accomplish two purposes. One is to provide experience in two of the methods used to influence decision makers: using the media and letter writing. The second purpose is to help identify the primary methods workers use in pursuing organizational and community change.

Exercise 4.1: Preparing a Press Release

A.   Brief description:
      In this exercise, you will prepare a press release about the opening of a new agency. You will work on this as a task group.
B.   Objectives:
      You will be able to:
      1.   Develop a news release suitable for dissemination to newspapers, radio, or television.
      2.   Identify the key items that should appear in every news release.
C.   Procedure:
      1.   There are a number of reasons why you might write a news release for your agency. These include announcement of a new service provided by the agency, the need to publicize an existing program, or a desire to recruit volunteers or foster parents. Working with and using the news media to publicize events, activities, and perspectives is an essential skill. News releases are one of the easiest and simplest ways to keep the media informed about your agency or activity. As in any news article, basic information is expected by the reader. This includes such items as who, what, where, why, when, and how.
      2.   Break down into work groups of two or three persons.
      3.   Read the following example of an agency news release. It was written to publicize the creation of a new program and provides information about services provided, hours of operation, and contact persons.

> Rural Mental Health Clinic
> 12 East North Street
> East North Overshoe, Vermont
> 802/658-0371
>
> For Immediate Release:
>
> Drug and Alcohol Program a First in State
>
> EAST NORTH OVERSHOE, VT—December 28, 2004, The Rural Mental Health Clinic has added a drug and alcohol program to its new service center in East North Overshoe.
> According to the Director, Jim Beam, the new program is the first in the state to offer both inpatient and outpatient service to chemically addicted individuals. The clinic has added three staff members and will be hosting an open house on Friday, January 14, from 1:00-3:00 p.m. The office for the new program is at 232 Spring Street.
>
> For further information, contact Jim Beam at 658-0371 or 658-9981.

4. Now prepare your own news release. Put yourself in the following role:

> **Scenario**
> You are the director of a new agency established to coordinate services to families in Clearwater City. Your agency was set up through the cooperative efforts of four existing agencies which felt they could better serve families in need by pooling their resources. You want the community to know about your agency and about the fact that several agencies acted cooperatively to launch this program. You also want them to know that taxpayers' money is being used in a positive fashion.
> There is only one newspaper in your city, the *Daily Planet*, and no other print media. There is a radio station that plays funeral dirges all day and does not have any news programs. Their only public service announcements cover the openings of new mortuaries and the daily obituaries. Plan your news release to convey information succinctly and in an interesting manner.

5. In the release, remember to include the following elements:
    a. *Who* (person or agency) is this news release about?
    b. *What* is important enough to deserve a news article?
    c. *When* did or will this event occur?
    d. *Where* or in what location did this event occur?
    e. *Why* is this being brought to the attention of the public?
    f. *How* did this event occur?
    The entire release should be no longer than one page. Take about 20 minutes to write it. Remember that, although this release will be handwritten for the purposes of this assignment, a real release would be typewritten, double-spaced, with margins of at least 1 ½ inches on each side of the page.

6. After you complete your release, your instructor may ask you to share what you've written with the entire class. The class may address the following questions:
   a. What are the similarities among the various releases?
   b. What are the differences?
   c. What did you find most difficult about writing the release?
   d. Describe in your own words how such a news release might benefit the agency for which you work.

Exercise 4.2: Letter Writing

A. Brief description:
There are many ways to influence decision makers. One method is to write to them, expressing your opinions and ideas. This exercise will give you practice in writing a business letter.

B. Objectives:
You will be able to:
1. Prepare a business letter that contains appropriate items such as the correct opening, closing, presentation of ideas, etc.
2. Recognize inappropriate format in a business letter.

C. Procedure:
1. Review the instructions for writing a letter shown below. They are taken from Highlight 4.7 in the text.

Letter Writing Strategies
To be effective, letters:
a. Are planned carefully, revised, polished, and proofread;
b. Include letterhead (with address), date, salutation (Dear ___), body, complimentary close (Sincerely), and both typed and written signature;
c. Are businesslike and pleasant;
d. Are brief (preferably one page) and discuss only one topic;
e. Open with a positive comment;
f. Are factual, and simply written;
g. Should have perfect grammar and spelling; and
h. Request a response.

Letters which are less likely to be effective include those that appear identical, those copied out of newspaper advertisements, or clearly mass-produced letters (e.g., duplicated copies instead of original). Letters which attack the reader are less likely to work and may backfire. Some people advocate handwritten letters, but the advantages of a clear, typed message outweigh the advantages of a handwritten communication.

If letters are to be mass-produced, as might be desired when a group is trying to sway the reader, at least vary the letters so that they don't appear identical. Written letters are helpful in certain situations and help create a record of communication with the decision-maker. They should be used as an adjunct to, and not instead of, other more personal forms of contact. Person-to-person communication is still superior to written messages as a means of influencing other people.

---

2. Now read the business letter shown below. In a number of ways, it is very poorly constructed.

January 31, 2005

Mr. Raul Prenner
Department of Aging
1492 Columbus Way
Santa Maria, NY 00923

Dear Mr. Prenner:

You've got your nerve telling my client she isn't eligible for your program. I don't know how you get off with your attitude. It's really poor. My client and I think you need to change your policy so that people like my client can use your agency.

I think we need to get together to talk about your silly policies at my earliest convenience. Please call my office and arrange for an appointment immediately.

Yours Truly,

Edgar J. Hoover
Social Worker

---

3. List the things that are wrong with this letter. This may include the tone of the letter and the absence of important information.

4. Now rewrite this letter using the same general information contained in the poorly written letter. This time, use your own name and address. Be careful to conform to the standards for effectiveness described.

5. After completing the letters, the entire class can discuss the results. Address the following questions.
   a. In what specific ways was the original letter poorly written?
   b. In what specific ways could the original letter be improved?
   c. What things were the most difficult about writing your own letter?
   d. What might be some of the reasons for writing letters in social work practice?

Exercise 4.3: Connecting Roles and Responsibilities

A. Brief description:
Social workers may assume many roles in organizational and community change. Roles involve expectations regarding how you should behave and what you wish to accomplish. Learning these roles is not always easy. This exercise is designed to assist you in understanding and distinguishing the various roles that you may be called upon to play.

B. Objectives:
You will be able to:
   1. Correctly identify several roles used by social workers pursuing organizational or community change.
   2. Recognize major responsibilities associated with each of these roles.

C. Procedure:
1. Review the two columns shown below. In one column are the role titles frequently associated with change efforts in communities and organizations. In the second column are descriptions of various roles.

Role Titles	Role Descriptions
A. Initiator	1. Decides what the client is entitled to and what is keeping the client from receiving what she needs. Requires worker to assess an adversary's strengths and weaknesses.
B. Negotiator	2. Represents an organization or group trying to gain something from another group. Seeks win-win situations and a middle ground that both sides can accept.
C. Advocate	3. Calls attention to an issue such as a problem existing in the community, an unmet need, or a situation to be improved.
D. Spokesperson	4. Helps two sides work out a compromise. The role player is neutral, not siding with either party. One task involves ensuring that both sides understand the other's positions.
E. Organizer	5. Provides advice, suggestions, or ideas to another person, group, or organization. Two characteristics are important: knowing more than the person being helped; and the ability to see her advice ignored without getting personally involved or hurt.
F. Mediator	6. Presents an organization's views to others without coloring them with his or her own opinions.
G. Consultant	7. Creates groups of people who share a similar concern. Tasks include developing the leadership potential of others, stimulating others to act, and identifying targets for change.

2. Match the Role Titles with the Role Descriptions.
3. Your instructor will supply you with the correct answers. Compare your answers with the correct ones.
4. Discuss the following questions with the entire class:
    a. What roles were the most difficult for you to understand?
    b. Describe possible agency situations where each role might be used.
    c. What are examples of practice situations in which workers might assume more than one role?
    d. Are there situations in which workers might have to assume roles that conflict with each other? If so, how might these roles conflict?

Chapter 5
Engagement and Assessment in Generalist Practice

I.   **Introduction**

II. **Engagement**

    A.   Greeting the Client

    B.   Demonstrating Effective Attending Skills

        1.   Listen carefully

        2.   Make eye contact—Be aware of cultural differences

        3.   Focus on client thoughts and feelings—Use open-ended questions

        4.   Use silence as necessary

        5.   Take notes of information you are unlikely to remember

    C.   Discussing Agency Services and Client Expectations

    D.   Deciding If the Agency and Worker Can Help

    E.   Offering Agency and Worker Services to the Client

    F.   Orienting the Client to the Helping Process

        1.   Client needs to know the rules and conditions

        2.   Negotiate with clients as to frequency of sessions, time and place, and total number of sessions

    G.   Completing Required Paperwork

III. **Assessment**

    A.   Assessment—Acquiring an understanding of a problem, what causes it, and what can be changed to minimize or resolve it

    B.   Four perspectives

        1.   Assess individuals and families considering such factors as transactions between and among clients, family members, friends, and other systems in the immediate environment

        2.   Focusing on functioning at different points in the life cycle

3.   Specific problems can be the focus

4.   The techniques and assessment methods used by social workers run the gamut from micro to mezzo to macro situations

C.   *Highlight 5.1: The Difference Between Diagnosis and Assessment*

    1.   From the 1920s to the 1960s, most social work programs used a medical model to understand human behavior and human problems

    2.   Medical model

        a.   Views clients as patients

        b.   Diagnosis—Seeking causes of a patient's problems and then providing treatment

    3.   In the 1960s, environmental factors were shown to be *at least* as important in causing a client's problems as internal factors, if not more. Attention shifted from individual pathology to problems in the client's environment

    4.   Social workers began to *assess* problems by viewing clients in their situations instead of *diagnosing* what was wrong with the clients themselves

    5.   Assessment differs from diagnosis in at least four major ways

        a.   Environmental surroundings (mezzo and macro aspects) are considered as important as the micro aspects when trying to understand any problem situation

        b.   Since problems may exist outside of the client, outside systems can become targets of change

        c.   Using the medical model, a client is diagnosed as having a problem; assessment in generalist practice emphasizes that practitioners work *with*, not *on*, clients

        d.   Diagnosis focuses on pathology; assessment targets not only the client's problems but also the client's strengths

D.   How to Approach Assessment

    1.   Micro

    2.   Mezzo

    3.   Macro

    4.   Human diversity

5.   Each dimension requires focus on clients' problems and needs and on clients' strengths

6.   *Figure 5.1: Assessment in the Generalist Intervention Model (GIM)*

7.   Five Major Points

      a.   Involvement of client is absolutely essential

      b.   Assessment always involves making judgments

      c.   Highlighting strengths is paramount

      d.   A single, clear definition of the problem may not exist

      e.   Assessment is a continuous activity

8.   *Figure 5.2: Assessment in Planned Change Is an Ongoing Process*

9.   Assessment involves critical thinking skills and should reflect best practice in social work

10.   *Critical Thinking Question 5.1*

E.   Goals of Assessment

1.   Articulate a clear statement of the need, problem, or situation

2.   Recognize the strengths, assets, skills, and abilities of clients

3.   Formulate a clear description of the client system

4.   Understand the client system's interactions with other systems

5.   Identify any missing information that is important

6.   Put all the information together

F.   Assessment From a Micro Practice Perspective

1.   Defining problems and issues

      a.   Recognize the client's unmet needs

      b.   Identify the barriers that prevent the client's needs from being fulfilled

      c.   Determine the capacities, strengths, resources, and motivations that are present in the client and/or environment

2. Types of problems

    a. Interpersonal conflict—Involves individuals having difficulty relating to each other

    b. Dissatisfaction in social relations—Involves inability to get as close to others as he or she would like, and/or lack of assertiveness

    c. Problems with formal organizations—Involves feeling they are not getting the resources they need

    d. Difficulties in role performance—Can best be distinguished from interpersonal conflict by the fact that role performance is more one sided

        1) Role—A culturally expected behavior pattern that characterizes people having a particular position and status in society

        2) Role performance involves family, student, employee, patient roles, etc.

    e. Problems of social transition—Difficulty dealing with some major change in their lives

    f. Psychological and behavioral problems—Emotional upheavals and inappropriate, self-defeating, criminal, or uncontrollable behavior

    g. Inadequate resources—Deprivations of basic needs

    h. Problems in decision making—Emotional dilemmas may create emotional turmoil and they see no positive solution

    i. Cultural and religious conflicts—Involve discrimination and oppression by majority groups

    j. Prioritizing problems—The number of potential problems may seem overwhelming and they need help in deciding which problem to work on first, second, etc.

3. Empowerment: Identifying Clients' Strengths

    a. Family and friends

    b. Education and employment background

    c. Problem-solving and decision-making skills

    d. Personal qualities and characteristics

    e. Physical and financial resources

f.   Attitudes and perspectives

g.   Religiosity and spirituality

h.   Miscellaneous other strengths

4.   Resistance in Assessment

a.   An important concept in assessment is to start where the client is

b.   *Critical Thinking Question 5.2*

5.   Which Problem Should You Work On?

a.   Client must recognize that the problem exists

b.   Problems should be clearly defined

c.   You and client should realistically be able to do something to remedy the problem

d.   Partialization—Breaking down a problem or series of problems into manageable parts

e.   Problems should be ordered in terms of their priority to the client

f.   *Highlight 5.2: Examples of Questions You Can Ask During Assessment*

6.   Gathering Information: Sources of Assessment Data

a.   Agency forms completed by client

b.   Responses by clients to your questions during interview

c.   Nonverbal behavior of client

d.   Client's interactions with other people

e.   Outside sources

f.   Psychological or other testing

g.   Your own interactions with client

7.   Assessment Instruments

   a.   Diagnostic and Statistical Manual (DSM)

      1)   Five major axes:

         a)   Clinical disorders and conditions not directly attributable to a mental disorder

         b)   Personality disorders

         c)   Physical conditions

         d)   Environmental and psychosocial problems

         e)   Global assessment of overall level of functioning

      2)   Four reasons why DSM is relevant to social workers

         a)   Provides means for variety of professionals to communicate with each other

         b)   Helpful in evaluating and treating clients with mental disorders

         c)   Utility in teaching about mental disorders

         d)   Provides better opportunities to do research on mental disorders

      3)   Reasons to be wary of using DSM

         a)   It only describes particular conditions

         b)   There can be some tendency to focus on individual pathology instead of client interactions with the environment

         c)   Imperfections in its categories

         d)   It is primarily focused on deficits, and is not a strength-based assessment tool, and gives little help in identifying client resources

   b.   Assessing Assertiveness

      1)   Rathus Assertiveness Schedule (RAS)—An instrument composed of 30 items that measure an individual's assertiveness

      2)   *Figure 5.3: The Rathus Assertiveness Schedule (RAS)*

c.   Assessing alcohol and other drug abuse

        1)   The National Institute on Alcohol Abuse and Alcoholism (2000) reports that alcohol-related problems include economic losses resulting from time off work owing to alcohol-related illness and injury, disruption of family and social relationships, emotional problems, impact on perceived health, violence and aggression, and legal problems

        2)   *Figure 5.4: College Alcohol Problems Scale-Revised*

G.   Family Assessment

    1.   Family—A primary group whose members assume certain obligations for each other and generally share common residences

    2.   Choosing to Work with Families

    3.   Family Assessment Skills

        a.   Family communication

        b.   Family structure—Involves the organization of relationships and patterns of interaction within the family

            1)   Assessment of five dimensions of family structure

                a)   Functioning as a system that is intact with appropriate boundaries and subsystems

                b)   Family norms

                c)   Family roles

                d)   Appropriate balance of power

                e)   Intergenerational aspects and the impact of family history upon current family functioning

        c.   Life-cycle adjustments

        d.   Impacts of the social environment

        e.   Key areas of family conflict

    4.   Family Relationships

        a.   Eco-map—Provides a graphic representation of the family's ecological system, and depicts family membership and relationships

        b.   *Figure 5.5: Eco-Map*

c. Genogram—Provides a means of depicting a family from one generation to the next, and provides a chronological picture of the family noting important events, additions and loses to the family, communication and relationship patterns, and occupational or work connections

d. *Figure 5.6: Genogram*

5. Home Visits

    a. Workers' reactions

        1) The shocking nature of what people must endure as a result of their impoverished environments or their state of physical or mental health

        2) Address own perceptions and reactions

        3) Be behaviorally or descriptively specific regarding what is considered dirty and what is not

        4) Be aware of the family environment

    b. Scheduling home visits

        1) Home visits should be at a time as convenient as possible for family members

        2) Home visits can be scheduled by phone

    c. Taking care of your own safety

        1) Suggestions for volatile situations

            a) Remain outwardly calm regardless of how you feel inside

            b) Remain respectful toward the individual who is threatening

            c) Continue to face the aggressor and do not turn away from them

            d) Use a calm voice in talking with the individual

            e) If the client is standing, ask them to sit down to talk with you

            f) Avoid defensiveness or taking the person's anger personally

g)   Be honest in what you say and do not try to promise something that you cannot deliver

h)   Use appropriate empathy toward the individual's feelings

i)   If de-escalation is not working, ask the person to stop or remove yourself from the situation

2)   *Highlight 5.3: Be Alert, Streetwise, and Safe*

     a)   Elementary street sense

     b)   Walking smart

     c)   Elevator sense

     d)   Defensive driving

     e)   Tips for buses

     f)   If you are threatened

H.   Assessment in Mezzo Practice: Assessing Groups

     1.   Potential sponsorship

     2.   Who should be members of the group?

         a.   *Highlight 5.4: Sociograms*

             1)   Sociometry—Involves asking children questions about their relationships and feelings toward other people

             2)   Sociograms—Extremely useful for assessing children's interactional patterns, such as for those who have low self-esteem and difficulty relating to peers

         b.   Selection criteria for treatment group membership

             1)   Motivation

             2)   Group purpose

             3)   Common communication skills

             4)   Group advantages versus disadvantages

        c.   Gathering information about potential treatment group members

             1)   Interviews with potential group members prior to beginning the group

             2)   Use of self-assessments

             3)   Those who referred a client to the group

        d.   Selection criteria for task group membership

             1)   Individual interests

             2)   Expertise

             3)   Homogeneity versus heterogeneity

             4)   Prestige in the community

             5)   Relationship with sponsoring agency

             6)   Diversity and demographic characteristics

             7)   Recruiting task group members

        e.   Ongoing group assessment

        f.   Ongoing assessment in treatment groups

             1)   Individual self-rating questionnaires

             2)   Clients may keep diaries of daily events

             3)   Charting their improvements

             4)   Role-playing

             5)   Bring in outside observers

I.   Assessment in Macro Practice

    1.   Assessment of community needs

        a.   Employing participatory research in a community assessment

        b.   Information

        c.   Resources available

        d.   Community attitudes

2.   An example of a community assessment—a five-step process

     a.   Step 1: Exploring the nature of the neighborhood or community

           1)   How people in the neighborhood function

           2)   Local centers of government

           3)   Maps

           4)   Telephone books

           5)   Newspapers

     b.   Step 2: Getting to know the area and its residents

           1)   Getting a general impression of the community is probably the most useful thing to do at this point

           2)   Establish the community's boundaries in your own mind

     c.   Step 3: Identifying the community's strengths

           1)   Healthy businesses

           2)   Homes kept in good repair

           3)   Social clubs and organizations

           4)   Churches

           5)   Friendly interaction with community residents

     d.   Step 4: Talking to people in the community

           1)   Identify major community figures

           2)   The elementary school principal

           3)   Community leaders

           4)   Vocal community members

           5)   Obtain information about a broad cross section of the community

           6)   Suggestions for interviewing persons in the community

                 a)   Take time for small talk

                 b)   Provide your interviewee with a clear definition of your purpose

                 c)   Clearly explain to your interviewee what community of people or neighborhood you are interested in

          d)   Ask interviewee for suggestions about others you should talk to

          e)   Make sure your interviewee feels comfortable with you by using your micro practice skills

          f)   Ask interviewee's opinion about what might happen

          g)   Make sure the interviewee has the opportunity to share opinions and to conclude the interview

    e.   Step 5: Gather other information

       1)   Databases

       2)   Public libraries

       3)   Internet

          a)   Economic Success Clearinghouses (ESC): www.financeproject.org/irc/win.asp

          b)   The Community Tool Box: http://ctb.ku.edu

3.   *Highlight 5.5: A Format for Analyzing a Community or Neighborhood*

    a.   Demographic factors

    b.   Economic factors

    c.   Communication systems

    d.   Social service organizations

    e.   Civic/service organizations

    f.   Health and medical services

4.   *Critical Thinking Question 5.3*

J.   Assessment, Client Empowerment, and Strengths

EXERIENTIAL EXERCISES AND SIMULATIONS

The following exercises address various aspects of engagement and assessment. Exercise 1 looks at some typical mistakes made during engagement. Exercise 2 provides a case example with which to practice the assessment process. Exercise 3 presents the opportunity to practice assessing minor personal problems. Established assessment mechanisms on assertiveness and alcoholism are employed respectively in Exercises 4 and 5. Exercises 6 and 7 provide opportunities to practice, respectively, making genograms and eco-maps. Finally, Exercise 8 provides the opportunity to do a community analysis.

Exercise 5.1: Engagement

A.   Brief description:

Working singly or as a group, students will identify problems in the engagement phase of a case example.

B.   Objectives:

You will be able to:

1.   Identify social worker errors in the engagement phase.

2.   Describe appropriate worker actions in the engagement phase.

C.   Procedure:

Read the brief vignette below. Identify at least five errors or problems on the part of the worker. Explain what the worker should have done to conduct an effective engagement.

Vignette

"Hi, Mary. I'm Derrick, your social worker here at the homeless shelter. I bet you really could use a shower and a meal." With those opening statements, Derrick Broder greeted Mary Livingston, a woman who had just sought shelter for herself and her child.

"As you probably know, we don't charge too much here and you'll be glad you came to the shelter. We help lots of people with your problems."

"Well, I don't know," said Mary. "I don't have much money."

"Don't worry about a thing, Mary. Now let's get you and your little boy a bed and a meal. In the morning, I'll have my colleague, Monica, meet with you to discuss ways you can improve your child-rearing skills, too. You'll like her."

Exercise 5.2: The Assessment Process

A.   Brief description:

Students will break up into pairs and role play as worker and client, following the prescribed assessment process.

B.   Objectives:

You will be able to:

1.   Identify the steps in the assessment process.

2.   Demonstrate a simulated case assessment.

C.   Procedure:

1.   Before beginning the exercise, review the material in the text on how to approach assessment, and on assessment from a micro practice perspective. A copy of the figure entitled "Assessment in the Generalist Intervention Model" is provided below. Follow these steps in your role play.

ASSESSMENT IN THE GENERALIST INTERVENTION MODEL

FOUNDATION FOR GENERALIST PRACTICE

KNOWLEDGE:
Fields of Practice
Practice Skills
HBSE
Research
Policy

SKILLS:
Common Generalist
  Micro
  Mezzo
  Macro

VALUES
Professional Ethics
Identification of
  Personal Values

ENGAGEMENT

ASSESSMENT

STEP 1: Identify your client.

STEP 2:
Assess the client-in-situation from the following perspectives:

STEP 3:
Cite information about client problems and needs.

STEP 4:
Identify client strengths.

MICRO:

MEZZO:

MACRO:

ASPECTS OF DIVERSITY:

2.　　Divide up into pairs. One student in each pair will role play the client and the other the worker. The worker's task is to do an assessment of an elderly client as described below. The worker's job is intake worker for Horseradish County Social Services Department.

THE CLIENT

A concerned neighbor referred Grafton, seventy-seven, to the Horseradish County Elderly Protective Services Unit. Grafton lives on his rundown family farm on the outskirts of the rural Midwestern county. The neighbor reported that twice he found Grafton had fallen while walking out to get his mail, and the elderly man lay helplessly on the ground. Both times the neighbor had to practically carry Grafton back into the house. Grafton has rheumatoid arthritis, which makes it very difficult to walk even with his two canes. Additionally, his eyesight is very poor. The neighbor also raised questions about Grafton's ability to shop and cook for himself.

Grafton's wife, Vicki, died two years ago after a long bout with intestinal cancer. Since her death, Grafton has remained isolated and alone. He has three sons. Only his oldest son, Ralph, forty-eight, lives nearby in a small town in Horseradish County. He owns a small pea canning factory. Ralph works long hours to keep his business afloat and has little time to spend with his own family, let alone with Grafton. Ralph and his second wife, Janet, have three teenage children.

Grafton's second son, Chuck, forty-two, is a pop artist in San Francisco. The youngest, Jim, thirty-five, is a worm farmer in Idaho. Both are single.

Grafton considers himself an intelligent, independent man who worked hard all of his life to make his farm successful. However, since his arthritis took a turn for the worse ten years ago, he has had to stop actively farming. He is now facing financial difficulties. He's experienced many years of little income and high health costs for both himself and his wife. He is becoming increasingly depressed at his failing health. However, he clings doggedly to the notion that he must remain on his farm. To do otherwise, he thinks to himself, would mean giving up and accepting certain death. Grafton is aware of the Happy Hunting Ground Health Care Center, the only nursing home in the area. He has sadly watched some of his friends enter it, and dreads the thought of having to go himself.

In summary, Grafton's problems include: failing health involving arthritis, poor eyesight, and intestinal distress (the last of which he does *not* like to talk about); loneliness; having few activities to keep him busy; and feeling unwanted and unimportant. Strengths include: intelligence; independence; ownership of the farm; having concerned children; and an outgoing, sociable personality. Some of Grafton's likes include: a love of reading classical novels (on bright days when his eyesight improves slightly); seeing his children; playing stud poker; and drinking beer.

3.　　The worker should follow the assessment process as described in the text. Notes should be taken as if the worker would have to write up an actual assessment report. The role-played interview should last from fifteen to twenty minutes. The worker may choose to focus on the following:

a.　　Acknowledgement of the specific problems and issues involved.

b.　　Identification of the actual pros and cons of remaining in his own home versus entering a nursing home.

c.　　Emphasis on Grafton's strengths and how he might best put them to use.

d.　　Micro, mezzo, and macro aspects of the situation and how they might be involved.

e.　　Aspects of diversity which might be important.

The worker might choose to ask questions resembling the following:

a. "What do you plan to do regarding your health problems?"

b. "What do you feel you need at this time?"

c. "Would you be interested in trying . . . ?"

d. "How could you structure your time so that you'd be more able to do what you want to?" (See the figure in the text for additional questions to ask during assessment.)

The person playing Grafton should feel free to elaborate on the information provided above and add detail. Grafton's description should be merely a starting point.

4. After fifteen to twenty minutes, your instructor will call you back for a class discussion. Focus on the following questions:

a. What information that you collected do you think would be the most helpful in planning with a client such as Grafton?

b. What information was the most difficult to obtain?

c. What were your feelings about doing the interview, either as client or worker?

d. What did you learn about assessment from participating in this role play?

Exercise 5.3: Peer Assessment

A. Brief description:

In pairs, you will take turns assessing minor problems using the model proposed in the text.

B. Objectives:

You will be able to:

1. Identify the steps in the assessment process.

2. Recognize how a personal problem can be assessed using the proposed process.

3. Demonstrate the assessment of a problem.

C. Procedure:

1. Before beginning the exercise, review the material in the text on how to approach assessment, and on assessment from a micro practice perspective. Pay particular attention to figure 5.1, which portrays a figure entitled "Assessment in the Generalist Intervention Model," as you will be asked to follow these steps. A copy of this figure is provided in Exercise 2 above.

2. Specify to yourself some minor problem you are currently experiencing. It should be nothing too personal as you will be asked to share it with a partner.

3. Divide up into pairs. Take turns portraying the person describing a problem and the person doing the assessment. Take fifteen minutes each to answer questions concerning your problem asked by the "assessor." The assessor in each instance should follow the assessment format provided in the text. She or he should take notes as if preparing to write up a report.

4. After fifteen minutes your instructor will ask you to switch roles. After another fifteen minutes your instructor will call you back for a full class discussion.

5. Address the following questions:

a. What information that you collected do you think would be the most helpful in planning a solution to the problem?

b. What information was the most difficult to obtain?

c. What were your feelings about doing the interview, either as assessor or client?

d. What did you learn about assessment from participating in this role play?

A. Brief description:
    You will complete the Rathus Assertiveness Questionnaire to evaluate your own assertiveness. You will then relate your findings to how similar assessment information may be used in actual practice.
B. Objectives:
    You will be able to:
    1. Identify some of the issues involved in assertive behavior.
    2. Relate this information to assessment in practice situations.
C. Procedure:
    1. Before beginning the exercise, review the material in the text on assessment instruments.
    2. Take the Rathus Assertiveness Schedule (RAS) printed below.[1]

The Rathus Assertiveness Schedule (RAS)

Directions: Indicate how characteristic or descriptive each of the following statements is of you by using the code given below.

+3   Very characteristic of me, extremely descriptive
+2   Rather characteristic of me, quite descriptive
+1   Somewhat characteristic of me, slightly descriptive
-1   Somewhat uncharacteristic of me, slightly nondescriptive
-2   Rather uncharacteristic of me, quite nondescriptive
-3   Very uncharacteristic of me, extremely nondescriptive

____ 1. Most people seem to be more aggressive and assertive than I am.
____ 2. I have hesitated to make or accept dates because of shyness.
____ 3. When the food served at a restaurant is not done to my satisfaction, I complain about it to the waiter or waitress.
____ 4. I am careful to avoid hurting other people's feelings, even when I feel that I have been injured.
____ 5. If a salesman has gone to considerable trouble to show me merchandise which is not quite suitable, I have a difficult time in saying "no."
____ 6. When I am asked to do something, I insist upon knowing why.
____ 7. There are times when I look for a good and vigorous argument.
____ 8. I strive to get ahead as well as most people in my position.
____ 9. To be honest, people often take advantage of me.
____ 10. I enjoy starting conversations with new acquaintances and strangers.
____ 11. I often don't know what to say to attractive persons of the opposite sex.
____ 12. I will hesitate to make phone calls to business establishments and institutions.
____ 13. I would rather apply for a job or for admission to a college by writing letters than by going through with personal interviews.
____ 14. I find it embarrassing to return merchandise.

---

[1] The Rathus Assertiveness Schedule and the accompanying scoring explanation are adapted from "Rathus Assertiveness Schedule: Normative and Factor-Analytic Data," by D.B. Hull and J.H. Hull, *Behavior Therapy*, 9 (September, 1978), p. 673. Reprinted with permission of the authors and the Association for the Advancement of Behavior Therapy, 15 W. 36th St., New York, NY 10018.

_____	15.	If a close and respected relative were annoying me, I would smother my feelings rather than express my annoyance.
_____	16.	I have avoided asking questions for fear of sounding stupid.
_____	17.	During an argument I am sometimes afraid that I will get so upset that I will shake all over.
_____	18.	If a famed and respected lecturer makes a statement which I think is incorrect, I will have the audience hear my point of view as well.
_____	19.	I avoid arguing over prices with clerks and salesmen.
_____	20.	When I have done something important or worthwhile, I manage to let others know about it.
_____	21.	I am open and frank about my feelings.
_____	22.	If someone has been spreading false and bad stories about me, I see him (her) as soon as possible to "have a talk" about it.
_____	23.	I often have a hard time saying "no."
_____	24.	I tend to bottle up my emotions rather than make a scene.
_____	25.	I complain about poor service in a restaurant and elsewhere.
_____	26.	When I am given a complaint, I sometimes just don't know what to say.
_____	27.	If a couple near me in a theater or at a lecture were conversing rather loudly, I would ask them to be quiet or to take their conversation elsewhere.
_____	28.	Anyone attempting to push ahead of me in a line is in for a good battle.
_____	29.	I am quick to express an opinion.
_____	30.	There are times when I just can't say anything.

3.   Score the RAS by following these procedures:

a.	Change the sign from positive (+) to negative (–) or from negative (–) to positive (+) for your answers to the following questions: 2, 4, 5, 9, 11, 12, 13, 14, 15, 16, 17, 19, 23, 24, 26, 30.
b.	Add up your total.

    1)   Scores of –90 to –20 means you're generally unassertive, and probably too much so. The lower your score, the less assertive you are.

    2)   Scores of –20 to +60 indicate you're within the realm of being appropriately assertive much of the time.

    3)   Scores of +60 to +90 mean you're very assertive or possibly aggressive. This is a warning category.

|--------------------------|------------------|-----------------------|
-90	-20	+60	+90
Unassertive	Assertive	Very Assertive
		Maybe Aggressive

4.   Join a class discussion that addresses the following questions:
    a.   How assertive does the RAS indicate you are?
    b.   Do you think the RAS is accurate?
    c.   What did you learn about assertiveness and assertive behavior by taking the RAS?

      d.   What did you learn about improving assertiveness and assertive behavior by taking the RAS?

      e.   For what types of client problems and needs might the RAS be used in practice?

Exercise 5.5: College Alcohol Problems Scale – Revised

A.   Brief description:

You will be asked to complete a test designed to provide a rough measure of alcoholism. You will then relate your findings as to how similar assessment information may be used in actual practice.

B.   Objectives:

You will be able to:

1.   Identify some of the issues involved in alcoholic behavior.
2.   Relate this information to assessment in practice situations.

C.   Procedure:

1.   Before beginning the exercise, review the material on assessment instruments provided in the text.
2.   Complete the following alcoholism test.

College Alcohol Problems Scale – Revised[2]

Use the scale below to rate <u>HOW OFTEN</u> you have had any of the following problems over the past year <u>as a result of drinking alcoholic beverages.</u>

1. Feeling sad, blue, or depressed

    (1) Never   (2) Yes, but not in the past year   (3) 1-2 times

    (4) 3-5 times   (5) 6-9 times   (6) 10 or more times

2. Nervousness, irritability

    (1) Never   (2) Yes, but not in the past year   (3) 1-2 times

    (4) 3-5 times   (5) 6-9 times   (6) 10 or more times

3. Caused you to feel bad about yourself

    (1) Never   (2) Yes, but not in the past year   (3) 1-2 times

    (4) 3-5 times   (5) 6-9 times   (6) 10 or more times

4. Problems with appetite or sleeping

    (1) Never   (2) Yes, but not in the past year   (3) 1-2 times

    (4) 3-5 times   (5) 6-9 times   (6) 10 or more times

---

[2] Maddock, J.E., Laforge, R. G., Rossi, J.S. & O'Hare, T. (2001). The College Alcohol Problems Scale. *Addictive Behaviors,* 26, 385-398.

5. Engaged in unplanned sexual activity

       (1) Never   (2) Yes, but not in the past year   (3) 1-2 times

       (4) 3-5 times   (5) 6-9 times   (6) 10 or more times

6. Drove under the influence

       (1) Never   (2) Yes, but not in the past year   (3) 1-2 times

       (4) 3-5 times   (5) 6-9 times   (6) 10 or more times

7. Did not use protection when engaging in sex

       (1) Never   (2) Yes, but not in the past year   (3) 1-2 times

       (4) 3-5 times   (5) 6-9 times   (6) 10 or more times

8. Illegal activities associated with drug use

       (1) Never   (2) Yes, but not in the past year   (3) 1-2 times

       (4) 3-5 times   (5) 6-9 times   (6) 10 or more times

The more questions you answered yes, the more likely you are to have a problem with alcohol.

3.   Join a class discussion that addresses the following questions:
      a.   What did you learn about alcoholism and alcoholic behavior by taking the test?
      b.   What practice situations might you envision where such a test might prove useful?
      c.   How do you think clients might react to such a test?

Exercise 5.6: Genogram

A.   Brief description:
      Working independently, students will prepare a genogram of their own families.
B.   Objectives:
      You will be able to:
      1.   Construct a genogram with appropriate symbols.
      2.   Increase your awareness of your family history.
C.   Procedure:
      Review the description and examples of a genogram contained in the text. Interview family members and other data sources to gather the information you require. Construct a genogram of your family. What can you conclude from your review of this genogram?

A. Brief description:
    Students will prepare an eco-map for themselves or a friend. This can be done in class or as an out-of-class assignment.
B. Objectives:
    You will be able to:
    1. Construct an eco-map.
    2. Increase your awareness of the information needed to construct eco-maps.
C. Procedure:
    Review the description of eco-maps in the text. Using yourself or a friend or fellow student, construct an eco-map using appropriate symbols. Describe any patterns or unusual characteristics you noted when preparing the eco-map.

A. Brief description:
    Small groups analyze the community your campus is in by following a prescribed format.
B. Objectives:
    You will be able to:
    1. Recognize the broad range of variables you need to assess in order to understand a community.
    2. Apply a format for community analysis to the community where your campus is located.
C. Procedure:
    1. Before beginning this exercise, review the material on assessment in macro practice provided in the text.
    2. Break up into small groups of four to six persons.
    3. Focusing on the community where your campus is located, take about forty-five minutes to begin answering the "Format for Analyzing a Community or Neighborhood" cited below. It addresses community characteristics and community life. Additionally, it assesses the public welfare and social service system available in the community.
        Answer the questionnaire to the best of your ability. One group member should be assigned to take notes so that results can be discussed later with the entire class.

    A Format for Analyzing a Community or Neighborhood
    Below is a format for analyzing a community. It addresses community characteristics and community life. Additionally, it assesses the public welfare and social service system available in the community. Suggestions for undergoing the process of assessing a community have already been provided. Now we will provide a format for the specific types of questions to ask and for how to organize that information.
        The questions asked in the various sections are not exhaustive nor all of equal importance. They are suggested as beginnings in a search for change. Some of them may not be useful or may not fit your particular local government. However, most can be adapted. Some may uncover issues that need more careful study than this format allows.
        One other important thing to remember is that a community is not an isolated entity. Rather, it is part of a much larger social, legal, and political system. What's decided at the national, state, and even county levels can have awesome impacts upon a community's functioning. The following format directs attention only to the community itself. It will at least, however, give you a jumping-off point for beginning to understand your community:

A Format for Analyzing a Community or Neighborhood

Understanding a neighborhood or community is an important ability for social work practitioners who work there. This often requires gathering information that helps paint a picture of the area's characteristics, its economic and political structures, communication systems, and quality of life. Below we have identified several categories of information that might be gathered in order to produce a complete community needs assessment.

Demographic factors—These include factors such as the age, gender, ethnicity, and cultural backgrounds of residents.

Economic Factors—Included here are major sources of employment, income of residents, unemployment rates, quantity and quality of housing, costs of housing, and patterns of home ownership.

Communication Systems—In this category we want to know about the major avenues of communication among community members. This includes newspapers, radio, television, and other media influences.

Social Service Organizations—It is important to know the range and quality of social services available to community residents as well as how they are funded. This can range from counseling services to financial aid, welfare, and other public assistance programs. It may also include programs such as foster care.

Civic/Service Organizations—These provide a wealth of functions for a community including financial, community building, socialization, and, sometimes, political.

Health and Medical Services—Availability of medical care, prevention services, and long term physical care is important to determine.

Gathering information on these areas should allow you to better understand the environment in which you live and work. It also will form a solid basis for efforts to intervene in the community.

---

4.   After about forty-five minutes your instructor will call you back for a large group discussion. Focus on the following questions:
   a.   What did you learn about your campus's community from doing this exercise?
   b.   What did you find out that you still don't know about the community?
   c.   What information about communities can be most helpful in serving clients?

Chapter 6
Planning in Generalist Practice

I. **Introduction**

II. **Steps in the Planning Process**

    A.   *Figure 6.1: Planning in the Generalist Intervention Model (GIM)*

    B.   Step 1: Work with Your Client(s)

    C.   *Critical Thinking Question 6.1*

    D.   Step 2: Prioritize Problems: Which Problem Should You Work On First?

        1.   Identify with client the range of problems that are most significant to the client

        2.   Restate each problem using explicit behavioral terms

        3.   Prioritize the problems in order of their importance to the client

        4.   Establish an initial agreement with the client regarding the problem you will attend to first

    E.   Step 3: Translate Problems into Needs

        1.   Problems—Involve any source of perplexity or distress

        2.   Needs typically fall into three categories

            a.   Items we depend upon for survival

            b.   Items we require in order to maintain a sense of well-being

            c.   Items we require to achieve a sense of fulfillment in our lives

        3.   *Figure 6.2: Examples of Related Needs Translated from Identified Problems*

    F.   Step 4: Evaluate Levels of Intervention—Selecting a Strategy

        1.   Suggestions for developing a strategy

            a.   Focus on the first need you and the client have selected to work on

            b.   Review the need and consider identifying micro, mezzo, and macro alternative strategies to arrive at a solution

            c.   Emphasize your client's strengths when establishing strategies

        d.   Evaluate the pros and cons of each strategy you have considered with your client

        e.   Select and pursue the strategy that appears to be most efficient and effective

2.   Unit of attention—The system you will focus on as a target of change

3.   Brainstorming—The process of generating as many options as possible

4.   Strengths

        a.   *Highlight 6.1: Potential Areas of Clients' Strengths*

              1)   Special interests and activities

              2)   Family and friends

              3)   Religion and values

              4)   Occupation and education

              5)   Reaction to professional services

              6)   Emotional and mental health

              7)   Physical condition

              8)   Support system

              9)   Other

5.   Pros and cons

        a.   Macro strategy

        b.   Micro strategy

G.   Step 5: Establish Goals—Benefits:

1.   Help ensure that clients and workers are in agreement about such matters as problem definition and the changes that must occur to produce a suitable outcome

2.   Validate the client's concerns and definition of the problem and facilitate client empowerment

3.   Suggest the direction and nature of the intervention which helps both client and social worker stay on course

4.   Lend themselves more easily to evaluation, which is a critical component of the planned change process

H.   Step 6: Specify Objectives

    1.   Objectives should be measurable

    2.   Sometimes goals and objectives are confusing

        a.   *Objectives* should <u>always</u> be clear, specific, and measurable

        b.   *Goals* are often too complex to be measurable

    3.   Setting objectives in micro practice

        a.   Establishing objectives

            1)   Objectives should meet three criteria

                a)   Specificity—Should be explicit enough that anyone can tell that they have or have not been achieved

                b)   Clarity—Others should be able to restate with precision

                c)   Completeness—Enough information should be given about how the objective can be attained

        b.   Ideal objectives can be measured

            1)   Performance—Involves what the client, worker, or other individual involved is to perform in order to attain the objective

            2)   Conditions—Involves the conditions or circumstances under which the behaviors involved in achieving the objective are performed

            3)   Standard of performance—Involves how well, how soon, or how often the performance, activity, or behavior should be done

        c.   *Highlight 6.2: Using the Concepts of Performance, Conditions, and Standards to Establish Goals and Objectives with Clients*

        d.   *Highlight 6.3: Clarifying Vague Goals and Objectives*

I.   Step 7: Specifying Action Steps

    1.   *Who* will do *what* by *when*

        a.   *Who*—the individual specified for accomplishing a task

        b.   *What*—the tasks the individual has to complete in order to achieve the goal

        c.   *When*—sets a time limit so that the task is not lost in some endless eternity

J.   Step 8: Formalize a Contract

      1.   Four major components

           a.   A contract specifies what will occur during the intervention process

           b.   A contract is established by a worker and client making an agreement together

           c.   A contract generally contains four types of information: (1) goals, (2) methods, (3) timetables, and (4) mutual obligations

           d.   A contract's format can be written, oral, or implied

      2.   The purpose of a contract

           a.   Contracts ensure the consumer's rights, to free the consumer, and to increase consumer control in developing and implementing the plan

           b.   Purchase of service agreement—A fiscal arrangement or contract between two or more organizations

      3.   Make contacts *with* clients

      4.   Culturally competent contracting

      5.   The format of a contract

           a.   The written contract

                1)   Advantages

                     a)   Clear, virtually indisputable record

                     b)   Participants sign the contract

                2)   Disadvantages

                     a)   Takes time to draw up

                     b)   Clients may feel uncomfortable or pressured into signing a contract

        b.   The oral contract

                1)   Advantages

                        a)   Can be done swiftly and easily

                        b)   Can be helpful with resistant clients who refuse to sign a
                                written document

                2)   Disadvantage: Forgetting the details is easy

        c.   Implicit contracts—Agreements that are implied or assumed but not
                actually articulated

    6. What to include in intervention contracts

        a.   Identifying information

        b.   Specified objectives and action steps

        c.   Signatures

        d.   Dates

        e.   Formats vary

        f.   Contracts often change over time

        g.   *Figure 6.3: An Example of a Written Contract Format*

        h.   *Figure 6.4: An Example of Progressively Changing Contracts*

III.   Planning in Mezzo Practice

    A.   The Complexity of Setting Objectives in Mezzo Practice

        1.   Clarifying Goals and Objectives

        2.   Input from Both Worker and Clients

        3.   Workers' Perspective

        4.   Group Members' Perspective

        5.   Variations in Goals

6.   Categories of Goals

        a.   Group-centered goals—involve nourishing the group and keeping it going

        b.   Common group goals—arrived at and shared by all group members

        c.   Individual goals—an individual member works to attain some specific goal for him- or herself

B.   Contracts in Mezzo Practice

        1.   Contracts between the sponsoring agency and the group itself

        2.   Contracts between the worker and the group

        3.   Contracts between the group and an individual group member

        4.   Contracts between the worker and a group member

        5.   Contracts involving two or more members of the group

C.   *Critical Thinking Question 6.2*

IV.   **Planning in Macro Practice**

A.   An Approach to Program Planning

        1.   Work with the client

        2.   Prioritize problems

        3.   *Highlight 6.4: Planning a Health Clinic*

        4.   *Critical Thinking Question 6.3*

        5.   Translate problems into needs

        a.   Get data and information to clarify need

        b.   Specify other agencies already addressing the identified need

        c.   Talk to other professionals involved with clients

        d.   Ask community residents how they perceive the problem and need

        e.   Consider a more formal needs assessment

        6.   Evaluate the levels of intervention

7.   Establish goals, specify objectives, and action steps

     a.   Determine whether the need exists

     b.   Marshal support for program development—Action group

     c.   Allocate responsibilities to a board or advisory council

     d.   Describe the purpose of the proposed program

     e.   Formulate clear objectives

     f.   Implement a feasibility study. Feasibility study—A systematic assessment of the resources needed to accomplish a specified objective and concurrent evaluation of an organization's existing and anticipated capabilities for providing those resources

     g.   Solicit financial resources needed to initiate the program

     h.   Describe how program will provide services

     i.   Get the program started

     j.   Establish how service will be provided on an ongoing basis

8.   Formalize a contract

EXPERIENTIAL EXERCISES AND SIMULATIONS

Four exercises in this chapter focus on various aspects of the planning process described by the Generalist Intervention Model. Exercise 1 addresses prioritizing problems, Exercise 2 deals with translating problems into needs, Exercise 3 provides practice in clarifying vague objectives, and Exercise 4 concerns making a contract.

Exercise 6.1: Prioritizing Problems

A.   Brief description:
Pairs will take turns helping each other prioritize an array of personal problems.

B.   Objectives:
You will be able to:
1.   Identify a variety of problems.
2.   Prioritize these problems in terms of the order in which they will be addressed.

C.   Procedure:
1.   Before beginning this exercise, review the material in the text on the steps in the planning process. The planning process is summarized in the accompanying diagram.

2.   Take a sheet of scratch paper and vertically list the letters *a* through *e*. Beside each letter, cite a problem you are currently having. Problems may range from the very broad (for example, not having any money or being depressed) to the very specific (for instance, setting up two different dates at the same time next Thursday night or forgetting to send your mother a birthday card). Do *not* list problems that you don't care to share (for example, you think you're pregnant). You will be asked to share the list of problems with your partner.

3.   Break up into pairs. Take turns playing the worker and the client. First, the worker asks the client about his or her problems for approximately fifteen minutes. The worker should:

    a.   Identify with the client the range of problems that are most significant to the client. (Problems should be included only when the client recognizes their significance, they can be clearly defined, and there is some possibility of finding a solution.)

    b.   Restate each problem using explicit behavioral terms.

    c.   Prioritize the problems in order of their importance to the client.

4.   After fifteen minutes, reverse roles and do the same thing.

5.   Return to the class for a full class discussion which addresses the following questions and issues:

    a.   How difficult was it to identify problems? Explain.

    b.   How difficult was it to use explicit behavioral terms? Explain.

    c.   How difficult was it to prioritize the array of problems? Explain.

    d.   What problems tended to take highest priority (for example, the most serious, the simplest, or the easiest to solve)?

    e.   How similar do you think this exercise is to prioritizing problems with real clients?

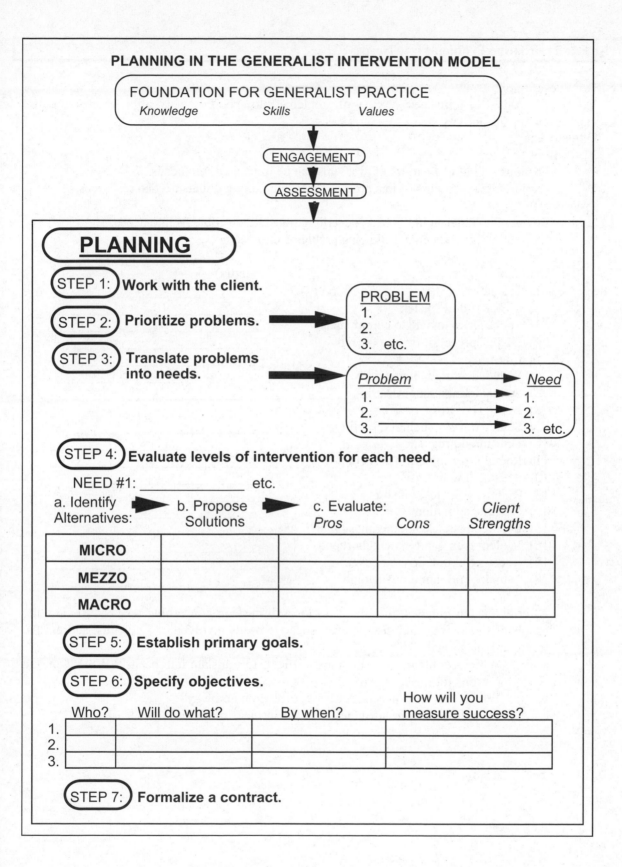

PLANNING IN THE GENERALIST INTERVENTION MODEL

FOUNDATION FOR GENERALIST PRACTICE
Knowledge   *Skills*   *Values*

ENGAGEMENT

ASSESSMENT

PLANNING

STEP 1: **Work with the client.**

STEP 2: **Prioritize problems.**

PROBLEM
1.
2.
3.   etc.

STEP 3: **Translate problems into needs.**

Problem   ⟶   *Need*
1. ⟶ 1.
2. ⟶ 2.
3. ⟶ 3. etc.

STEP 4: **Evaluate levels of intervention for each need.**

NEED #1: _____ etc.

a. Identify Alternatives: b. Propose Solutions   c. Evaluate:

		Pros	Cons	*Client Strengths*
MICRO				
MEZZO				
MACRO				

STEP 5: **Establish primary goals.**

STEP 6: **Specify objectives.**

	Who?	Will do what?	By when?	How will you measure success?
1.				
2.				
3.				

STEP 7: **Formalize a contract.**

Exercise 6.2: Translating Problems into Needs

A. Brief description:
    You will be asked to translate a variety of problems into specific needs, after which the entire class discusses the activity.

B. Objectives:
    You will be able to:
    1. Demonstrate how a variety of problems can be translated into needs.
    2. Explore the usefulness of this process regarding getting clients needed resources.

C. Procedure:
    1. Review the material in the text concerning translating problems into needs.
    2. By yourself, translate the following problems into needs:

Problem	Need(s)
1) Truancy	_____
2) Children don't listen	_____
3) Spouses are unable to communicate	_____
4) No resources for paying the rent	_____
5) Infertility	_____
6) Wife is battered almost daily	_____
7) Sexual harassment at work	_____
8) Being HIV positive	_____
9) Severe developmental disability	_____
10) Unwanted pregnancy	_____
11) Racial discrimination at work	_____
12) Rheumatoid arthritis	_____
13) Runaway adolescent son	_____
14) Cocaine addiction	_____
15) Divorced spouse not paying support	_____
16) Violent teen gang in neighborhood	_____
17) Received drunk driving ticket	_____
18) "Stuck" in minimum wage job	_____

3. After about ten minutes, join the class for a discussion concerning results. Review the problems one by one and discuss the respective needs involved. Afterwards, address the following questions:
    a. Which problems were the most difficult to translate into needs? What were the reasons for this?
    b. Which problems needed further clarification and why?
    c. How do needs provide clues for what services might be useful?

Exercise 6.3: Clarifying Vague Objectives

A. Brief description:
    Via class discussion, address a series of vague objective statements, explore the reasons for their vagueness, and propose improved restatement of the objectives.

B. Objectives:
    You will be able to:
    1. Evaluate a number of value objective statements.
    2. Explain the reasons why they are vague.
    3. Propose improved objective statements using the performance/conditions/standards format.

C. Procedure:
    1. Review the material in the text concerning establishing goals and objectives.
    2. In a class discussion, address the vague objective statements given below, one by one. Discuss the reasons why each statement is vague and establish improved objective statements. Use the performance/conditions/ standards formula discussed in the text to formulate new objectives. Finally, clearly identify what portions of the new objectives reflect performance, conditions, and standards.

Vague Objective Statement	Reasons for Vagueness	Improved Restatement: Performance/Conditions/Standards
1. Promote emotional well-being		
2. Increase self-awareness		
3. Find adequate housing		
4. Facilitate adequate functioning		
5. Accept physical disability		
6. Dress appropriately		
7. Increase motivation		
8. Show interest		
9. Respond appropriately		
10. Improve self-concept		
11. Develop a relationship		
12. Decrease hostile attitude		

A.   Brief description:

        Volunteers are asked to role play a family and worker. The worker then develops a contract specifying an initial intervention plan.

B.   Objectives:

        You will be able to:

        1.   Examine the contracting process.

        2.   Assess the specificity of objectives established in the contracting process.

        3.   Analyze the usefulness of contracting in the planning and intervention process.

C.   Procedure:

        1.   Review the material in the text on formalizing a contract.

        2.   In preparation for a role play, read about the following characters:

Role Play Characters

Lucinda, sixteen, is referred to the Oconomowoc County Social Services Department by a local hospital. She just delivered Rosanna there two days ago and doesn't know what to do or where to go. Her parents, Frannie and Darryl, refuse to let her come home. They insist that she give the baby up for adoption. Lucinda adamantly refuses. Lucinda, a high school junior, is a C+ student. She has never presented her parents with major behavioral problems before her pregnancy. Gavin, seventeen, Rosanna's father, wants nothing to do with the situation and has not been in contact with Lucinda for five months.

Frannie, thirty-eight, Lucinda's mother, is distraught by her daughter's "sinful" behavior. She doesn't want Lucinda to "ruin her life" by giving up her childhood to be a mother herself. She feels that if she refuses to let Lucinda come home, she will force her daughter to give the baby up for adoption because she lacks other options. Frannie does not want "to start all over again" and help Lucinda with the many parenting tasks Frannie knows are involved. Frannie is very outspoken about her feelings.

Darryl, forty-four, Lucinda's father, agrees with Frannie, although less adamantly. On the one hand, he wants Lucinda to give Rosanna up. On the other, he loves his daughter dearly and worries both about what she will do now and about how she will feel in the future about losing Rosanna. However, he tends to be cowed by Frannie's strong will and volatile temperament. Darryl finds it much easier to agree with Frannie than to fight her, especially on major issues such as this.

The Worker, Ms. DeWitt, is an intake worker at the Oconomowoc County Department of Social Services. Her job is to work with initial referrals and establish beginning plans of action. Ms. DeWitt has read the initial referral information and has spoken with all three family members on the phone. This is her first face-to-face meeting with them. She needs to help Lucinda, Frannie, and Darryl come to some agreement and establish an initial contract regarding what they will do about Rosanna. She feels that foster placement is a viable temporary solution until the family can come to a decision concerning Rosanna's permanent placement. Rosanna remains temporarily at the hospital.

---

3. Volunteers are needed to play the various roles. They should assume places in the front of the class where other class members can easily see them. The worker's task is to establish an initial contract with the family following the "Contract for Intervention Plan" cited below. Note that the number of objectives can vary. That is, there don't have to be exactly five. The role play should last no longer than twenty minutes.

Contract for Intervention Plan

Client Name: _____

I.   Brief description of the problem:

II.   Primary goals:

III.   Objectives:
        A.   _____
        B.   _____
        C.   _____
        D.   _____
        E.   _____

_____
(Signature of Worker)   (Date)

(Signature[s] of Client[s])   (Date)

_____

---

4. The Class should observe the role play until a contract is established or twenty minutes have passed (whichever comes first). The instructor should record on the blackboard the contract as it has been developed so that it's easier to discuss, even if the contract has not yet been completed. Discussion will focus on the following questions and issues:
    a.   Summarize what occurred during the role play.
    b.   What difficulties did the worker encounter?
    c.   To what extent are the objectives clearly stated?
    d.   What did you learn from the role play that you might be able to apply to contracting with your own clients in practice?

I.   **Introduction**

    A.   *Figure 7.1: Implementation in the Generalist Intervention Model*

II.   **Child Maltreatment and Protective Services**

    A.   Child Maltreatment

    B.   *Highlight 7.1: A Profile of Child Maltreatment*

        1.   Definitions and indicators

            a.   Physical abuse

                1)   Bruises

                2)   Lacerations

                3)   Fractures

                4)   Burns

                5)   Head injuries

                6)   Internal injuries

            b.   Behavioral indicators

                1)   Extremely passive, accommodating, submissive behavior aimed at preserving a low profile and avoiding potential conflict with parents that might lead to abuse. Hypervigilence—Avoiding playing because it draws too much attention to themselves

                2)   Notably aggressive behaviors and marked overt hostility toward others caused by rage and frustration at not getting needs met

                3)   Developmental lags—Because abused children are forced to direct their attention and energy toward coping with their abusive situation, they will frequently show developmental delays. These may appear in the form of language delays, poorly developed social skills, or lags in motor development

            c.   *Critical Thinking Question 7.1*

d. Child neglect—A caregiver's failure to meet a child's basic needs that may involve deprivation of physical, emotional, medical, mental health, or educational necessities

    1) Physical health care

    2) Mental health care

    3) Educational neglect

    4) Supervision

    5) Abandonment and substitute child care

    6) Housing hazards

    7) Household sanitation

    8) Personal hygiene

    9) Nutrition

    10) Social and attachment difficulties

    11) Cognitive and academic deficits

    12) Emotional and behavioral problems

e. Psychological neglect—Passive or passive/aggressive inattention to the child's emotional needs, nurturing, or emotional well-being

f. Psychological abuse—More aggressive and negative than emotional neglect. It is belittling, humiliating, rejecting, undermining a child's self-esteem, and generally not creating a positive atmosphere for a child

g. Sexual abuse—Any sexual activity with a child where consent is not or cannot be given. This includes sexual contact that is accomplished by force or threat of force, regardless of the age of the participants, and all sexual contact between an adult and a child whether the child is aware of the sexual nature of the contact or not

    1) Physical indicators

    2) Emotional indicators

    3) Increased or inappropriate sexual behaviors

    4) Difficulties in social relationships

h. Incest—Sexual intercourse between people too closely related to legally marry (usually interpreted to mean father-daughter, mother-son, or brother-sister combinations)

2. Incidence of child maltreatment

   a. The actual number of child maltreatment cases is difficult to determine

   b. One study found that 63 percent of reported cases were due to neglect, 20 percent to physical abuse, 10 percent to sexual abuse, and 8 percent to psychological abuse or neglect

3. Characteristics of perpetrators

   a. Serious need for support and nurturance that remains unfulfilled from their own childhoods

   b. Social isolation—their own self-confidence is low. They feel that no one will like them, so they isolate themselves

   c. Communication and relationship difficulties. Relationships abusers do have with family, significant others, and others are often stormy

   d. Not knowing how to raise children in a nurturing family environment. Their own family environment of origin may have been hostile and abusive

   e. Poor general coping skills. Perpetrators may be unable to cope with stress, lashing out at their children instead

      1) Lack anger management skills

      2) Inappropriate delineation of responsibility

      3) Lack decision-making or problem-solving skills

      4) Lack skills in how to delay their own gratification

   f. Extreme external stress and life crises

   g. Parents who neglect their children appear to have characteristics similar to physically abusive parents, although poverty can also contribute to the potential for neglect

   h. No clear-cut description characterizes people who sexually abuse children other than that most are male and are known to the victim. Some tend to be shy, lonely, poorly informed about sexuality, and very moralistic or religious

117

C.   Family Preservation Philosophy: Empowering Families

      1.   Family preservation philosophical perspective

           a.   Problem is seen as a social issue

           b.   Condemning and punishing parents who maltreat their children does no good

           c.   Intervention should not interfere with the family's dynamics and ongoing activity any more than is absolutely necessary to ensure a partnership role

           d.   Concentrate only on working constructively with the families

           e.   Coordinate intervention efforts with other professionals

           f.   Most maltreating child caretakers can improve their conduct with support and assistance

           g.   Keep maltreated children within their own families if at all possible

           h.   Clients should always be integrally involved in the intervention

D.   The Generalist Intervention Model: Engagement

      1.   The child protective service worker should have a forthright and candid approach, making a clear statement on the agency's behalf that it has learned that the child is in potential danger and that, representing the community, it would like to enlist the aid of the parents in determining what is happening

      2.   The worker should emphasize that the process is a joint process where both worker and family are trying to address and resolve the problem

      3.   The worker should assume an approach of helper rather than authoritative investigator

      4.   The worker should reflect the agency's concern for the well-being of the entire family

E.   The Generalist Intervention Model: Assessment

      1.   Family assessment: Interviewing the child

           a.   Be aware of how a child's perception might differ from that of adults in at least three dimensions

                1)   Children often use metaphors or stories representing what they want to say instead of using literal facts as adults do

2)   Time—Specific numbers of days or weeks may have little meaning to children

   3)   A child's attention span is usually much more limited

         a)   Use activities such as role playing, play therapy, or drawing

         b)   Play therapy—The child can use toys or dolls to act out situations that are difficult to talk about

b.   Pay attention to the interview setting. Select a familiar room where they feel comfortable and where there is some privacy

c.   Be especially sensitive to the child's emotional perspective in view of the turbulent context of abuse

   1)   Abused children are not easy clients—they have learned not to trust themselves, other people, or their environment

   2)   Withdrawing from this painful world is safer than chancing relationships

d.   Introduce yourself and inform the child about the purpose of the interview and your own role—must be done carefully so as not to frighten the child or imply blame

e.   Use some initial small talk about the child's favorite toys, television shows, or what the child is wearing

f.   Help the child anticipate what will happen in the future

2.   Family assessment: Understanding the family

3.   Risk assessment

a.   Risk assessment—To determine the degree of risk and the need to further involve the family with social services or law enforcement

b.   Five forces that can either contribute to or diminish risk in a home

   1)   Maltreatment force—Involves the type and severity of maltreatment that are occurring in the home

   2)   Child force—Involves the maltreated child's personal characteristics

3) Parent force—Entails the characteristics of the parents in the family

    a) Characteristics of the parents—how do they feel about themselves

    b) Parents' child management skills

    c) Parents' own upbringing and past

4) Family force—Concerns three elements

    a) What variables characterize the family in terms of demographics

    b) How can family function, interact, and communicate

    c) What overall support and nurturance does the family receive from the surrounding social environment

5) Intervention force—Concerns the workers' anticipation of how the family will react to intervention

6) Assessing the forces of risk

F. The Generalist Intervention Model: Planning

1. Eight dimensions upon which goals are frequently based for families in risk management

    a. Self-sufficiency

    b. Communication skills

    c. Parenting knowledge

    d. Stress management

    e. Impulse control

    f. Problem-solving skills

    g. Interactive nurturing

    h. Resource enhancement

G. The Generalist Intervention Model: Implementation

H. The Generalist Intervention Model: Evaluation, Termination, and Follow-Up

I. Empowerment, Child Maltreatment, and Mezzo Practice

J. Empowerment, Child Maltreatment, and Macro Practice

    1. Five areas for improvement at the macro level

        a. Focus on providing services aimed at prevention instead of emphasizing the reporting of child maltreatment

        b. A more supportive system geared toward improving resources and services for families in general is essential to maintain family strengths

        c. More resources should be directed at treatment instead of case finding

        d. Focus on treatment outcomes and improvement rather than on treatment process

        e. Locate and develop more community and neighborhood supports

    2. *Critical Thinking Question 7.2*

III. Crisis Intervention

A. Crisis intervention—A brief and time-limited therapeutic intervention where a social worker or other mental health professional helps a client system in crisis recognize the precipitating problem and identify potential coping methods

B. The Crisis Process

    1. An individual is exposed to a heavy amount of stress over some period of time

    2. This stress acts to make the person exceptionally vulnerable to intimidation and assaults from outside

    3. Some precipitating factor acts as a turning point to push the individual into a state of active crisis, marked by disequilibrium, disorganization, and immobility

    4. The person experiences surging anxiety and such accompanying troublesome emotions as depression or grief. At this point, the individual will probably be most receptive to help

C. *Highlight 7.2: Major Concepts in Crisis Intervention*

    1. The primary goal is to help the client return at least to the pre-crisis level of functioning

    2. Crisis intervention is relatively short term

    3. Specific, current, observable difficulties are the target of the intervention

4.   Crisis intervention strategies generally work better than other approaches when dealing with crises

5.   The practitioner in crisis intervention assumes a more active role which is often more directive than that assumed in other approaches to generalist practice

D.   Steps in Crisis Intervention

1.   Step 1: Engagement

    a.   The foundation of crisis intervention is the development of rapport

    b.   *Critical Thinking Question 7.3*

2.   Step 2: Assessment

    a.   Five specific areas of questioning

        1)   Why did the person called or came to you on that particular day?

        2)   How does your client view the crisis situation and precipitating event?

        3)   Does your client have access to support from others?

        4)   What is your client's history in solving similar problems?

        5)   To what extent is your client either suicidal or homicidal?

3.   Step 3: Planning

    a.   Evaluate the extent the crisis has interfered with client's ability to function

    b.   Review potential alternatives, evaluate pros and cons, and determine course of action to pursue

4.   Step 4: Implementation

    a.   Four suggestions for what to address during the implementation phase of the process

        1)   Help the client look at the crisis situation more objectively

        2)   Help the client express hidden feelings

        3)   Use past coping methods in resolving the crisis

        4)   Re-establish old or develop new social support systems

5. Step 5: Anticipatory planning

    a. Evaluation

    b. Termination

    c. Follow-up

E. A Case Example of Crisis Intervention in Micro Practice

1. Step 1: Engagement

2. Step 2: Assessment

3. Step 3: Planning

4. Step 4: Implementation

5. Step 5: Anticipatory planning

F. *Highlight 7.3: A Few Words about Helping People Cope with Grief and Loss*

1. Encourage clients to talk about their loss, both with you and supportive others

2. Understand that many negative feelings may surface when a person is struggling to cope with a crisis

3. Convey verbally and nonverbally that you are willing to talk about any concerns of the client

4. Do not discourage crying. Rather, people should be encouraged to cry as they feel the need

5. Answer questions as honestly as you can

6. If the crisis involves a dying person, help that person become the *star* of his or her own death

7. *Critical Thinking Question 7.3*

G. Crisis Intervention at the Mezzo Level

H. Crisis Intervention at the Macro Level

1. *Highlight 7.4: Crisis Intervention at the Macro Level: Disaster Relief and Trauma Counseling*

    a. Disaster relief work versus individual crises

    b. Assessment in disaster relief

　　　　c.　　Intervention in disaster relief

　　　　　　1)　　Welcoming

　　　　　　2)　　Framing

　　　　　　3)　　Educating

　　　　　　4)　　Grieving

　　　　　　5)　　Integrating

　　　　　　6)　　Reflecting

　　　　　　7)　　Empowering

　　　　　　8)　　Terminating and revisiting

　　　　d.　　Provision of long-term help

　　　　　　1)　　Four phases that communities often experience following a disaster

　　　　　　　　a)　　Heroism phase—Helpers rally to respond to the crisis and help those in need

　　　　　　　　b)　　Honeymoon phase—People work together to begin rebuilding their community

　　　　　　　　c)　　Disillusionment phase—The burdens of accessing adequate resources and trying to rebuild become extremely difficult and frustrating

　　　　　　　　d)　　Reconstruction phase—Community residents take on the long-term, grueling task of rebuilding the best they can

　　　　e.　　Taking care of yourself in disaster relief

　　　　f.　　Social work and disaster relief

　　2.　　Crisis intervention in most macro situations requires a multidisciplinary approach

IV.　Practice Issues with Populations-at-Risk

　　A.　　Generalist Practice: Empowerment, and Older Adults

　　　　1.　　An empowerment orientation to practice can assist older people to utilize their strengths, abilities, and competencies in order to mobilize their resources toward problem solving and ultimately toward empowerment

2.	*Highlight 7.5: Spirituality and Religion as Potential Sources of Strength for Older Adults*

    a.	Spirituality—The individual search for meaning, purpose, and values that typically rises above everyday physical limitations and connects one to something greater than oneself

    b.	Religion—Involves people's spiritual beliefs concerning the origin, character, and reason for being, usually based on the existence of some higher power or powers, and implies membership in a spiritual organization with customs, traditions, and structure

    c.	Social work assessment of older adults' spirituality

3.	Terms used for older adults—older adults, older persons, or elders instead of elderly, as elderly reflects a descriptive term more than a noun

4.	Potential aspects of decreased power

    a.	Physical health tends to decline

    b.	Functional limitations and subsequent reliance on external support

        1)	Activities of daily living (ADL)—refers to the ability to perform these basic personal care tasks

        2)	*Critical Thinking Question 7.4*

    c.	Labor force participation—approximately 12 percent of adults over age 65 continue to be employed

    d.	Economic status

        1)	About 12 percent of older adult households fall below the poverty line

        2)	*Critical Thinking Question 7.5*

5.	Essential concepts in empowerment

    a.	Adaptation—To new experiences, issues, and even losses

    b.	Competence—Focus on and emphasize what they *can* do instead of what they *cannot* do

    c.	Relatedness—Strengthen older adults' relationships with others, including friends, family members, and professional caregivers

    d.	Autonomy—Helping people to live as independently as possible

6. Strategies for working with older adults

    a. Identify and face any preconceived notions and stereotypes you might harbor about older adults

    b. Appreciate the different life situations experienced by people from different age groups within the senior population

    c. Understand that older adults are individuals with unique characteristics, experiences, and personalities just like anybody else

    d. Learn about how both gender and cultural background influence the aging experience

    e. Understand the developmental aspects of later life such as people's physical, mental, living, and socioeconomic conditions

7. *Highlight 7.6: Empowerment in Micro Practice with Older Adults*

    a. Listen carefully to what clients are saying and work to understand what they mean

    b. Help clients identify their coping skills and their abilities to implement planned change

    c. Show clients videotapes of other older adults talking about how they have learned to cope with similar issues

    d. Share newspaper articles, stories, or other informative materials with clients, especially those about older adults who have initiated service activities and political action (e.g. Gray Panthers—an advocacy organization for the rights and socioeconomic needs of older adults)

    e. Connect clients with other older people to provide mutual support and education

    f. Encourage clients to help others

8. Empowerment in mezzo practice with older adults

9. Empowerment in macro practice with older adults

B. Generalist Practice, Empowerment, and People Having Other National Origins

1. National origin—Involves individuals', their parents', or their ancestors' country of birth, and often is an important factor in people's cultural values and expectations

2. Refugees—People who have crossed national boundaries in search of refuge. People who flee to another country out of a fear of persecution because of religion, political affiliation, race, nationality, or membership in a particular group

3. Immigrants—Individuals who have been granted legal permanent residence in a country not their own

4. Migrants—People, usually workers, who have temporary permission to live in a country, but plan to return to their country of origin

5. Illegal immigrants—People who migrate illegally to another country

6. Approximately 1,122,000 immigrants were admitted to the United States in 2005, with 645,000 to 1,059,000 admissions during the decade prior to that

7. Approximately 12 million illegal immigrants currently reside in the United States

8. Asian and Latino immigrants arriving after 1965 account for more than 80 percent of the immigration to the United States

9. By 2040 one in four Americans will be an immigrant or the child of immigrants and by 2010 children of immigrants will account for 22 percent of the school-age population

10. Acculturation—The process wherein the ethnic values, behaviors, and rituals clients hold from their traditional culture change over time and integrate with the values, behaviors, and rituals of the majority or host culture

11. *Highlight 7.7: Critical Issues in Working with People Having Another National Origin*

    a. Cultural heritage

    b. Maintaining ties with the country of origin

    c. Linkages with the ethnic community

    d. Language

        1) Suggestions for maximizing effectiveness when using interpreters

            a) Interpreters should be competent in both understanding professional terminology and their fluency or literacy in English and the target language

            b) Clear standards for confidentiality should be established

    c)   Workers should strive to clarify information when interpreters make short summaries of prolonged communication

    d)   Social worker should always address the client (not the interpreter) directly and use culturally appropriate and respectful nonverbal reinforcement such as body language, eye contact, and gestures

    e.   Learning about the U.S. system

    f.   Advocacy

V.   Alcohol and Other Substance Abuse

    A.   Reasons substance abuse background is needed

        1.   Social workers may be employed by agencies specializing in treatment for substance abuse

        2.   Social workers may also function as administrators or analysts with local or state government bureaus responsible for substance abuse services and as aides to legislative committees

        3.   Social workers will probably have clients or the client's family members with alcohol and other substance problems and you must be capable of making appropriate referrals

    B.   *Highlight 7.8: Definitions of AODA Terms*

        1.   Alcohol—Refers to any type of fermented or distilled liquor containing alcohol

        2.   Drug—Refers to a wide range of materials that alter mood or consciousness when ingested including amphetamines, cannabis, cocaine, and hallucinogens

        3.   Substance—Is commonly used to refer to mind-altering drugs, including alcohol

        4.   Intoxication—Linked to drug abuse and dependence, is the development of a series of symptoms, often involving psychological or behavioral changes, directly related to intake of the substance and its influence on the central nervous system

        5.   Abuse—Maladaptive pattern of substance use manifested by recurrent and significant adverse consequences related to the repeated use of substances

6.   Substance dependence—A cluster of cognitive, behavioral, and physiological symptoms resulting from continued use of the substance despite significant resulting problems. It occurs when three or more of the following happen within a one-year period:

a.   Tolerance—The user requires increasingly more of the substance to reach the same level of mood alteration or the substance's effects diminish significantly with continued use

b.   Withdrawal—Symptoms that develop as a result of discontinued use of the substance or the compulsion to absorb the substance to avert these symptoms

c.   The user takes greater amounts of the substance over a longer time period than he or she meant to

d.   The user expresses an ongoing desire or failed attempts to decrease or control substance use

e.   The user spends huge amounts of time participating in activities aimed at obtaining or using the substance and recuperating from its aftermath

f.   The user curtails or avoids significant social, work, or recreational involvement due to substance use

g.   The user continues to use the substance despite being aware that the substance is causing or intensifying continued physical or psychological difficulties

7.   Substance abuse—A maladaptive pattern of substance use manifested by recurrent and significant adverse consequences related to the repeated use of substances.

a.   Substance abuse is reflected by one or more of the following criteria in any 12-month period:

1)   Repeated failure to accomplish major work, educational, or social responsibilities due to substance use

2)   Repeated use of the substance at times when it could cause physical harm

3)   Repeated use of the substance that results in legal problems

          4)   Continued use of the substance despite the fact that it causes frequent interpersonal problems

          5)   Substance abuse involves people who have never been diagnosed with substance dependence

     b. .   Substance abuse might be regarded as less problematic than substance dependence because many of the physical and psychological symptoms associated with dependence are not yet evident

8.   Intoxication—The development of a series of symptoms, often involving psychological or behavioral changes, directly related to intake of the substance and its influence on the central nervous system

9.   Addiction—Dependence on some substance, having the same consequences as those described for substance dependence, the term that is now commonly replacing addiction

10.   Professionals working with alcohol and other substance abusers may be referred to as substance abuse, AODA, or chemical dependency counselors

C.   *Highlight 7.9: Your Role as Referral Agent*

1.   Resources available

     a.   Detoxification—Short-term treatment designed to oversee the client's safe withdrawal from the substance to which he or she is addicted

     b.   Outpatient treatment—That received by participating in a program without staying overnight at a treatment facility

     c.   Inpatient treatment—That received by remaining at the facility all day and night. It provides a comprehensive, structured environment that maximizes control of the treatment process

     d.   Therapeutic communities—Residential programs where clients remain for one to three years, although some require only a six-month stay

     e.   Halfway houses—Temporary residences to assist in the transition from an inpatient program to the real-life community

     f.   Mutual self-help groups—Composed of nonprofessional people with a common problem or life predicament who voluntarily gather together to provide mutual support and share information aimed at improving their lives (AA, Narcotics Anonymous, Al-Anon, Alateen)

     g.   Pharmacological adjuncts—Some alcohol or other substance-dependent people need the help of prescribed medications (e.g., Antabuse) to help them begin the recovery process

D.   People with Alcohol Problems

   1.   Alcohol problem—If someone's drinking causes problems for him or her, or for someone else, in any area of their lives, then that drinking is problematic

   2.   *Figure 7.2: The Continuum of Alcohol Use and Resulting Problems*

      a.   Complete abstinence

      b.   Occasional use of alcohol with no problems

      c.   Frequent use of alcohol with no or few problems

      d.   Frequent use of alcohol with increasing problems

      e.   Increasingly serious use of alcohol and escalating problems

      f.   Seriously heavy use of alcohol and multiple, severe problems

   3.   Typical defense mechanisms used by people who abuse alcohol or other drugs to protect themselves from having to deal with the problems caused by the abuse

      a.   Minimization—Assigning little importance to drinking or its consequences

      b.   Rationalization—Making excuses for the problems caused by the dependence on alcohol

      c.   Denial—Insisting to oneself that nothing is wrong (the most prevalent defense)

E.   Alcohol Abuse and Family Relationships

   1.   Themes that characterize the families of people dependent on alcohol (and other substance abuse)

      a.   Alcoholic's alcohol use becomes the most important thing in the family's life

      b.   Family members strive to keep the family together even when conditions are deteriorating due to the abuser's behavior

      c.   Family members often act as enablers for the abuser's alcohol use

      d.   Family members often feel incredible guilt

      e.   Family members often do not know what they want—their lives are centered around the chemically dependent individual

      f.   Family members feel worthless—they feel as though no one cares for how they feel or for what they want

g. Family members don't trust others—they have been disappointed so many times by the dependent person's behavior that they can't afford to dream about things getting better

h. Family members have poor communication skills—they learned the credo of the chemically dependent family—don't talk, don't trust, and don't feel

F. The Effects of Alcoholic Parents on Their Children

1. Children may risk experiencing problems in four areas

a. Anti-social behavior and conduct disorder

b. School environment problems

c. Emotional

d. Adolescence

2. Recent evidence indicates that children will not automatically experience such negative effects

3. Children of alcoholics must be involved in the treatment process, including being the recipients of individual and/or group counseling

G. Your Role in Intervention with Alcoholics

H. Treatment Approaches for Alcoholism

1. Four principles important in treatment

a. Engagement with the social worker in a trusting and open relationship is essential for successful treatment

b. A multiple-system approach should be used

c. Follow-up care after primary treatment has ceased is critical to maintain progress

d. Clients need help in developing a social network of people or groups to call upon for support, guidance, and recreation

2. A four-stage recovery model

a. Stage 1: Abstinence

b. Stage 2: Confrontation

c. Stage 3: Growth

d. Stage 4: Transformation

3.   The strengths perspective on alcohol abuse and dependence treatment

      a.   Harm reduction treatment approach emphasizing means to reduce the harm caused by the addiction

      b.   A more traditional disease model espoused by AA may experience success with extraverted, severely addicted, structure seeking people

      c.   A harm reduction approach provides more flexibility in terms of treatment planning and goals. A key component is <u>choice</u>

      d.   The practitioner assists clients in understanding the costs of drinking and exploring what options they have to gain greater control of their lives if that is what they desire

4.   *Highlight 7.10: Helpful Techniques in the Harm Reduction Approach*

      a.   Express empathy

      b.   Develop discrepancy

      c.   Avoid argumentation

      d.   Roll with resistance

      e.   Support self-efficacy

5.   *Critical Thinking Question 7.6*

6.   Other issues

      a.   Early screening for abuse and dependence

      b.   The problem of denial

      c.   What if your client has a relapse?

            1)   Remain calm and be empathic

            2)   Treat the ordeal in as beneficial a light as possible

            3)   If the relapse was related to stress, address how to manage stress better in the future

      d.   What if your client arrives drunk?

            1)   Counseling cannot proceed effectively if a client comes to an interview drunk

            2)   The worker's main goal should be to minimize the disruption and send the client safely home

I.   Empowerment at the Mezzo Level

J.   Empowerment at the Macro Level

       1.   Adequacy and effectiveness of treatment programs

       2.   Accessibility of alcohol and other substances to abusers

       3.   Prevention of alcohol and other substance abuse

       4.   *Critical Thinking Question 7.7*

K.   *Highlight 7.11: Integration of Policy and Practice: Ethical Dilemmas in Managed Care*

       1.   Managed care is an integral aspect of social work practice in many settings

       2.   Capitation—The managed care organization pays a fixed, per-person amount to its providers for a given time period, regardless of the number of services rendered

       3.   Two primary principles—Retention of quality and access, and controlling cost

       4.   It reduces utilization rates, but direct patient costs are not total costs

       5.   Traditional relationships between clients and workers in mental health settings has been fundamentally transformed

       6.   Ethical issues concerning managed care

              a.   Potential conflict between the gatekeeping role of the managed care organizations and client self-determination

              b.   Managed care may destroy informed consent

              c.   Potential to violate client confidentiality

       7.   Advocacy is an important role for social workers

This chapter focuses on the three major thrusts of chapter 7. Exercise 1 asks you to assess an alleged child maltreatment case according to the five major forces of risk discussed in the chapter. Exercise 2 describes a crisis intervention role play which the class evaluates. Exercise 3 asks you to assess your own perspective on spirituality and religion as a potential for personal strength and the extent to which these dimensions can serve as potential sources of strength for clients. Exercise 4 provides four role plays of possible alcoholics where class members take turns asking questions and trying techniques.

Exercise 7.1: Risk Management

A.   Brief description:
        You are presented a case involving alleged child maltreatment, and are asked during a class discussion to assess the five forces of risk involved. Finally, you are asked to discuss what goals might be established for the family members and which specific service might be useful.

B.   Objectives:
        You will be able to:
        1.   Assess the five forces of risk present in a simulated case situation.
        2.   Formulate potential goals to work toward with the family.

C.   Procedure:
        1.   Prior to doing this exercise, review the material in the text on risk management in protective services.
        2.   Assessment of the five forces of risk is an integral part of the risk management process. You will be asked to assess these forces (maltreatment, child, parent, family, and intervention) in the Ashton case situation.[1]

The Ashton Case[2]

The Presenting Problem

        A concerned neighbor calls Milwaukee County Protective Services to report that Tiffany Ashton is abusing her eight-year-old daughter Dominique. A Protective Services worker named Ms. Stalwart reviews Ms. Ashton's records and visits the Ashton home to investigate the situation.

        Ms. Stalwart finds Ms. Ashton extremely disoriented and depressed. Her sister recently died in a car accident due to her being drunk while driving. Apparently, this seriously affected Ms. Ashton's emotional stability. Ms. Stalwart takes Ms. Ashton to a Milwaukee Public Hospital and places Dominique in emergency foster care until Ms. Ashton's mental health improves.

---

[1] The five forces of risk and suggestions for their evaluation are based on that described in *Child Protective Services Risk Management: A Decision-making Handbook* (1991). Charlotte, NC: Action for Child Protection, developed by Holder and Corey.

[2] This case is based loosely on a case study entitled "Case History #3: The Heller Family," in *Resource Materials: A Curriculum on Child Abuse and Neglect,* published by the U.S. Department of Health, Education, and Welfare, DHEW Publication No. (OHDS) 79-30221, 1979.

Prior Agency History

Agency records indicate that nine months ago, Dominique's teacher had referred Dominique to Protective Services because she missed eight consecutive days of school without an excuse. The school could not reach Ms. Ashton by phone to find out what was wrong. Dominique's teacher indicated that Dominique's school performance has increasingly deteriorated over the past several months.

A Protective Services worker visited the home and found no evidence of habitation. A next-door neighbor indicated that Ms. Ashton and Dominique hadn't been around for several weeks. She said they had moved in with Ms. Ashton's boyfriend, Jagger, in a small flat a block away. The neighbor gave the worker the new address.

When the worker arrived at Jagger's apartment, Ms. Ashton appeared surprised but allowed her in to talk. The worker noted that Dominique had numerous bruises on her arms and legs. Ms. Ashton acknowledged that she had beaten Dominique with a stick three days earlier. Ms. Ashton continued that the beating resulted from Dominique starting a fire in her bedroom while Ms. Ashton and Jagger were out. Ms. Ashton said she had been so shocked that she beat Dominique to emphasize how dangerous firesetting was. Ms. Ashton and Jagger often left Dominique alone to fend for herself when they were gone.

After a number of interviews, the Protective Services worker determined that the beating was a singular occurrence. Furthermore, Ms. Ashton regretted the beating deeply and expressed eagerness to cooperate with the worker. Ms. Ashton evidently did not understand that leaving an eight-year-old daughter alone for substantial periods of time was inappropriate and potentially dangerous. Ms. Ashton indicated that in the future she would make certain she found a babysitter before going out.

Four months later (and five months before Ms. Stalwart found her disoriented in her apartment), Ms. Ashton tried to kill herself by taking an overdose of sleeping pills. After she had spent several days in the hospital, her physician referred her to the local mental health center for treatment. However, she never followed through on this recommendation.

Two months later (and three months before Ms. Stalwart found her), Jagger beat Ms. Ashton up and threw her out of his apartment. She returned to her current apartment.

Prior Family History

Ms. Ashton's own personal history was turbulent. She was one of nine children raised in a poverty-stricken, multiproblem family. Her parents were alcoholics. They were divorced after her father was found guilty of committing incest with two of her sisters. Subsequently, Ms. Ashton and several of her siblings were removed from the home and placed in foster care for several years.

After becoming pregnant at age seventeen, she married Dominique's father, who deserted her shortly thereafter. She contemplated giving Dominique up for adoption but decided against it. She never divorced Dominique's father because she still "really loves him." She became pregnant twice more with different boyfriends and gave both children up for adoption.

Since Dominique's birth, Ms. Ashton has been receiving public assistance. At Ms. Ashton's request, the County Department of Social Services enrolled her in three job training programs over the years. However, she soon dropped out of each, and so never neared completion. She experienced several bouts of depression for which she received medication. Until Dominique was three, Ms. Ashton lived with her own prior foster parents who provided Dominique with satisfactory care.

> *Dominique's History*
>   Dominique achieved her developmental milestones within normal limits. Her childhood was healthy with the exception of common childhood diseases.
>   Dominique's teachers describe Dominique as a pleasant, likable child. However, she does poorly in school, especially in math and English. They indicate that Dominique has been seriously distressed by her mother's mental state, which has detracted from Dominique's school performance.
>   A recent report by a consulting psychologist indicates that, despite Ms. Ashton's emotional difficulties, she and Dominique have a "close, loving relationship." They care deeply for each other and, according to his recommendation, should not be permanently separated.

3. Your instructor will lead the class in a discussion regarding how the five forces (maltreatment, child, parent, family, and intervention) contribute to or diminish risk in the Ashton family. Your discussion should first focus on each force, briefly defined below. Address the questions relating to each force, note those areas where you need additional information, and arbitrarily evaluate the amount of risk you feel is present. Subsequently, evaluate the risk for each force as great, moderate, or small.

    It is beyond the scope of this workbook to undertake an extensive risk assessment as a worker would conduct in real life. This exercise is designed to help you focus on those variables contributing to risk in any particular family and make an arbitrary judgment about what should be done. In a real case situation, the assessment would assume much greater depth.

> a. *Maltreatment Force* involves the types and severity of maltreatment that are occurring in the home, and the conditions under which maltreatment usually occurs.
>   1) Are the children being neglected, burned, beaten, or sexually molested?
>   2) Is the abusive parent drunk, depressed, or explosive?
>   3) Does the maltreatment occur randomly or only in times of crisis?
>   4) What amount of risk does maltreatment force generate within the home—great, moderate, or small?
> b. *Child Force* involves the maltreated child's personal characteristics and the extent to which you as the worker perceive the child as being susceptible to maltreatment.
>   1) Is Dominique extremely withdrawn, brashly aggressive, or exceptionally slow to respond?
>   2) Is Dominique a very young child or physically disabled (which would make her exceptionally vulnerable)?
>   3) What amount of risk does child force generate within the home—great, moderate, or small?

c. *Parent Force* entails the characteristics of parents in the family, the parents' child management skills, the parents' own upbringing and past experiences, and the interactional patterns of the parents with others.

    1) *Ms. Ashton's Characteristics:*
        a) How does Ms. Ashton feel about herself?
        b) Does she feel guilty after maltreatment occurs?
        c) How does she cope with external stresses?

    2) *Ms. Ashton's Parenting Skills:*
        a) To what extent does Ms. Ashton rely on physical punishment to control Dominique?
        b) How responsive is Ms. Ashton to Dominique's wants and demands?

    3) *Ms. Ashton's Own Upbringing:*
        a) How was Ms. Ashton treated by her own parents?
        b) Do they have a prison record or record of legal convictions?
        c) Do they have health difficulties?

    4) *Ms. Ashton's Parents' Interactions:*
        a) How do Ms. Ashton's parents communicate with other people?
        b) Do they have friends or neighbors with whom they associate?
        c) To what extent are they isolated from others?

In summary, what amount of risk does parent force generate within the home—great, moderate, or small?

d. *Family Force* concerns family demographics, family functioning and communication, and the overall support and nurturance the family receives from the surrounding social environment.

    1) *Family Demographics*:
        a) What variables characterize the family in terms of demographics?
        b) Are one or both parents involved?
        c) How many children are there?
        d) Is the family a blended stepfamily?
        e) What levels of education, job training, and work experience do the parents have?
        f) What is the family's income level?
        g) Is unemployment a problem?
        h) What are there housing conditions like?

    2) *Family Function and Communication:*
        If the parents are married, how do they get along?
        a) How involved is Jagger or other boyfriends with Dominique?
        b) How do family members talk to each other?
        c) How would you describe the family's lifestyle?
        d) Is the family prone to crises?

    3) *Environmental Supports*
        a) What relationships does the family have with extended family members?
        b) Does the family have access to adequate transportation?
        c) Is the family socially isolated?

In summary, what amount of risk does family force generate within the home—great, moderate, or small?

4. Now address the following questions:
   a. What do you feel is the overall amount of risk to Dominique in the Ashton home—great, moderate, or small?
   b. In a real treatment situation, what types of goals might you as a worker pursue? Consider the following (Berry, 2005; Crosson-Tower, 2005; Holder & Cary, 1991):

   1) *Self-Sufficiency*
      Parents and families frequently need to enhance their ability to function independently. This dimension has to do with families being better able to fend for themselves and satisfy their own needs. Specific objectives often involve increasing self-esteem and confidence.

   2) *Communication Skills*
      Goals focusing on improved communication skills among family members are common. Members can be encouraged to identify and express their feelings openly and honestly. Listening skills can be enhanced. Family members' ability to understand each other's point of view can be improved.

   3) *Parenting Knowledge*
      Parents may not know how to handle and control children. They may have been brought up in emotionally deprived environments themselves. They may resort to force for controlling children's behavior because they've never been taught any other behavior management techniques. They can be taught not only to control, but to play with and enjoy their children.

      Additionally, parents may need knowledge about normal development. They need to know what to expect in terms of normal behavior at each age level. Appropriate expectations may reduce the frustrations parents feel when children don't behave the way the parents think they *should*.

   4) *Stress Management*
      Parents can be taught to better manage their stress levels. They can be taught to release their feelings more appropriately, instead of allowing emotional pressure to build up and explode. Learning specific stress management techniques such as relaxation approaches can also help them cope with stress.

   5) *Impulse Control*
      Many parents in families at risk have poor impulse control. They are under tremendous stress. They often need to learn how to direct their energies in more fruitful ways than by violently lashing out at children.

   6) *Problem-Solving Skills*
      Parents in high-risk families may be so frustrated and stressed that they feel they have little control over their lives and their behavior. They can be taught how to analyze problems, translate these problems into needs, establish potential alternatives for meeting these needs, evaluate the pros and cons of alternatives, and, finally, select and pursue their most promising options.

7)   *Interactive Nurturing*

Many times family members need to be taught how to express their positive feelings, on the one hand, and accept affection, on the other. They can be taught how to empathize with each other, verbalize their feelings, and, hence, reinforce their support and caring for each other.

8)   *Resource Enhancement*

A primary means of increasing the strength of families at risk is to increase their resources. Adequate employment, income, housing, food, and clothing all contribute to a family's wellbeing.

Exercise 7.2: Crisis Intervention

A.   Brief description:

Volunteers are asked to role play two social workers and members of a family experiencing a crisis. Social workers focus on the planning and intervention phases of the crisis intervention model.

B.   Objectives:

You will be able to:

1.   Identify the steps in crisis intervention.
2.   Demonstrate the application of these steps to a crisis situation.
3.   Evaluate the approaches used during a role play.

C.   Procedure:

1.   Before beginning this exercise, review the material in the text on crisis intervention.
2.   Volunteers are needed to participate in a role play involving crisis intervention. Otherwise, your instructor will assign roles. The roles are as follows:

Role Play: Crisis Intervention

Social Work Role: Two social workers are intake workers in a crisis intervention unit of a community mental health center. Their job is to meet with people who phone for help because of a current crisis, assess the situation, and make the appropriate referrals. They have already gathered the following information about the clients.

The Situation: The workers are meeting with Farrah, Francine, and Felicity. Farrah's husband, Festus, was killed in a car accident five weeks earlier. Francine, sixteen, and Felicity, twelve, are Farrah's daughters. One other child, Fulbert, four, is not present at the interview.

Farrah, thirty-four, had been happily married to Festus for eighteen years. Having married right after high school, she has never worked outside the home. She loves her children very much and is very concerned about what will happen to them now.

Farrah is a quiet, pleasant, soft-spoken woman who is overwhelmed with grief and with the terror of being alone. She loved Festus dearly and had a very close relationship with him. He tended to make most of the family's decisions. Farrah had gone from being dependent on her parents to being dependent on Festus. She felt relatively comfortable and settled in that role.

Festus, thirty-eight, had been an assistant at the Morbid Misty Eye Mortuary for the past seventeen years. He had been earning $42,000 per year.

The family has a small home with only ten years remaining on the mortgage at 9 percent interest. Although the family had never been wealthy, they had lived comfortably and adequately. Farrah was exceptionally good at managing the household finances. Now Farrah has the following major concerns:

1. Grief at the loss of her husband.
2. Fear of loneliness.
3. Financial worries—house payments, food, clothing, etc.
4. Worry about the children—both their emotional and physical needs.
5. What she will do.

Francine (nicknamed Foofy), sixteen, is an outgoing, friendly young woman who maintains a B+ average in school. She is fairly well adjusted in school, participates in a number of class activities (including cheerleading and chess club), and has many friends.

Francine is suffering from terrible grief at the loss of her father. She had a very good relationship with him and misses him very much.

It seems things in her life have gone pretty well up until now. But now everything has fallen apart. She doesn't know what to do. She's worried about her mother and siblings. She doesn't know what will happen to the family. It seems her father was always the strong one who held things together. She can't even concentrate on her schoolwork much anymore. She'd like to help her mother, but just doesn't know what to do.

In summary, Francine has the following major concerns:

1. Grief at the loss of her father.
2. Questions about what her mother is going to do now.
3. Worry over her siblings and what will happen to them.
4. Worry about what will happen to her.

Felicity, twelve, is a pretty yet shy and withdrawn girl. She lacks self-confidence and generally has had difficulties in school, both with grades and with making friends.

She, too, is very upset by her father's death. She feels he was the only family member she could talk to.

Felicity feels that Francine, unlike herself, always seems to do well and have things come easily for her. Felicity resents this and often finds herself becoming angry at Francine. She feels guilty about these negative feelings toward her sister.

Felicity loves her mother but feels that her mother sides with Francine on most issues. Felicity especially resents how her mother tends to speak for her and answer questions addressed to her.

In summary, Felicity has the following major concerns:

1. Grief at the loss of her father.
2. Resentment towards her sister Francine for "being better at everything" than she is.
3. Resentment towards her mother Farrah for never listening to her opinion.
4. Low levels of self-confidence.
5. Lack of friends.

3.   Volunteers should seat themselves in front of the class where they can be observed easily. Each volunteer should display an 8" x 5" note card with the client name marked boldly so that observers can better remember which volunteer is playing which role.

4.   The workers should focus on the planning and intervention steps in the crisis intervention model presented in the text. Assessment, of course, is an ongoing process. The role play should continue for twenty to thirty minutes. Your instructor will indicate to the role players when it's time to stop.

5.   During the role play, observers should take notes on the form shown below as they address the following questions:

Role Play Feedback Form

A.   What do you think are particularly *good techniques* used by the social workers? How did the *clients react* to these techniques? (Please be specific.)

B.   Do you see any weaknesses or areas in which improvement would be helpful? (Specific suggestions for how to improve are beneficial.)

C.   Do you have any additional thoughts or comments?

---

5.   After the role play, your instructor will lead a discussion which focuses on the following questions:

    a.   What feedback did you note on your feedback forms? Strengths? Suggestions for improvement? Other comments?

    b.   What did you feel were the critical points in the role play?

    c.   To what extent did you feel the workers followed and applied the steps inherent in crisis intervention?

    d.   How did the workers feel while doing the role play?

    e.   How did the clients feel in reaction to what the workers said?

Exercise 7.3: Spirituality As Strength

A.   Brief description:

You are asked to answer a questionnaire designed to evaluate your own perspective of spirituality as a potential source of strength. Small groups then discuss and compare findings.

B.   Objectives:

You will be able to:

1.   Assess the extent to which you perceive of spirituality as a potential source of strength for yourself.

2.   Compare and contrast your own beliefs with others.

3.   Examine the potential of spirituality as a source of strength for clients.

C.   Procedure:

1.   Before beginning this exercise, review the material on spirituality and religion as potential sources of strength for older adults (and others including yourself).

2.   Answer the questions posed on the questionnaire below.

Questionnaire: Your Personal Perceptions of Spirituality as a Potential Source of Strength

1.   How would you differentiate spirituality from religion?

2.   What are your personal beliefs about spirituality and religion as they apply to your own life?

3.   What level of involvement, if any, do you have with a religious institution such as a church, synagogue, or mosque?

4.   What role, if any, do you see this institution as having in supporting you in your daily and spiritual life?

5.   How important, if at all, is this affiliation to you?

6.   How would you describe your own philosophy of life?

7.   What helps you most when you are afraid or need special help?

8.   What do you feel is most meaningful to you in your life at this time?

9.   What gives you hope for the future?

3. After completing the questionnaire, form small groups of 4 to 6 persons. Your instructor will give you time to compare your answers on the questionnaire with each other.
4. After about 20 minutes, your instructor will have you join a full class discussion concerning your findings. At least one member of each group should summarize what conclusions and differences were reached. Your instructor will then ask the entire class to address the following questions:
    a. In summary, to what extent do you perceive spirituality and religion as a potential source of strength?
    b. To what extent do you think spirituality and religion might serve as a potential source of strength to clients?
    c. How difficult do you feel it might be for you not to impose your own beliefs on your clients?
    d. What approaches might help you separate your own beliefs from those of your clients?

Exercise 7.4: What Do You Do with a Drunken Sailor (or an Alcoholic Client)?

A.   Brief description:
      Volunteers are asked to role play possible alcoholics. The remainder of the class then responds concerning assessment information, potential referral sources, and addressing the role player's denial.
B.   Objectives:
      You will be able to:
      1.   Recognize the symptoms of alcoholism.
      2.   Propose and evaluate potential referral sources.
      3.   Demonstrate some techniques used to address denial in alcoholics.
C.   Procedure:
      1.   Before beginning this exercise, review the material on alcohol and other drug abuse presented in the text.
      2.   Volunteers are needed to play the various roles cited below. Your instructor will first read them to you.

Roles

Stephanie, twenty-one, is a college junior who majors in education and loves to "party." She has been known to label herself a "party animal." She goes out drinking almost every night (after some studying, of course). She drank occasionally at parties during high school and even got drunk a dozen or two times. When she first got to college, she limited herself to going out and "getting plastered" only on Friday and Saturday nights. However, as time passed, she's found herself wanting to go out every night.

She has fun, all right. But twice last month she found herself waking up in bed with some guy she didn't remember ever seeing before. Those guys were pretty "sleazy-looking," too. How embarrassing! Each time she surely got out of there in a hurry. She hopes she remembered to use condoms.

After all, she's doing okay in school. Sure, her grades have slumped a little bit. She's dropped from a B+ to a straight C average. But that's because the older she gets, the more difficult her courses get. For example, that stats course is pure misery. She often tells herself she's doing fine.

She's not crazy about the headaches she has most mornings. It takes her a while to get going. But she's only missed six or seven mornings of class since the semester started. She's doing okay. She surely isn't an alcoholic or anything like that.

The problem is that as she was driving from one bar to another the other night, a cop (who must've come out of the Twilight Zone because she surely didn't see him) busted her for drunk driving. Rats. What a bummer. What a fine. She also has to take a series of drug education courses. Crummy.

Carlo, thirty-three, works on the line at Darley Havidson Motorcycle Manufacturing Company making "hogs" (a slang term used by motorcycle enthusiasts to refer to "awesome" cycle machines.) He married Blair nine years ago after he "knocked her up." They now have four children whom he frequently refers to as "ye olde wailing brats." Sometimes, he thinks it's too bad he doesn't like children very much.

He works second shift so he doesn't have to see too much of the family. Blair works first shift at George Webb's hamburger parlor. Carlo sometimes thinks that people who work there are required to have bad complexions and a hundred extra pounds of fat. That's Blair, all right.

Carlo's one joy in life is going down to Heck's Tavern and having a few "brewski's" after work. He and his cronies inevitably close it down and stagger home. Carlo even volunteers for overtime whenever possible so he won't miss weekend nights. Otherwise, he contents himself with a few twelve-packs and TV (football when in season).

In a vague way, Carlo thinks he's not very happy with his life. But he doesn't like to think about it too much. It's too depressing. The job's boring and he's never completely sure he won't get laid off. Yet, he can't afford to quit and start over somewhere else. Blair's constantly "bitchin'" about his drinking when he does see her. She says he slaps her around when he's drunk. Maybe, just a little, but not much. It's a good thing they work different shifts.

Day after day, week after week, he waits patiently for closing time when he can "belt down a few" and forget all his humdrum problems.

The problem is that last week that crazy town cop gave him a drunk driving ticket as he was trying to drive home. Carlo wasn't really drunk. He only had a few beers. How do you expect a guy to be able to relax, anyhow?

Viki, fifty-seven, is an executive for an accounting firm. She's been married to Alex, a sixty-year-old engineering consultant, for thirty-four years. Their three adult children live with their own families in various peripheries of the country.

Viki's job is extremely demanding. She usually works eleven-hour days, often including weekends. Alex's job is also demanding, so they don't see much of each other. They never were much for socializing, anyway. In the free time he does have, Alex keeps busy with fishing, reading, and doing projects around the house.

Although Viki often states that she loves her job, she typically comes home exhausted. Her high-level position makes her feel very important. She feels she needs to keep striving for greater and greater accomplishments in order to keep up with her very competitive colleagues.

Upon entering the door as she gets home, Viki can't wait to mix her first very dry martini. Then she can't wait to mix her next one . . . and the next. Finally, after a couple of hours, she passes out on the couch watching television. Meanwhile, Alex goes to bed by himself. Viki will usually wake up at 2:00 or 3:00 a.m. and crawl into bed. A few hours later, her alarm sounds and she's soon off to work again.

Martinis help Viki relax. It's tough to "wind down" after a whirlwind day at the office. She's not an alcoholic, though. She only drinks to relax, and then only a few martinis.

The problem is, she had to attend a going-away party for one of her colleagues two weeks ago. She only had a couple of martinis. That cop must've been parked outside the bar where the party was held, just waiting for her to come out. Anyway, he gave her a ticket for drunk driving. How mortifying. And to think she usually only drinks a little at home.

Mortimer, sixteen, isn't into school very much. His parents are always on his back, so he does go. But they can't make him pay attention. He is passing. What do they want? He even got a C in shop last term.

Mortimer's got a part-time job, working after school at the local Sentry supermarket. It's not much of a job. It only pays minimum wage, but it does keep him in funny money.

Mortimer mostly likes to go out with his friends. They'll go to a game, watch TV, or "scope cherubs" (that is, look for gorgeous younger women who adore "older" men). Occasionally, he and his friends will really "get down and party heavy." Maybe every month or so, he'll really "tie one on." So what? He's just trying to have a little fun. He's only young once, right?

It worries him just a tad, however, how he can never remember what happened after a major party. He just wakes up the next morning with a major hangover to match. So what? It only happens once in a while. He's just having some fun. He doesn't *have* to drink. He just does it to have some fun with his friends.

The problem is that last Saturday morning, his dad entered his bedroom with the most somber expression on his face. Mortimer wondered how anybody could be beet red in anger and yet resemble a hard, cold stone statue like that. That's when his dad stated in a deathly, steel-like calm, icy voice, "How'd you annihilate the right front fender on the Lexus last night?"

"Oh, s _ _ _," Mortimer thought to himself. He didn't remember a thing.

3. Using the suggestions for working with alcoholics and other drug abusers presented in the text, the remainder of the class should take turns approaching each client about his or her behavior and situation. Role players should be addressed in turn, one at a time. The discussion for each client should take about 10 minutes. Your instructor will tell you when it's time to talk to the next client.

    Class members should ask questions and make comments targeting three aspects of the situation:

    a. Assessment of whether each role player is an alcoholic.
    b. Addressing the problem of denial.
    c. Determining what resources, if any, may serve as appropriate referrals.

4. Following this discussion, your instructor will help you summarize your conclusions.

I.   **Introduction**

    A.   *Figure 8.1: Evaluation in the Generalist Intervention Model (GIM)*

II.   **Evaluating Social Work Practice**

    A.   Evidenced-based practices—Ensures that we use only knowledge that has been adequately tested using some degree of scientific rigor

    B.   Authority-based practice—Relies on opinion and testimonials to support specific interventions

    C.   Definition and Purposes of Evaluation

        1.   Evaluation—A process of assessing the success or worthwhile

        2.   Micro level—Determine to what extent our work with a specific client was successful

        3.   Mezzo level—Determine if the treatment or educational group achieved its purposes

        4.   Macro level—Determine whether entire programs accomplished their purpose

        5.   *Highlight 8.1: Evaluating Programs*

            a.   Provides data that will assist current program improvement

            b.   Helps agency administrators keep track of new programs still in the development stage

            c.   Assists agencies in determining which programs are most effective and should be continued

            d.   Identifies programs with limited effectiveness to be considered for elimination

            e.   Demonstrates to funding bodies that their money is being spent in accordance with their expectations

            f.   Provides donors, legislators, and other organizational supporters reassurance that their support is justified

D. External Factors in Evaluation

    1. Economic

    2. Political

    3. Consumer

    4. Accountability—In social work it involves being responsible for and answerable to others for the quality and effectiveness of one's efforts

E. Obstacles to Evaluation

    1. Reasons evaluation has not been an ongoing concern for workers

        a. Leaves practitioner vulnerable

        b. Workers often too busy

        c. Many agencies have not emphasized its importance

        d. Most social workers lacked training in use of evaluations

    2. Thrusts of evaluations

        a. Monitoring—Looks at the process of giving service

        b. Evaluation—Looks at the effectiveness of the service provided

        c. Effectiveness—Involves succeeding at what you set out to accomplish

        d. Efficiency—Concerns doing it at a reasonable cost

F. The Evaluation Process

    1. Key terms and ideas

        a. Formative evaluations—Focus on the process of providing help instead of the end product of help giving (e.g. PERT charts)

        b. Summative evaluations—Provide information about whether or not the outcome we anticipated at the beginning of our planned change process has been achieved

        c. Differences between formative and summative evaluations—Formative evaluations occur while a planned change process is continuing, and summative evaluations occur at the conclusion of the planned change process, looking backward

        d. Baseline A measure of the frequency, intensity, or duration of a behavior

e. Validity—Refers to the extent to which you are measuring what you think you are measuring

    1) Face validity—Professional judgment about whether the measure actually measures what it is supposed to

    2) Concurrent validity—Exists when scores on one instrument correlate well with scores on another instrument that is already considered valid

    3) Predictive validity—Exists when a measure can be used to predict future events (e.g., SAT test scores)

    4) *Critical Thinking Question 8.1*

f. Reliability—The extent to which an instrument measures the same phenomenon the same way each time it is used

g. Data-gathering methods

    1) Surveys or interviews

        a) Structured (specific set of questions in a structured format)

        b) Unstructured (open-ended questions in an informal discussion)

    2) Observations

        a) Direct (person-to-person)

        b) Recorded

            (1) Videotape

            (2) Self-reports (subjective)

                (a) Depression scales

                (b) Assertiveness schedules

    3) *Highlight 8.2: Finding Valid and Reliable Instruments*

    4) Products—Achievement of a specific task or change in behavior

    5) Observational measures—Rely on others to observe a change in the client's behavior

h.   Independent and dependent variables

    1)   Independent variable—The factor we think is responsible for causing certain behaviors, reactions, or events

    2)   Dependent variable—The outcome or end product of the helping process (outcome is dependent upon the helping efforts)

i.   Generalizability—The ability of a set of results in one situation to fit another circumstance or instance

    1)   Substantial number of cases is necessary

    2)   Members of group must be representative

j.   Generalization across the globe

2.   *Critical Thinking Question 8.2*

III.   Evaluation Designs for Generalist Practice

A.   Single-Subject Designs—Research methods aimed at determining whether or not an intervention was successful, and are frequently used with a single case or client

    1.   AB design—The outcome of the intervention is compared to the state of affairs prior to intervention

        a.   The A represents the preintervention state, and B the intervention

        b.   *Figure 8.2: Single-Subject (AB) Design*

        c.   Steps in implementation

            1)   Identify an easily measured goal

            2)   Baseline established showing frequency of the behavior prior to intervention (Phase A)

            3)   Record kept of frequency of behavior during and following intervention

    2.   B Design—Used when there is no opportunity to establish a baseline

        a.   Only the behavior occurring during and at the end of the intervention phase can be measured

        b.   It is relatively simplistic to consider results that occur in Phase B to be caused by the intervention

        c.   *Figure 8.3: B Design Without a Baseline*

3. ABC Design

    a. Phase A: Period prior to intervention

    b. Phase B: When social worker begins to provide an intervention

    c. Phase C: Additional treatment prescribed

    d. *Figure 8.4: ABC Design*

4. ABAB Design

    a. A: Baseline

    b. B: Intervention runs its course and is discontinued

    c. A: Based on the measurement level when the last intervention stopped

    d. B: Intervention is begun again

    e. *Figure 8.5: ABAB Design*

    f. The Rathus Assertiveness Scale is an example

B. Additional Perspectives on Single-Subject Design

1. BAB Design—Multiple baselines

2. *Figure 8.6: BAB Design with Multiple Baselines*

C. Goal-Attainment Scaling—A method used when achievement of the goal is sufficiently important to be used as the primary outcome criterion

1. *Table 8.1: Goal-Attainment Scaling*

2. *Table 8.2: Modified Goal-Attainment Scaling*

D. Task-Achievement Scaling—A method of evaluating the degree to which an identified set of tasks has been accomplished

1. Typically a five-point scale is used

2. *Table 8.3: Task-Achieving Scaling*

E. Client Satisfaction Questionnaires—A series of questions designed to learn the reactions of the client to various aspects of a product

1. *Figure 8.7: A Client Satisfaction Questionnaire*

2. Disadvantage: Potential for misuse

F. Target-Problem Scaling—A process where a problem is identified, a plan is implemented, and changes in target problems are measured to determine if the problem has changed in severity or seriousness

   1. The original problems are rated by degree of severity

   2. *Table 8.4: Target-Problem Change Scale*

   3. Peer review—A formal evaluation by a relevant peer group of an individual's general competence or specific actions

IV. Evaluation Designs for Programs

A. Needs Assessments—Systematic efforts to help an agency determine whether, and to what extent, a program is needed. A form of front-end analysis

B. Evaluability Assessments—Methods designed primarily to answer the questions: "Can this program be evaluated?" and "Is the agency evaluation ready?"

C. Process Analysis—Designed to evaluate the way interventions in an agency are carried out (formative evaluations)

D. Program Outcome Analysis—An evaluation designed to tell us whether or not a program is working

E. Continuous Quality Assurance Evaluations—Evaluations focused on measuring attainment of previously identified program goals

   1. Program goals are usually specific indicators that the agency has accepted as evidence of best practices

   2. *Table 8.5: Continuous Quality Assurance Evaluation*

F. Program Monitoring—An ongoing activity designed to provide information to the agency on all aspects of its operation

G. *Table 8.6: Evaluation Designs for Programs*

V. Issues and Problems in Evaluation

A. Problems in Generalizability

   1. Random sample—One in which all elements in a population have an equal probability of being included in a sample

   2. Stratified random sampling—A method of sampling that ensures some important subset or strata of a population is not accidentally left out of a typical random sample

B. Wrong Choices of Evaluation Tools

C.   Failure to Involve Clients in the Evaluation Process

D.   Staff Distrust of Evaluation

E.   Evaluation Process Interference with Service-Giving

F.   Alternative Explanations for Program Outcomes

       1.   *Highlight 8.3: Alternate Explanations for Outcomes*

             a.   History—Any event that occurs prior to the end of an intervention

             b.   Maturation—The process of aging

             c.   Mortality—The loss that occurs when some of the people in the sample begin to drop out

             d.   Creaming—The tendency of some programs to take only the very best candidates for a program

             e.   Regression towards the mean—The tendency for extreme scores to move toward the mean over time

             f.   Reactance—The reaction or change of behavior that occurs simply because of a new situation or environment

G.   Unanticipated Consequences

       1.   Side effects—When a program has had consequences or outcomes we did not envision. These may be classified as harmful to clients, neutral in their impact, or beneficial

       2.   Regressive effects—A situation gets worse as a result of the intervention (e.g., *Scared Straight* programs

H.   *Highlight 8.4 Cultural Competence and Evaluation*

       1.   Ensure that samples chosen for research accurately reflect the diversity and characteristics of the entire population

       2.   Be sensitive to data gathering approaches that may be less effective with some groups

       3.   Recognize that language differences and facility with English may place respondents from other cultures at a disadvantage in terms of understanding either written or oral interview questions

       4.   Whenever possible, involve members of minority groups, people of color, women, and gay and lesbian people in the planning stages of research that affects them

5. Recognize that questionnaires and other data sources that have worked well with men or white people may not work as well with women or people of color

6. Use culturally sensitive language when developing instruments

7. Where needed, use interpreters to ensure that respondents understand the question and the researcher understands the response.

8. Avoid unnecessary emphasis on problems with oppressed populations. Focus on strengths to the extent possible

9. Avoid generalizing findings to any other group than that represented in the study

10. Look for differences among participants that may help understand differential outcomes

11. Ensure that all questions are gender-neutral and not biased toward the life experiences of any particular group

12. When giving choices on questionnaires make certain that you have not overlooked critical options such as ethnic group or forced choices that do not apply

VI. **Termination and Follow-Up**

A. *Figure 8.8: Planned Change Steps in the Generalist Intervention Model (GIM)*

B. Ethical Practice and Critical Thinking About Termination

1. Termination must be based on clear evidence that the goals and objectives have been achieved

2. *Critical Thinking Question 8.3*

C. Terminating Professional Relationships

D. Tasks of termination

1. Decide when to terminate the professional worker-client relationship

2. Evaluate achievement of objectives

3. Maintain and continue progress

4. Resolve emotional reactions of the worker and client

5. Make appropriate referrals

6. Ultimately, the goal at termination is to empower the client system

E. Planned terminations

F.   Unplanned terminations

    1.   Terminations may occur because no progress has been made or because problems are getting worse, not better

    2.   Client is being referred to another agency

    3.   Clients may simply quit coming without notifying the worker

    4.   The area being probed is too sensitive and the client cannot tolerate opening the matter up

    5.   *Highlight 8.5: Unplanned Terminations in Groups*

        a.   Lack of motivation

        b.   Changes in life that reduce interest in the group

        c.   Problems with group meeting schedules

        d.   Feeling out of place in the group

        e.   Inability to form appropriate relationships with other group members

        f.   Discomfort with strong feelings expressed in the group

        g.   Insufficient orientation to therapy

        h.   Feeling scapegoated in the group

        i.   Problems arising from concurrent individual and group therapy

        j.   Lack of financial resources to continue

        k.   Satisfaction with current changes that have occurred

    6.   Other points about termination

    7.   Reactions and feelings in terminations

        a.   Extent and range of emotional reactions

        b.   Amount of contact

        c.   Size and type of system

        d.   *Table 8.7: Factors Affecting Reactions to Termination*

        e.   Mixed feelings

        f.   Worker reactions to termination

G.	Helping Clients at Termination

1.	Planning for termination

2.	Addressing feelings about termination

a.	Worker should help the client express any feelings associated with termination

b.	Sometimes sharing the worker's own feelings about the approaching termination can be helpful

c.	*Highlight 8.6: Termination Feelings of Family and Group Members*

3.	Summarizing progress

H.	Stabilization of Change

1.	Suggestions to help clients maintain and generalize changes

a.	Help clients select relevant and appropriate situations to work on

b.	Help clients build confidence in their own abilities

c.	Use multiple situations and settings when helping members learn new behaviors

d.	Use naturally occurring consequences rather than creating artificial ones

e.	Extend treatment through use of follow-up sessions

f.	Reduce setbacks in other environments

g.	Help members confront future problems by teaching them a problem-solving process

2.	Stabilizing change in small groups

a.	Vary use of group activities

b.	Ceremonies (graduations) help intensify the sense of ending and acknowledge progress of client

3.	Stabilizing change in large systems

a.	Routinize procedures and processes

b.	Clarification of policies and procedures

c.	Reducing the influence of the change agent

4.	Addressing ongoing needs of clients

VII. **Client Follow-Up**

    A. Follow-up—The act of acquiring information about a client following termination

    B. *Highlight 8.7: Possible Tasks for the Worker at Follow-Up*

        1. Actively represent the consumer

        2. Discuss problems

        3. Straighten out difficulties

        4. Prepare the consumer

    C. Possible intervention outcomes that may be discovered during follow-up

        1. The client may be functioning at the same level in follow-up as at termination

        2. The client may have shown more improvement since termination

        3. There may be a gradual deterioration that is a result of premature withdrawal of the intervention or of other unknown factors

        4. Rather than a gradual deterioration, there may be a complete relapse

    D. Doing the Follow-Up

    E. Overcoming Barriers to Follow-Up

EXPERIENTIAL EXERCISES AND SIMULATIONS

There are four exercises in this chapter, each intended to help illustrate a major idea appearing in chapter 8. The first three exercises involve evaluation of practice. The first asks you to select an appropriate evaluation design for assessing effectiveness of a small program. The second activity requires you to apply your knowledge of several key concepts described in chapter 8. The third exercise asks you to determine which of several alternative explanations might account for the apparent "success" of an intervention. The final exercise involves applying your knowledge both of feelings associated with termination and of how to respond to client comments or behaviors during the termination phase.

Exercise 8.1: Evaluation of Practice

A. Brief description:
Working as a task group member in a role-play, you will apply your knowledge concerning evaluation of practice to a case situation.

B. Objectives:
You will be able to:
    1. Select an appropriate evaluation design for direct practice,
    2. Identify data that will be needed for that evaluation design and the sources of that data.
    3. Identify the program evaluation design that is most appropriate to a given case situation.

C.   Procedure:
   1.   Review the four evaluation designs for generalist practice discussed in the text. They are single-subject designs, task-achievement and goal-attainment scaling, and client satisfaction questionnaires. Also review the five types of evaluation designs for programs (needs assessments, evaluability assessments, process analysis, program outcome analysis, and program monitoring).
   2.   The instructor will assign students to task groups of four to six people. Each group will participate in a role play. Identify one person to serve as recorder for each group.
   3.   Below is a case situation describing the need for evaluation within a social agency. Read the case carefully.

Case Situation: The Morningside Center

Marian Edwards is the coordinator of juvenile services for the Morningside Center, a small private agency that has a contract with the Department of Human Services. Under the terms of the contract, the Morningside Center provides after-school recreational and group activities for adolescent males and females. The Department of Human Services is requiring an evaluation component in all future contracts, and the Morningside Center's contract is up for renewal. Marian has been asked to design an evaluation mechanism that will help determine whether Morningside Center is achieving its purpose of giving adolescents a place to go so that they can stay out of trouble. Many of the adolescents in the Morningside area are at-risk for involvement in delinquent behavior. It is this behavior that the Department of Human Services is most interested in preventing. Marian is meeting with her staff to discuss the need to design an evaluation program. You are part of that staff for purposes of this exercise.

---

   4.   Assess the four evaluation designs to establish which one seems appropriate for use in this situation. Use the following format for your assessment:

Design	Pros	Cons
Single-subject design:		
Goal-attainment scaling:		
Task-achievement scaling:		

Client satisfaction questionnaire:

5. Select the design that seems most appropriate to this situation and list three reasons why this design is best.

    a.   Most appropriate design: _____

    b.   Reasons why this design is best:

         1) _____

         2) _____

         3) _____

6. Identify at least two types of information that might be gathered for use in this evaluation. Identify the sources or methods by which this information might be acquired.

    a.   Types of information:

         1) _____

         2) _____

         3) _____

    b.   Methods for gathering information:

         1) _____

         2) _____

7. Assume that the evaluation design you select has been in use for two years. Of the five types of evaluation designs for programs mentioned in the text (needs assessments, evaluability assessments, process analysis, program outcome analysis, and program monitoring), which is best suited to the task of determining whether the Morningside Center is effective?

_____

_____

Why is it the most suited?

_____

_____

8. Record your responses to items 5 through 7 and report them back to the larger class at the direction of the instructor.

9. Your instructor will lead a class discussion focusing on the following questions:

    a.   Why do social workers seem more interested in "doing" social work than in "evaluating" it?

    b.   Why is evaluation of social work practice important? To whom is it important?

    c.   Does a funding body such as the Department of Human Services have a right to require an evaluation component in contracts they sign with other agencies? Why or why not?

A.   Brief description:
       You will test your knowledge of key concepts used in the evaluation of practice. You will be
       given a list of statements, some or all of which may be incorrect. Your task will be to distinguish
       between those which are incorrect and those which are correct. You are to work alone on this
       project.

B.   Objectives:
       You will be able to:
       1.   Identify key terms used in the evaluation of practice and connect them with their
              meanings.
       2.   Recognize when such terms are being used incorrectly or misinterpreted.

C.   Procedure:
       1.   Review the section of Chapter 8 entitled Key Terms and Ideas.
       2.   Listed below are several statements regarding some of the key concepts described in
              Chapter 8. Read each of them carefully.
       3.   For each statement, use the space provided to answer the questions posed.

Key Concept Statements

a.   Frank says an assertiveness program which has proven successful with six
       nonassertive clients can be utilized for *all* nonassertive clients. He states the
       success of one program can be *generalized* to *all* clients with the same problem.
       Is he right? Why or why not?

       _____

       _____

       _____

b.   A paper-and-pencil questionnaire seems to accurately distinguish between clients
       who are depressed and those who are not. Clients with a score over 30 on the
       questionnaire are usually given both anti-depression medication and counseling
       when they are seen by a psychiatrist. Would this suggest that the questionnaire is
       a *valid* measure of depression? Why or why not?

       _____

       _____

       _____

c.   Mary and John are arguing about the meaning of *dependent* and *independent*
       variables. John says that the interventions he is doing with a family constitute
       the *dependent variable* and the changes the parents have made, such as praising
       the children more and communicating feelings to one another, are the
       independent variables. Mary says John has the concepts backward. Who is right
       and why?

       _____

       _____

       _____

---

d. Alice has been using an at-home pregnancy test to determine if she is pregnant. The test has given different results on three occasions. Alice says the test does not seem *reliable*. Is she right? Why or why not?

_____

_____

_____

e. At the conclusion of each group session, Ed, the social worker, asks the group members to give their opinions about how well the group functioned during the session. Ed commented to a colleague that he does this as one type of *formative evaluation*. Has Ed correctly described this type of evaluation?

_____

_____

_____

Exercise 8.3: Alternative Outcome Explanations

A. Brief description:
    You will be given three case situations involving clients. Following each you will need to identify a possible alternative explanation for the successful outcome of the case.

B. Objectives:
    You will be able to:
    1. Identify alternative explanations for outcomes in various case situations.
    2. Recognize when apparent success of an intervention might be explained by factors unrelated to your intervention.

C. Procedure:
    1. Read each of the following case situations.
    2. Select an alternative explanation for the outcome which seems most probable given your knowledge of evaluation.

Case Situation #1

A group for twelve delinquent adolescents was begun ten weeks ago by the Juvenile Probation Department. The group was voluntary and involved regular sessions with a probation officer who asked the members to talk about their feelings. Six of the members dropped out along the way. Each of the six that remained evaluated the group experience very positively. Which of the following explanations might better explain the "successful" outcome?

a. History
b. Maturation
c. Mortality
d. Reactance

What is the reason for your answer?

Case Situation #2

Five very nonassertive adults joined a group to teach them to be more assertive. The group met for twelve weeks. Each person in the group was given an assertiveness test before joining and during the twelfth session. All showed more assertiveness on the last test. Other than an effective assertiveness training program, what might account for the change in their scores from the first session to the last?

a.　　Maturation
b.　　Regression toward the mean
c.　　Mortality
d.　　Creaming

What is the reason for your answer?

Case Situation #3

You see an advertisement for a new program which claims a high rate of success in treating anorexia (an eating disorder). The only people admitted to the program are those who have been through a battery of tests and interviews. All candidates are evaluated on their motivation to change, and only those with the highest motivation are admitted to the program. What might explain the very positive outcomes claimed by this program?

a.　　Maturation
b.　　History
c.　　Mortality
d.　　Creaming

What is the reason for your answer?

Exercise 8.4: Addressing Feelings About Termination

A.　　Brief description:
　　　　In this exercise, you will be considering the cases of three clients with whom separate social workers have been working for six months. In each case, the worker-client relationship has focused on helping the client get back on her feet after she left a physically abusive spouse and acquired a job to support herself.

B.　　Objectives:
　　　　You will be able to:
　　　　1.　　Recognize feeling expressions associated with termination;
　　　　2.　　Identify possible techniques useful in helping clients deal with termination.

C.　　Procedure:
　　　　1.　　Read each of the following excerpts from a worker-client interview.
　　　　2.　　For each vignette, select one worker response which appears to be the most appropriate and circle your choice.
　　　　3.　　Compare your answers with the class.

Vignette #1

Joan is meeting the worker for the last time. She appears a bit red-eyed near the end of the session as they finish their discussion about how much as happened in the past six months. Ann, the worker, is unsure of what might be going on in Joan's mind since they have talked about termination at previous meetings. Which of the following might be an appropriate response on Ann's part?

a.   Let's not get too choked up now; you are doing fine.

b.   You seem a little teary just now. What are you feeling?

c.   You seem upset. Should we meet once more to talk about how things are going?

Vignette #2

Jan has just gotten a new job as a nurse's aide. She seems happy and expresses her glee to her social worker, Dorothy, at their last session together. What should Dorothy say?

a.   I am so happy for you and delighted that you have found something that really interests you. You really look excited.

b.   You are happy now but I worry about how you will get along after our sessions are over. This has been an important part of your life and I would think you might miss it. Many others have.

c.   Let's talk about how you're feeling about the ending of our relationship. I feel a bit blue that we won't be seeing each other every week.

Vignette #3

Susan appears distraught and anxious at the beginning of the next-to-the-last session. She states that she really does not feel that she has made much progress in her work with Mark, and wonders aloud whether this has all been a waste of time. Now Mark is confused. What might he say?

a.   You seem pretty upset today. I wonder what's going on.

b.   We have accomplished a great deal together and I wonder how you can say we haven't made much progress.

c.   Susan, something is troubling you today. I sense that you may be reacting to the ending of our sessions. A common reaction to termination is to be fearful of the future. People often question whether they've accomplished anything. Perhaps you are a bit angry with me. Do any of these strike a chord with you?

Chapter 9
Understanding Families

I.   **Introduction**

II.   **Families and the Generalist Intervention Model**

III.   **Family Assessment**

    A.   Families—A primary group whose members assume certain obligations for each other and generally share common residences

    B.   Families—Can include two or more people who assume responsibility for each other's well-being over time (e.g., caring for children, providing economic support, or giving help and support during illness)

    C.   Assessing Family Communication

        1.   Verbal and nonverbal communication

            a.   Intent—What the sender means to say

            b.   Impact—What the receiver understands the sender to be saying

            c.   *Highlight 9.1: An Example of Conflict Between Verbal and Nonverbal Communication*

            d.   Family interaction and communication

                1)   What one family member might say in words to another one may not be what that sender really means

                2)   Nonverbal behavior can provide important clues regarding what a sender really wants to convey

                3)   Critical nonverbal communication may involve any number of seemingly petty behaviors

                4)   Nonverbal behaviors often transcend trivial behaviors

                5)   Many times a generalist practitioner will be called upon to disentangle confused verbal and nonverbal communications

2.   Avenues of communication

    a.   Consonance—Refers to the extent to which the receiver accurately hears and understands the sender

    b.   Condemnation—Involves regular patterns of family members severely criticizing, blaming, negatively judging, or nagging other family members

    c.   Submission—Involves feeling so downtrodden, guilt-ridden, or incapable that you succumb to another's will

    d.   Intellectualization—The process of staging all communication within a strictly logical, rational realm

    e.   Indifference—Involves remaining unconcerned, not caring one way or another, and appearing detachedly aloof

3.   *Critical Thinking Question 9.1*

D.   Assessing Family Structure

1.   Family structure—The organization of relationships and patterns of interaction occurring within the family

2.   The family as a system

    a.   Boundaries and subsystems

        1)   Boundaries—Invisible lines of demarcation that separate the family from outside non-family environment. Inside the family system, they differentiate subsystems, and help achieve and define the separate subunits of the total system

        2)   Subsystem—A secondary or subordinate system (system within a system)

3.   Family norms—The rules that specify what is considered proper behavior within the family group

    a.   In families with problems, the family rules usually do not allow the family or the individual members to function effectively and productively

    b.   Social workers need to identify and understand family norms so that inappropriate, ineffective norms can be changed

    c.   *Highlight 9.2: Family Norms Vary Dramatically from One Family to Another*

4. Family roles—Individually prescribed patterns of behavior reinforced by the expectations and norms of the family

5. Balance of power within the family system

   a. Power—The ability of prevailing family members to have authority and control over the perspectives or actions of other family members

   b. Power is relative—one individual has more or less power than other individuals

   c. In assessing a family, the important question is whether or not the balance of power as perceived by each individual is adequate and fair

6. Assessing intergenerational aspects of family systems

7. *Critical Thinking Question 9.2*

E. Assessing Life-Cycle Adjustments

   1. Traditional family life cycle concept

      a. Stage 1: Involved an unattached young adult separating from his or her family of origin

      b. Stage 2: Concerned marrying and realigning life's joys and responsibilities within a couple's framework

      c. Stage 3: Entailed having children and meeting the children's needs

      d. Stage 4: Concerned dealing with adolescent children, whose needs and strivings for independence called for very different types of interaction than that appropriate for younger children. It also marked refocusing the couple's relationship and addressing the needs of their own aging parents

      e. Stage 5: Involved sending children forth into their own new relationships, addressing midlife career issues, and coping with the growing disabilities of their own parents

      f. Stage 6: Entailed adjustments to aging themselves and addressing the inevitability of one's own death

   2. Today no single list of stages (for a typical family life cycle) is sufficient or inclusive

   3. Poverty can pose immense consequences upon the life cycle of families

   4. Social class standing in the context of a family's surrounding community has huge implications regarding development of self-esteem and the ability to function effectively

5.   Culture affects the life cycle of families at every stage

6.   Workers will need to focus both on the individualized life transitions of clients and their dynamic interactions with the social systems enveloping them

F.   Impacts of the Impinging Social Environment

     1.   Assessing a family's access to resources

         a.   *Figure 9.1: Family Access to Basic Resources (FABR)*

         b.   Be aware that the poverty line established by the U.S. government is probably significantly lower than what a family actually needs to thrive

         c.   Poverty line—A yearly cash income [minimum] (based on family size) set by the federal government to determine if an individual or household can be classified as poor

         d.   Food Stamp Program—Administered by the United States Department of Agriculture (USDA) and paid for by the federal government, was established in 1964 to supplement the ability of impoverished families to obtain food

         e.   WIC—The Special Supplementary Feeding Program for Women, Infants, and Children administered by the USDA. The intent is to provide low-income women and their children at risk of insufficient nutrition with food subsidies

     2.   *Critical Thinking Question 9.3*

     3.   Difficulties in soliciting personal information

         a.   Acknowledge the fact that solicitation may be difficult

         b.   Be a warm, giving, and dependable person who uses an appropriate dose of self-disclosure to help the client see you as a real and genuine person

         c.   Start out with asking less-sensitive questions

         d.   Be tactful

         e.   If clients refuse to provide information, follow up with an effort to engage the client in a discussion of general reasons why some topics might be hard for people to discuss and why people often want to withhold and protect certain information

IV.   Family Conflicts, Problems, and Their Resolutions

    A.   Partner Difficulties

          1.   Enhance the congruence between intents and impacts as individuals communicate

          2.   *Highlight 9.3: An Example of Communication Problems Within a Marriage*

    B.   Parent-Child Relationship Difficulties

          1.   Approaches include applications of learning theory and communication techniques involving the use of active listening and the sending of "I" messages

          2.   Behavior modification—Involves the application of learning theory principles to real-life situations

          3.   Active listening—Involves the receiver of the message trying earnestly to understand the sender's feelings and messages, and the receiver putting this understanding into his or her own words and feeding it back for the sender's verification

          4.   "I-messages"—Involve responding to another person's verbal and nonverbal behavior by clearly stating your feelings and reactions to that behavior. Instead of using a blaming "you-message," structure your verbal response to use an "I-message"

    C.   Personal Problems of Individual Family Members

          1.   Scapegoating—The process of identifying one member as the problem

          2.   Treatment goals will most likely involve the restructuring of various family relationships

    D.   External Environmental Stresses: The Impact of Social and Economic Forces

    E.   *Critical Thinking Question 9.4*

V.   Variations in Family Structures

    A.   Single-Parent Families

          1.   More than 28 percent of U.S. families with dependent children are supported by single parents

          2.   A substantial majority (over 80 percent) of single parents are women

          3.   Over 65 percent of single women and over 60 percent of married women age 16 or older work outside the home. Over 68 percent of single mothers with children under age 6 are employed

4. Although over 73 percent of white families with children under age 18 have both parents living within the home, only about 35 percent of African American families and almost 65 percent of Hispanic families have both parents living there

5. Whereas almost 12 percent of all white women are living below the poverty level (compared to almost 10 percent of white men), 26.5 percent of African American women and 24 percent of Hispanic women live below the poverty level

6. The median income for all married-couple families is $63,630. In contrast, the median income for female family heads with no husband present is about 42 percent of that (or $26,964). This compares with a median income of $40,293 for male family heads with no wife present

7. Women earn about 76 percent of what men earn; for women of color, this figure drops to 64 percent

8. Almost 36 percent of babies are born to unmarried women in the United States

B. Single-Teenage Parents

1. Although the rate of teen pregnancy in the United States has declined during the last 40 years, the U.S. rate is significantly higher than those in other industrialized nations

2. The disproportionately high rate of pregnancies and births to African American and Latina teens has been linked to the higher rates of poverty and lower levels of academic success among these populations

3. Suggestions for working with single adolescent parents, focusing on a continuum of services

   a. Preventing pregnancy

      1) Research indicates that sound sex education programs can delay first intercourse, reduce the frequency of intercourse, decrease the number of partners, increase condom use, and reduce pregnancy and sexually transmitted diseases

      2) Ready access to contraception

      3) Promotion of chastity has been proposed; however, research has not established that this approach works

   b. Help during pregnancy

   c. Helping adolescent fathers

d. Helping mothers after the pregnancy

    1) Thcy may need help in learning about positive parenting and child management skills

    2) Adolescent mothers often need help in avoiding more pregnancies

    3) Young mothers often need assistance in their future life planning

4. Assessment and personal values—Clarifying your own personal values and prohibiting these values from interfering with assessment and other aspects of practice is critically important

C. Remarriage and Blended Families

1. Blended families—One or both spouses have biologically parented one or more children with someone else prior to the current marriage

2. Issues to address with blcndcd families

    a. Loyalty conflicts may arise

    b. Defense of territoriality

    c. Search for identity as a family unit

3. Aspects characterizing blended families

    a. Change and loss

    b. Unrealistic belief systems

    c. Insiders versus outsiders

    d. Power

    e. Loyalty conflicts

    f. Boundary problems

    g. Discrepant life cycles

4. *Highlight 9.4: An Example of Life Within a Blended Family*

5. *Critical Thinking Question 9.5*

VI. **Enhancing Cultural Competency: Family Assessment and Keys to Empowerment**

    A.   Immigration and Acculturation

        1.   How long ago newcomers arrived

        2.   The circumstances of their arrival

        3.   The support system they found upon arrival

        4.   The degree of acceptance they found here

    B.   School Adjustment

    C.   Employment

    D.   Questions for Assessing Culturally Diverse Families

    E.   *Critical Thinking Question 9.6*

    F.   *Highlight 9.5: Assessment of Diverse Families and Empowerment*

        1.   Respect the unique, culturally defined needs of various populations

        2.   Acknowledge the role that culture plays in shaping behaviors, values, and view of the society

        3.   Recognize that primary sources of support for minority populations are natural helping systems

        4.   Acknowledge differences in the concepts of *family* and *community* among various cultures and even subgroups within cultures

        5.   Remember that minority populations are usually best served by people who are part of that culture

        6.   When working with minority families, know that process is as important as outcome

        7.   Understand and recognize when values of minority families are in conflict with dominant society values

        8.   Practice with the knowledge that some behaviors are adjustments to being different

EXPERIENTIAL EXERCISES AND SIMULATIONS

The exercises in this chapter address various aspects of assessing and understanding families. Exercise 1 asks you to assess the roles in your own family. Exercises 2 and 3 employ an assessment instrument which specifies and clarifies a family's access to a wide range of resources. Exercise 4 provides a role play involving problem solving with a married couple. Finally, Exercise 5 asks you to propose policies which are supportive of positive family functioning.

Exercise 9.1: Family Roles

A. Brief description:
    You will identify the roles in your own family, share this information in pairs, and relate this information about roles to families you are likely to encounter in practice.

B. Objectives:
    You will be able to:
    1. Identify a variety of family roles.
    2. Discuss how family roles are important in practice with families.

C. Procedure:
    1. Prior to the exercise, review the material in the text on family assessment skills, especially that concerning family roles.
    2. Focus either on your family of origin or on your current family configuration. Take about ten minutes to write down answers to the questions below about family roles[1].

Family Roles

a. What specific roles does each family member occupy?

    _____
    _____
    _____
    _____

b. Do the various roles played work well together for the family's benefit?

    _____
    _____
    _____
    _____

c. Are any of the roles ambiguous, redundant, or left empty? Please explain.

    _____
    _____
    _____
    _____

d. Is there flexibility among family roles so that the family is better able to adjust to crisis situations? Please explain.

---

[1] These questions are used when assessing families. See A.M. Holman, *Family Assessment: Tools for Understanding and Intervention* (Beverly Hills, CA: Sage, 1983), p. 30.

    e.   Do the family's roles conform with basic social norms? (For example, society
          does not condone a criminal role.)

          _____

          _____

          _____

          _____

    f.   Do the family's roles function to enhance the family's feelings of self-worth and
          well-being or detract from these feelings? Please explain.

          _____

          _____

          _____

          _____

          _____

3.   Separate into pairs and discuss your answers to each question with your partner.
4.   After about ten minutes your instructor will call you back to join a full class discussion
      addressing the following questions:
      a.   What roles are most pronounced in your family?
      b.   What value judgments did you find yourself making about your family's roles?
      c.   What roles do you think are most pronounced in families generally?
      d.   What roles do you think emphasize the uniqueness of your family?
      e.   Can you think of a dysfunctional family you know?
      f.   What, if any, problems regarding roles did the family members experience?
      g.   What types of role problems do you think you will be most likely to confront in
            practice?

Exercise 9.2: Family Resources

A.   Brief description:
      You will be asked to complete a portion of a family resource assessment instrument and discuss
      the experience with the class.
B.   Objectives:
      You will be able to:
      1.   Assess the resources available to your own "family".
      2.   Relate this experience to real practice situations.
      3.   Recognize the variety of resources potentially available to families in need.
C.   Procedure:
      1.   Before beginning the exercise, review the information provided in the text concerning
            assessing a family's access to resources.
      2.   Take about 10 minutes to fill out the form presented below, which is the first section of
            "Family Access to Basic Resources (FABR)."[2]   Before beginning, establish the
            boundaries of your family. Focus on your current family, your family of origin, or
            yourself if you are single. It doesn't matter which family group you decide is
            appropriate. The important thing is to have a specific family group in mind.

_____

[2] Reprinted from Nancy R. Vosler, "Assessing Family Access to Basic Resources: An Essential Component of
Social Work Practice," in *Social Work*, 35(5) (1990), pp. 436-37. Reprinted with permission of the author and of the
National Association of Social Workers, Silver Spring, MD.

Family Access to Basic Resources (FABR)

Part 1—Monthly expenses for a family of this size and composition

Work expenses		Health care	
Transportation:	$___	Medical:	___
Child care:	___	Dental:	___
Taxes:	___	Mental health:	___
Purchases for basic needs		Special (e.g., substance abuse):	___
Decent housing:	___	Education:	___
Utilities:	___	Family & developmental	
Food:	___	(counseling) services:	___
Clothing:	___	Procurement of resources/	
Personal care:	___	services (e.g., transportation):	___
Recreation:	___		
		Monthly Total:	$___

Part 2—Potential monthly family resources

Money income
        Wages (if parents' occupations are known, what are average
           monthly wages for these types of jobs?): $___
        Child support (if applicable):   ___
        Income transfers (for those unemployed or not expected
        to work)
                Unemployment insurance: ___
                Worker's compensation: ___
                Social Security: ___
                Supplemental Security Income (SSI):   ___
                Aid to Families with Dependent Children (AFDC)[3]:   ___
                Other (e.g., general relief, emergency assistance):   ___
Credits, goods, and services (free or sliding scale):
        Housing
                Section 8:   ___
                Other housing assistance (e.g., public housing,
                      shelter, hotel/motel):   ___
                Utilities assistance: ___

---

[3] AFDC was "a public assistance program . . . funded by the federal and state governments to provide financial aid for needy children who are deprived of parental support because of death, incapacitation, or absence" (Barker, 1999, p. 15). The Personal Responsibility Act (PRA) passed by Congress in August, 1996, abolished AFDC "which had provided support for poor children and their mothers since its inception at Title IV of the 1935 Social Security Act;" AFDC was replaced by "block grants for Temporary Assistance to Needy Families (TANF) which "put a cap on federal funds provided to the states" and allowed states greater discretion in benefit distribution (Abramovitz, 1997, pp. 311-312). The purpose of the FABR questionnaire is to determine resources regardless of their source. Therefore, you might replace the AFDC category with other new programs providing benefits to children and families.

Food
　　　Food stamps:　　　　　　　　　　　　　　　　　　　　　　＿＿
　　　Women's, Infants', and Children's Supplementary
　　　　　Food Program (WIC):　　　　　　　　　　　　　　　　＿＿
　　　Food bank, food pantry, and other food assistance:　　　＿＿

　　　　　　　　　　　　　　　　　　　　Monthly Total:　　　$___

Clothing: Access to used clothing store?　　　　　　　Yes ☐ No ☐
Personal care and recreation:
　　　Access to free recreational facilities?　　　　　Yes ☐ No ☐
Health care
　　　Medicare?　　　　　　　　　　　　　　　　　Yes ☐ No ☐
　　　Medicaid?　　　　　　　　　　　　　　　　　Yes ☐ No ☐
　　　Health clinic?　　　　　　　　　　　　　　　Yes ☐ No ☐
　　　Dental clinic?　　　　　　　　　　　　　　　Yes ☐ No ☐
　　　Mental health services?　　　　　　　　　　　Yes ☐ No ☐
　　　Special services (e.g., drug abuse treatment)?　Yes ☐ No ☐
Education
　　　Public education?　　　　　　　　　　　　　Yes ☐ No ☐
　　　Special education?　　　　　　　　　　　　　Yes ☐ No ☐
　　　Tutoring?　　　　　　　　　　　　　　　　　Yes ☐ No ☐
　　　General Equivalency Diploma (GED)?　　　　　Yes ☐ No ☐
　　　Job Training?　　　　　　　　　　　　　　　Yes ☐ No ☐
Family and developmental (counseling) services
　　　Family services?　　　　　　　　　　　　　　Yes ☐ No ☐
　　　Support groups?　　　　　　　　　　　　　　Yes ☐ No ☐
　　　Family life education?　　　　　　　　　　　Yes ☐ No ☐
Procurement
　　　Transportation?　　　　　　　　　　　　　　Yes ☐ No ☐

Part 3—Current Resources

Access to resources last month

Money income
　Wages (use net pay; then subtract　　　　Clothing:　　　　　　　　$___
　　other work expenses from Part I　　　　Personal care and health care:　＿＿
　　including child care, transpor-　　　　　Education:　　　　　　　　＿＿
　　tation, etc.):　　　　　　　$___　　　Family & developmental
　Child Support:　　　　　　　　＿＿　　　　services:　　　　　　　＿＿
　Income transfers:　　　　　　　＿＿　　Procurement:　　　　　　＿＿
Credits, goods, & services:　　　　＿＿
　Housing:　　　　　　　　　　　＿＿
　Food:　　　　　　　　　　　　＿＿　　　　　　　Monthly Total:　　＿＿

3. For about ten minutes, address the following questions in a class discussion:
   a. How did it feel to fill out the FABR?
   b. To what extent was it uncomfortable to share such personal information?
   c. To what extent could you remember all of the detailed information requested?
   d. Were there resources mentioned on the form that you didn't know about or didn't understand? If so, which ones and why?
   e. How useful do you think the FABR might be in real worker/client practice situations?
   f. What did you learn from this experience?

Exercise 9.3: Clarifying Family Resources

A. Brief description:
   After completing Exercise 2, you will divide into pairs to complete the worker/client portion of the FABR.

B. Objectives:
   You will be able to:
   1. Employ a portion of a family resources assessment instrument in a simulated situation.
   2. Clarify and collect detailed resource information.

C. Procedure:
   1. Before beginning the exercise, review the information provided in the text concerning assessing a family's access to resources.
   2. Complete Exercise 2 above.
   3. Divide into pairs. Arbitrarily determine who will be the "worker" (that is, the person who will do the assessment) and who will be the "client" (that is, the person providing information).
   4. The worker should take about twenty minutes to complete the portion of the Family Access to Basic Resources (FABR) questionnaire provided below. This involves clarifying some of the information already gathered in Exercise 2.

Resource Stability[4]

How stable was each resource over the past year (very stable, somewhat stable, somewhat unstable, very unstable)? Discuss for each type of resource.

Wages: Overall access to wages through employment? Types of jobs available? Part-time or full-time? Wage levels? Benefits? How would/do you deal with child care or supervision of youth? Quality of child care? Do you have choices? How would/do you deal with an ill child? How would/do you get to and from work? What education and training are needed for good jobs? What education and training opportunities are available? Have you been laid off or terminated or experienced a plant closing? Number of times unemployed? Length of time unemployed?

---

[4] Reprinted from Nancy R. Vosler, "Assessing Family Access to Basic Resources: An Essential Component of Social Work Practice," in *Social Work* 35(5) (1990), pp. 436-37. Reprinted with permission of the author and of the National Association of Social Workers, Silver Spring, MD.

Housing: Rent or own? Choice? Maintenance a problem? Are utilities adequate? Have you been put on a waiting list or been dropped from Section 8 or other housing assistance? Have you had to move or been evicted because the landlord converted to higher rents, condominiums, etc.? Have you experienced homelessness?

Clothing: Variety for different roles?

Personal care and recreation: What kinds of recreation? Individual? Family?

Health Care: High quality? Choice? Available in a crisis? Have you been dropped from health care coverage with an employer or from Medicaid? If so, why? Have you or another family member been put on a waiting list, for example, for medical or dental care, for counseling for a mental health problem, or for treatment for alcohol or drug abuse? If so, how long did the person have to wait for services?

Other comments and reflections:

5. Rejoin the class for a ten minute discussion focusing on the following questions and issues:
    a. For the worker, how difficult was it to clarify the resources?
    b. What areas, if any, did you have difficulty understanding?
    c. Did you find yourself making value judgments in any areas?
    d. For the client, how did it feel to participate in the interview process?
    e. What information, if any, did you feel the worker misunderstood or missed?
    f. How useful do you feel such a resource assessment instrument would be in real practice situations? Why or why not?
    g. To what extent do you feel such an instrument might give you clues to undertaking macro and mezzo interventions? What are your reasons?

Role Play: Problem Solving with Couples

Social Work Role:
Two social workers do intake and provide some problem-solving counseling for Oshkosh County Social Services Department. The county is primarily rural so the workers assess a wide range of problems, provide help, and make referrals where appropriate.

Client Role:
Fred, twenty-seven, is a pleasantly attractive, slender person with an outgoing, likable personality. He works second shift in a donut factory, and has an annual salary of $22,000.

Client Role:
Ethel, twenty-five, is a nervous, intense person who frequently has a worried expression on her face. She refers to herself as being "very shy." She has a pretty face and is about twenty-five pounds overweight. Since before her marriage she has worked as a secretary for an Internet company. She earns approximately $23,000 annually. She also appears basically likable and eager to please.

The Presenting Problem:
Fred and Ethel have been married for four years. They come to Social Services because they are experiencing "marital problems."

Fred says that the problem is that he and Ethel fight all the time when they're together. He says he loves his wife and is committed to making his marriage work. He does not believe in divorce for moral and religious reasons. He and Ethel both want to have a family in a few years. He says Ethel always nags him about going out for a few beers after work with the boys and about how he really doesn't love her. No matter how much he tells her he loves her, she doesn't seem to believe him.

Ethel says the problem is that Fred ignores her all the time. He doesn't seem very interested in talking to her or spending time with her. She says she loves him very much and is committed to making the marriage work. She does not believe in divorce for moral and religious reasons. She and Fred both want to have a family in a few years. Ethel says she's getting more and more depressed about their marital situation and lack of communication. She constantly criticizes herself and wonders what she's doing wrong.

---

3.   Fred and Ethel also have hidden agendas which are recorded at the end of this chapter's exercise section. *Do not look at them at this time.* Only Fred and Ethel should read them before the role play. One intent of this exercise is for the workers to seek out information and identify problems. The hidden agendas will be shared later after the role play.

4.   The role play will begin in the middle of the interview. It is assumed that the workers have already gathered the information cited above. Their task now is to complete their assessment, prioritize problems, and make referrals as appropriate.

5.   During the role play, observers should take notes as they address the following questions:

6.   The role players should sit in the front of the room where other students can clearly observe them. The role play should last no longer than thirty minutes.
7.   After thirty minutes, your instructor will stop the role play and read Fred and Ethel's hidden agendas described at the end of this chapter's Exercise section.
8.   The class will then participate in a discussion addressing the following issues and questions:
    a.   What feedback did you note on your forms? Strengths? Weaknesses? Other comments?
    b.   How much of the clients' hidden agendas surfaced during the interview?
    c.   To what extent were the issues and future plans clear by the end of the interview?
    d.   To what extent do you think this role play might relate to the issues of real client couples?
    e.   What did you learn from participating in or observing this role play?

Exercise 9.5: Policies Impact Families

A.   Brief description:
You will break up into small groups and propose policies which would foster positive family environments.
B.   Objectives:
You will be able to:
    1.   Evaluate several policy areas directly impacting families.
    2.   Propose improved policies conducive to positive family life.
C.   Procedure:
    1.   Break down into groups of four to six persons.
    2.   For thirty minutes, discuss the policy questions listed below in six major policy areas impacting families. A volunteer should take notes so that your results can be shared later with the entire class. You should make specific suggestions when appropriate, and answer "yes" or "no" to closed-ended questions.

Policy Areas Impacting Families

a. *Employment*

1) What policies do you think would increase employment and decrease unemployment?

2) Should government subsidize industry in order to hire new workers or prevent laying off current workers?

3) Should taxes be levied on foreign imports?

4) Should the government expand old and set up new job training programs?

5) What would the costs of such policies be?

6) What can you do to help your clients gain adequate employment under such circumstances if few or no programs and policies exist to help you?

b. *Direct provision of income or substitutes for income*

1) What do you do when your clients aren't eligible for enough cash and in-kind (for example, food stamps) income transfers to survive?

2) What do you do if policies neglect clients who are slowly starving to death?

c. *Health care* (Millions of poor underemployed and unemployed people in this country are not covered.)

1) What health care policies should this country adopt to cover your clients who are poor and not currently covered?

2) Who should pay for such programs?

d. *Homeless people*

1) What can you as a social worker do if there are no programs with policies to provide your clients temporary shelter, food, and longer-term housing?

2) What can you do if families are living literally on the streets?

e. *Day care* (Most women work. More specifically, most women with children work. Adequate day care for their children is often difficult to find. It's also expensive and the quality is highly variable.)

1) Should the federal, state, and/or local governments establish policies to provide resources for day care so that parents can work?

2) Are you and others willing to pay taxes to finance these services?

3) What if your client is a single parent who receives public assistance payments barely allowing her to subsist below the poverty level? When benefits cease and she is forced to seek employment outside of the home, what if she can't afford the available day care? What policy changes might help her?

f. *Child support maintenance* (Policies dictate how much support divorced fathers provide their children. [Of course, mothers may also be required to provide support to children living with their fathers; however, this occurs infrequently.] Policies also mandate how the receipt of that support is monitored.)

    1) What if your single-parent, female client is not receiving the child support payments she needs to survive?

    2) Do existing policies indicate that a portion of the father's salary can be garnisheed, that is, legally removed from his pay and sent to his family before he receives his paycheck?

    3) Will policies mandate that this happens automatically, or must the mother seek legal counsel to advocate for her?

    4) What happens if the father moves to another state?

    5) Will that state's policies allow the garnishment of wages?

    6) What if your client, a single parent and mother of two, works for a minimum wage, can't afford adequate housing on that income, and desperately needs support payments to subsist?

3. After thirty minutes, your instructor will call you back into a full class discussion where you will share and address your group's findings.

HIDDEN AGENDAS FOR EXERCISE 4

Fred's Hidden Agenda

Fred has very high expectations for himself concerning being a good provider and husband. He gets very threatened both when Ethel criticizes him and when he feels that he's losing control of his marriage.

Fred's also afraid that Ethel's secretly drinking too much. Sometimes he smells liquor on her breath. Sometimes he finds her passed out. He's also found empty liquor bottles in the garbage. He hasn't said anything about this to her. He's afraid to confront her with it because he thinks it will move them closer to a divorce.

At this point, Fred doesn't know what to do, so he has withdrawn from Ethel. He tries to be pleasant to her but really doesn't talk to her very much. Sometimes to avoid her he goes out for a beer after work with his male friends at the factory.

Ethel's Hidden Agenda

Ethel is a very insecure person with a fairly poor self-concept. She is an expert on what is wrong with herself and sometimes wonders what Fred really sees in her. Her weight also bothers her. Sometimes she just can't stand it anymore and withdraws into drinking. She knows this is wrong and feels very guilty about it. She's drinking just about every day now. She doesn't want Fred to find out and doesn't want to talk about it.

Ethel's really afraid that Fred is turning to other women. There are several attractive women at the donut factory that she's met at parties and that Fred has casually mentioned in the past. She's terrified of losing Fred. Fred works six second-shift days a week and goes out almost every night "with the boys." Ethel thinks he's secretly having an affair. This hurts Ethel terribly. However, she is following her typical pattern of avoidance and has avoided mentioning this to Fred. Frustration has built up and she finds herself nagging and yelling at him a lot for little things.

Chapter 10
Working with Families

I.   **Introduction**

II.   **Generalist Practice with Families**

III.   **Family Treatment and the Planned Change Process**

       A.   *Highlight 10.1: Adopting a Strengths Perspective with Families*

            1.   Traditional Problem-Solving versus Strengths-Based Approaches

                   a.   Strengths perspective emphasizes that people have strengths, capabilities, coping potential, knowledge, and resources that only need be identified and tapped to help clients address their issues and needs

                   b.   The traditional problem-solving approach assumes that problems are a naturally occurring part of people's lives

            2.   Strengths-Based Strategies for Working with Families

                   a.   Build on the family's strengths and inherent desire to meet needs and reach goals

                   b.   Work collaboratively with families who are experts on their lives, their strengths, resources, and capacities

                   c.   Help the family formulate a vision of how life will be when they no longer have the problem

                   d.   Boost family participation and involvement

                   e.   Utilize environmental modification that may take the form of educating other people in the client's environment

                   f.   Model high expectations for family participation

            3.   A Case Example

IV.   **Strategizing for Family Intervention: Do You Always Have to See the Entire Family?**

       A.   Advantages to seeing the entire family together

            1.   Observing entire family in interaction can give great insight to understanding its dynamics

2. It enhances the worker's ability to assess and understand the problem from the perspective of all family members

3. The opportunity to see communication patterns

B. It is not always possible or appropriate

C. *Critical Thinking Question 10.1*

V. **Engagement, Assessment, and Planning with Families**

A. Three primary goals when beginning the intervention process with families

1. The worker needs to get a clear picture of the family's interaction, the problem itself

2. The worker must gain the family's consent to begin treatment and the family's commitment to participate

3. The worker needs to set procedures for change in motion

B. Five phases to beginning treatment

1. Phase 1: Alleviate or At Least Minimize Early Apprehension

a. A warm, cordial greeting and introduction is a pleasant way of initiating the worker-family system relationship

b. Complete family introductions

c. Clarify relationships during this phase

d. The practitioner may relate a brief history of contacts with the family and what information about the family is at his or her disposal

e. Fill in the scary unknown with concrete information

2. Phase 2: Ask Family Members to Explain What Is Wrong

a. There will likely be a wide variety of different perceptions

b. Allow the family to act as naturally as possible at this point

c. Worker may establish rules, such as family members must not interrupt each other

d. The worker may attempt to draw out quiet family members

3.   Phase 3: Establish Agreement about What Is Wrong

    a.   It is usually impossible and fruitless to search for the one problem that has some quintessential reality

    b.   Many families will verbalize superficial issues that are related to underlying problems

    c.   Instead of concentrating on solving specific problems, work with families often involves changing the way family members communicate with each other

        1)   Techniques for engineering a problem consensus

            a)   Attempt to focus on a problem or some aspect of a problem over which the family will concur

            b)   Reframe problems expressed in individual terms as problems of interactions between family members or as problems of the family as a whole

            c)   Help the family to articulate problems you observe in their interaction during the interview, problems that they are not able to express verbally themselves

            d)   If several problems have surfaced, present them to the family in the order you consider them important, ask the family members to rank the problems, then compare and contrast the results

            e)   Prevent family members from pointing their fingers at some individual and making that person the family scapegoat. Scapegoat—A family or group member who is made to bear the blame for others or to suffer in their place

    d.   Suggestions for targeting the family's problems

        1)   Limit the initial list of problems to three

        2)   Even a vague problem about which the family has a consensus is better than a list of minor, specific complaints

4.   Phase 4: Concentrate on How Family Members Relate to Each Other

    a.   Three structured ways the worker can orchestrate discussion of the problem by family members

        1)   The worker directs questions to members that further explore the problem

2) The worker instructs the family members to talk to each other about the problem

3) The worker instructs only two family members to talk about how to solve the problem with each other

    b. *Highlight 10.2: Four Ways of Exploring a Target Problem*

        1) The situation

        2) Exploration of the problem

            a) How long has the problem existed?

            b) How intense has the problem become in the last two weeks?

            c) What have family members done to solve the problem in the past?

            d) What barriers have been operating both inside and outside the family that have prevented the problem's solution until now?

        3) Summary

        4) So what happens?

    5. Phase 5: Establish Commitment to a Plan of Action

VI. Implementation of Family Intervention

    A. Empowerment by Emphasizing Family Strengths

        1. Emphasize positive statements reported by family members

        2. Encourage family members to share stories about themselves

        3. Note family interactions that reflect strength and competency

        4. Investigate times that family members enjoy together

        5. Emphasize what families do well

    B. Reframing—A strategy that helps family members view a problem or issue with a different outlook or understand it in a different way

C.	Teaching Families Problem Solving Techniques

    1.	Problem solving—A family's ability to resolve problems at a level that maintains effective family functioning

    2.	Families with problems usually require help in improving communication among members before they can master other problem solving skills

D.	Teaching Child Management Methods

    1.	Positive reinforcement—A procedure or consequence that increases the frequency of the behavior immediately preceding it

    2.	Negative reinforcement—The removal of a negative or aversive event or consequence that serves to increase the frequency of a particular behavior

    3.	Punishment—The presentation of an aversive event or the removal of a positive event that results in the decreased frequency of a particular behavior

    4.	Modeling—The learning of behavior by observing another individual engage in that behavior

E.	Offering Families Support

F.	Role Playing—Having a person assume a different role or part than she or he normally would

G.	Recording

H.	Homework Assignments—Tasks given to clients to be completed at home

    1.	Homework assignments should incorporate at least one of the following elements

        a.	Directions regarding specifically what is to be done

        b.	Specification regarding frequency or amount of times the homework should be done

        c.	Specification of how the homework is to be counted or kept track of

        d.	Directions regarding what is to be brought to the next interview or meeting

        e.	Indications of what will happen under specified circumstance

    2.	Social workers are not required to give homework assignments to families

VII. **Evaluation, Termination, and Follow-Up with Families**

    A.   One facet of evaluation is determining when longer term goals have been met in preparation for termination

    B.   Preparing the family for the end of contact with the worker and the agency is important

    C.   One aspect of follow-up is the identification of resources to continue maintenance of the family's homeostasis; another aspect concerns contacting the family to review its status and maintenance of achieve goals

VIII. **Family Issues and Services**

    A.   Multiproblem Families

        1.   Do not get overwhelmed yourself

        2.   Follow the planned change process as you would with any other situation

        3.   Partialize and prioritize the problems involved

        4.   Determine which, if any, problems you can work on yourself

        5.   Identify and use community resources

    B.   Family Preservation

        1.   Family preservation services—Intensive services generally delivered in the client's home over a brief, time-limited period

        2.   Family-based services—Reflects most of the same principles involved in family preservation, but services are not quite as intense (i.e., they involve longer timeframes and larger caseloads)

        3.   Six goals of family preservation services are to:

            a.   Protect children

            b.   Maintain and strengthen family bonds

            c.   Stabilize the crisis situation

            d.   Increase the family's skills and competencies

            e.   Facilitate the family's use of a variety of formal and informal helping resources

            f.   Prevent unnecessary out-of-home placement of children

4. Major themes in family preservation

    a. Crisis orientation

    b. Focus on family

    c. Home-based services

    d. Time limits

    e. Limited, focused objectives

    f. Intensive, comprehensive services

    g. Emphasis on education and skill building

    h. Coordination

    i. Flexibility

    j. Accessibility

    k. Accountability

5. Family preservation and planned change

    a. Four criteria for inclusion in family preservation services

        1) One or more of the children in the family is at imminent risk of out-of-home placement

        2) The family, or at least one of the adult members of the family, agrees to the service

        3) A less obtrusive community resource such as a parent aide or family counseling is either unavailable or not considered potentially effective

        4) It is determined that the children's safety will not be compromised by having them remain in the home during service provision

    b. Engagement

        1) The worker should use active listening and a nonjudgmental tone of voice when attempting to connect with the family and understand their perspective and their wants and desires

        2) Frequently the worker looks for some concrete way to help the family

c. Assessment

    1) Special emphasis is placed on safety issues for children and others in the family in addition to the family's access to necessary resources

    2) Emphasizing clients' strengths is critical

d. Planning—Suggestions for goal formulation:

    1) The client must feel that goals are significant

    2) Goals should emphasize social interaction both among family members and between them and others in the social environment

    3) Goals should be small, simple, and realistically achievable

    4) Goals should be viewed in terms of what can be done positively instead of focusing on problems

    5) Emphasize that goals are difficult to achieve

e. Implementation

f. Evaluation

g. Termination

    1) It is important to determine not only whether a program worked, but also how it worked

    2) In view of family preservation's time-limited approach, termination is actually introduced during the first family visit when the date is set

h. Follow-Up

C. Enhancing Cultural Competency: Diversity and Families

1. Lesbian and gay families

a. Homophobia—Extreme and irrational fear and hatred of lesbian and gay people

    1) Sexual orientation—A person's erotic and romantic attraction to one or both sexes

    2) *Highlight 10.3: Confronting Homophobia*

    3) *Critical Thinking Question 10.2*

b.   Coming out to oneself and others

    1)   Coming out—The process of acknowledging to oneself, and then to others, that one is gay or lesbian

        a)   Initial step is usually a person's realization that she or he feels different from the mainstream heterosexual model

        b)   The next step is accepting one's homosexuality

        c)   The decision must be made whether to be secretive or open

            (1)   Outing—Public disclosure of someone's secret homosexual orientation by someone else

            (2)   Disclosing one's gay or lesbian identity has been found to increase self-esteem, self-worth, and overall psychological adjustment

        d)   Questions to ask a client who is coming out: Who, what, why, where, and when

        e)   Referrals can also be made at the mezzo and macro levels to help people who are coming out

c.   Lesbians and gay men as parents

    1)   It is estimated that millions of lesbian and gay people reside in the United States and that millions of children are raised by lesbian and gay parents

    2)   Children raised by gay or lesbian parents are no more likely to "become gay" than children raised by heterosexual parents

    3)   Perhaps children with gay parents are raised to be more aware and acceptant of individual human differences in general

d.   Parents coming out to children

    1)   Gay and lesbian people are recommended to come out to their children at the earliest opportune time when their children are old enough to understand and ask questions for four reasons

        a)   Hiding one's homosexuality creates an atmosphere of secrecy

        b)   Evading the issue hinders positive, straightforward communication between parents and children

<ol type="c" start="3">
<li>Avoidance of the issue runs the risk that children may be informed about their parents' homosexuality from others and may be conveyed in a negative and critical manner</li>
<li>The effort of maintaining such secrecy may put pressure on family relationships</li>
</ol>

2) Suggestions for social workers to help parents come out to their children

<ol type="a">
<li>Gay and lesbian parents need to be comfortable with the fact that they are gay or lesbian</li>
<li>Gay and lesbian parents need to plan exactly what to tell their children about sexual orientation</li>
<li>If possible, coming out to their children who are young is probably least difficult</li>
<li>Teach children contextual alertness—evaluate each situation and the potential reactions of specific individuals involved</li>
</ol>

e. Social and economic oppression of lesbian and gay people

1) The right to marry

<ol type="a">
<li>The partner of a gay or lesbian person who becomes critically ill and needs hospitalization may be denied visiting privileges. Legal power of attorney documents are recommended</li>
<li>Although same-gender marriage is legal in Canada, it is only legal in Massachusetts, with civil union laws available in Vermont, New Jersey, and Connecticut</li>
<li>Thirty-nine states and the federal government have adopted defense of marriage acts, which define marriage as applying only to a man and a woman and bar recognition of same-gender marriage from other states</li>
<li>A Time/CNN poll conducted in late 2003 found that 62 percent of those interviewed opposed making gay marriages legal</li>
<li>*Critical Thinking Question 10.3*</li>
</ol>

	f)	Gay partners have no rights at all to any inheritance if there is no will
	g)	At the macro level, practitioners can advocate for new laws that forbid discrimination on the basis of sexual orientation

f. *Highlight 10.4: Empowerment of Lesbian and Gay People*

1)		Suggestions for empowering lesbian and gay people at the micro level
	a)	Don't assume that all people are heterosexual
	b)	Be sensitive to the language and terminology you use
	c)	Have a work environment that's friendly to gay and lesbian people
	d)	Become more knowledgeable about lesbian and gay life, issues, and culture
	e)	Be aware of the wide range of diversity within the lesbian and gay communities
	f)	Develop a list of local resources for gay and lesbian clients
2)		Suggestions for empowering lesbian and gay people at the macro level
	a)	Understand the many legal issues associated with lesbians and gays
	b)	Confront institutional homophobia at the state and federal levels
	c)	Become an expert in the field of gay and lesbian issues
	d)	Join and support pro lesbian and gay organizations
	e)	Support political candidates who have pro lesbian and gay agendas
	f)	Become politically active on the behalf of lesbian and gay rights by building gay-friendly support networks, coalitions, and constituencies

2.   Working with African American Families

    a.   The many strengths of African American families

        1)   Strong kinship system and support network developed beyond the simple nuclear family

        2)   The flexibility of family roles

        3)   Dedication to spirituality and serious involvement in their churches

    b.   Social work practice with African American families

        1)   Roles for social workers to assume when helping African American families

            a)   The worker needs to develop empathy for the cultural context saturated with the oppression in which African American families must live

            b)   The worker must maximize the use of practice skills and available resources to improve the social and economic conditions of African American families

            c)   The worker must advocate on behalf of African American families to change the policies, regulations, and expectations that act to discriminate against African Americans

    c.   Engage the client/family

        1.   Understand the initial silence and apparent lack of communication often posed by African American family members

        2.   Don't be defensive if family members express anger

        3.   Realize that most African American families will react most positively to an intervention process with clearly identified goals and with constraints on how long it will take to get results

    d.   Assess the family in past and present

    e.   Set mutual goals

    f.   Identify the target system for change

D.   The Current Status of Family Services

    1.   The types of family services available in any particular community depend on what the community needs and what it can afford

    2.   There is a definite macro practice aspect to the family service agency

    3.   *Highlight 10.5: An International Perspective: Policies and Programs for Families and Youth in Korea*

E.   Macro Practice with Families: Promoting Social and Economic Justice

    1.   *Highlight 10.6: Families, Macro Practice, and the Integration of Policy and Practice*

        a.   Employment

        b.   *Critical Thinking Question 10.4*

        c.   Direct provision of income or substitutes for income

        d.   *Critical Thinking Question 10.5*

        e.   Health care

        f.   *Critical Thinking Question 10.6*

        g.   Homeless people

        h.   *Critical Thinking Question 10.7*

        i.   Day care

        j.   *Critical Thinking Question 10.8*

        k.   Child support and maintenance

        l.   *Critical Thinking Question 10.9*

    2.   Poverty is a major stumbling block obstructing the progress of multitudes of American children and families

EXPERIENTIAL EXERCISES AND SIMULATIONS

Three detailed role plays are described for exercises in this chapter. They include a nontraditional family, a lesbian parent who wants to come out to her children, and a multiproblem family. Exercise 1 targets beginning techniques with families for the focus of the role play; Exercise 2 explores approaches for coming out to children; and Exercise 3 discusses specific techniques for working with multiproblem families. Exercise 4 structures the application of reframing or role-playing to one of the role-plays described earlier.

A. Brief description:

Volunteers role play a nontraditional family while the rest of the class observes and records feedback. Class discussion follows.

B. Objectives:

You will be able to:

1. Recognize initial goals and treatment phases in working with families.
2. Evaluate a family role play.
3. Formulate suggestions for effective treatment.

C. Procedure:

1. Before beginning the exercise, review the material in the text on beginnings with families. It emphasizes information that will be the focus of the exercise.[1] Initial goals include:

    a. Get a clear picture of the problem.
    b. Gain the family's consent to treatment.
    c. Set procedures for change in motion.

    The five phases for beginning treatment include:

    a. Alleviate or at least minimize early apprehension.
    b. Ask family members to explain what's wrong.
    c. Establish agreement about what's wrong.
    d. Concentrate on how family members relate to each other.
    e. Establish commitment to a plan of action.

2. Read the role-play described below. Volunteers are needed for each role. Otherwise, your instructor will assign roles.

Role Play: A Nontraditional Family

Social Work Role:

The social workers are counselors at a family services clinic. They accept call-in referrals and provide short-term counseling, emphasizing problem solving, primarily to families. On occasion, they provide individual counseling to family members in order to work on specific issues or problems.

The Situation:

This is the first interview with June Cleaver, her daughter, Waleeta, sixteen, and son, Beaver, eleven. June and her ex-husband Ward have just completed the divorce process. June called the agency in panic because of pain and confusion resulting from the divorce. You received the information presented below from the intake worker's report.

---

[1] The initial goals and five phases presented here are primarily based on material found in *Family Treatment in Social Work Practice* (4th ed.) by C. Janzen and O. Harris (Itasca, IL: F.E. Peacock, 2006).

Client Role:

June, thirty-eight, is a mild-mannered, friendly, responsive, attractive woman who is overwhelmed and confused by her recent divorce. After graduating from high school, she worked three years as a secretary and married Ward. Since her marriage, she has not worked outside the home. She has been involved in many civic organizations such as Kiwanis and the Society for Aid to the Homeless.

June thought everything in the marriage was fine—granted, a bit dull, but fine. She and Ward had a nice house and raised two fine children. People had often commented on what a fine relationship they had. They virtually never fought with each other. As a matter of fact, things were so comfortable between them that they rarely even talked with each other anymore.

Suddenly Ward broke the news to her that he had met another woman. He told June that he loved this woman and wanted to marry her. Six months later, June found herself divorced.

Ward, forty-two, is a relatively well-to-do small businessman who owns and runs a small Pac-Man outlet store. He fell in love with Barbie, twenty-six, his attractive secretary. Ward told June that he has much more in common with Barbie than he ever had with June. He told June that he loved his children and respected her, but could no longer stay in the marriage.

June is especially concerned about her present financial status. The divorce agreement mandated that she and Ward sell their home and divide the equity. This amounted to only $8,500 for each. Her total current income is $795 per month from child support. She questions whether she can do anything other than housework. She has little confidence in her own abilities.

She always thought she would grow old with Ward, living in a nice, secure, middle-class home. Now she feels her world has been shattered.

Client Role:

Waleeta is a pleasant yet assertive young woman. She has many friends and has always been a loving, well-behaved child.

Waleeta is angry and disappointed with her parents. She feels they've been keeping a big secret from her. She's angry at her father for running off with another woman and angry at her mother for letting him.

She especially has difficulties when she visits her father on weekends. She resents her new stepmother, Barbie, and has frequent arguments with her.

Although Waleeta has always been a B+ student in school, her grades have been slipping recently. She can't seem to concentrate anymore. She's worried about her parents, her lack of money for clothes and activities, herself, and relationships in general. She feels that the world has let her down.

Client Role:

Beaver is really Theodore, but everybody calls him the Beaver because he's so cute. Beaver has always been a happy, active (although a bit feisty) child. He's been well-behaved, although he has had a tendency to get into minor trouble like accidentally breaking windows or losing report cards on the way home from school. Although many of his friends have tried smoking Camels and drinking Rot-a-gut apple wine, Beaver always felt this was bad and avoided "going along with the crowd."

His father's leaving really confused him. He doesn't know quite what to do. He feels frightened and insecure. He feels more tempted now to do some of the "bad" things his friends do.

3.	The role-players should position themselves where the rest of the class can observe them clearly.
4.	The role-play should last no longer than twenty-five minutes. Your instructor will tell you when it should stop. The workers should focus on the goals and phases cited above. The clients should do their best to play the roles assigned.
5.	Observers should note their reactions during the role play on the role-play feedback form.

Role-Play Feedback Form

a.	What do you think are particularly *good techniques* used by the social workers? How did the *clients react* to these techniques? (Please be specific.)

b.	Do you see any weaknesses or areas in which improvement would be helpful? (Specific suggestions for how to improve are beneficial.)

c.	Do you have any additional thoughts or comments?

6.	After the role-play is finished, your instructor will lead a class discussion for approximately fifteen minutes focusing on the following questions:
   a.	What feedback did you note on your forms?
   b.	What were the strengths of the role-play?
   c.	What were some of the critical points during the role-play?
   d.	What techniques did the workers use that were exceptionally helpful?
   e.	What weaknesses were evident in the role-play?
   f.	What suggestions do you have for improvement? Please be specific.
   g.	How did the workers feel about how the role-play progressed?
   h.	How did the clients feel at the critical points of the role-play?
   i.	To what extent did the workers achieve their initial goals?

Exercise 10.2: A Lesbian Parent Coming Out

A.	Brief description:
	Volunteers role play a worker and a gay parent who is struggling with telling her children she's a lesbian while the rest of the class observes and records feedback. Class discussion follows.
B.	Objectives:
	You will be able to:
	1.	Recognize some of the issues involved when lesbian or gay people come out to their children.
	2.	Evaluate the effectiveness of a role-play addressing the issue of coming out.
	3.	Propose suggestions for dealing with this issue.
C.	Procedure:
	1.	Before beginning this exercise, review the material in the text on gay/lesbian families.
	2.	Read the role play described below. Volunteers are needed for each role-player. Otherwise, your instructor will assign roles.

Role-Play: A Lesbian Parent Coming Out

Social Work Role:

> The worker is a social worker at Happy Hoppy Tots, a large day care center. Her role is to address family adjustment problems involving the center's children, provide consultation regarding children's behavior to the center's "teachers," and help parents get the resources they need.
>
> The worker has been working with Frieda for the past six months. Frieda, thirty-one, is the mother of Angelo, four, a client at the center. The problem involved Angelo's temper tantrums. Specifically, the worker helped Frieda apply behavior modification techniques at home (for example, time-outs) and coordinated Angelo's behavior management with his teachers at the center. Improving control at home is related to improved control at the center. Angelo's behavior has significantly improved. The worker and Frieda have developed a good rapport.

Client Role:

> *Frieda* is a quiet, inconspicuous woman who works as a claims adjuster for an insurance company. Frieda also has another son, Harry, eight, living with her at home. She divorced Angelo and Harry's father six years ago.
>
> Frieda is grateful to the social worker for helping her with Angelo's temper tantrums. She is not usually one to talk about herself a lot or share her feelings. However, she has come to trust the worker and to appreciate the worker's competence.

The Situation:

> Frieda approaches the worker one day during one of their meetings. The two have been meeting regularly to discuss Angelo's progress.
>
> Suddenly, Frieda blurts out to the worker, "I can't stand hiding anymore. I'm a lesbian. How can I tell my children? Can you help me?"

---

3. The role-players should position themselves where the rest of the class can observe them clearly.

4. The role-play should last no longer than twenty-five minutes. Your instructor will tell you when it should stop. The worker should focus on helping Frieda decide what to do about coming out to her children. The person playing Frieda should feel free to make up and elaborate things about her role-play life.

5. Observers should note their reactions during the role-play on the role-play feedback form.

Role-Play Feedback Form

a. What do you think are particularly *good techniques* used by the social workers? How did the *clients react* to these techniques? (Please be specific.)

b. Do you see any weaknesses or areas in which improvement would be helpful? (Specific suggestions for how to improve are beneficial.)

c. Do you have any additional thoughts or comments?

---

6. After the role-play is finished, your instructor will lead a class discussion for approximately fifteen minutes focusing on the following questions:
   a. What feedback did you note on your forms?
   b. What were the strengths of the role-play?
   c. What were some of the critical points during the role-play?
   d. What techniques did the workers use that were exceptionally helpful?
   e. What weaknesses were evident in the role-play?
   f. What suggestions do you have for improvement? Please be specific.
   g. How did the worker feel about how the role-play progressed?
   h. How did Frieda feel at the critical points of the role-play?
   i. To what extent did the worker help Frieda make a decision about telling her children that she is a lesbian?

Exercise 10.3: Working with Multiproblem Families

A. Brief description:
Volunteers role play workers and members of a multiproblem family, while the rest of the class observes and records feedback. Class discussion follows.

B. Objectives:
You will be able to:
1. Recognize some of the issues involved in multiproblem families.
2. Evaluate the effectiveness of a role-play focusing on such a family.
3. Propose suggestions for effective interventions.

C. Procedure:
1. Before beginning this exercise, review chapter 10 in the text, especially the material on multiproblem families. Primary suggestions include:
   a. Don't get overwhelmed yourself.
   b. Follow the problem solving process as you would in any other practice situation.
   c. Partialize and prioritize problems.
   d. Determine which, if any, problems you can work on yourself.
   e. Identify and use relevant community resources.
2. Read the role-play described below. Volunteers are needed for each role-player. Otherwise, your instructor will assign roles.

> **Role-Play: Multiproblem Families**
>
> Social Work Role:
> The social workers are part of the family services unit in a large public welfare department in an urban county. The workers' job includes assessing the family's problems and needs, making referrals to community resources, and providing some short-term family counseling when necessary.
>
> The Situation:
> This is the third meeting with a six-person family that has come to the department because it is plagued with a multitude of problems and doesn't know where else to turn. Individual characters and problems are described below. This information was gathered during the two prior meetings when all family members were present. The workers are now at the point of establishing a plan of action.

Client Roles:

Ozzie, forty, spouse and father, is partially disabled in his legs because of a car accident. He can only walk for short distances and stand for short periods of time. He says he's depressed, feels useless, is unhappy, and has become quite "crabby." He describes himself normally as being rather quiet and reserved.

Ozzie is a high school graduate who had worked as a clerk in the city garbage collection department's office for nineteen years. He got laid off twenty-seven months ago due to departmental budget cuts. At that time, his annual salary had been $29,000.

Ozzie feels detached from his family and out of control. He has never been very involved with the children as he felt that was mostly Harriet's job.

Ozzie has defined the family's problems as follows (in unprioritized order):

- General lack of money.
- Inability to pay the rent or buy food.
- The leg is "acting up" and he needs medical attention for it, but has neither money nor insurance to pay for it.
- Almost constant fighting with Harriet.
- Feelings of inadequacy as a provider and as a husband.
- Recent sexual impotence.
- Not even enough money for booze.
- Annoyance with Grandma Hildegarde.

Harriet, thirty-two, spouse and mother, is a quiet, attractive person who has devoted her life to her family. She has an 11th grade education as she dropped out of high school to marry Ozzie. She does not consider herself to be very bright. In school, she had been placed in special education classes. She now works part-time at the Choosy Chunky Chicken Packing Plant, packing Chunky Chicken for minimum wage. Harriet has some trouble organizing household tasks and planning ahead, so she relies a lot on her mother (Grandma Hildegarde, who lives with the family) to help her make decisions.

Harriet perceives the family's problems as being the following (again in unprioritized order):

- Lack of money.
- Because of inability to pay the rent, the landlord's threatening to evict them.
- Worry over Ozzie's drinking (recently when he gets drunk, he's threatened to hit the kids).
- Fighting with Ozzie.
- Having trouble controlling the kids' behavior.
- Generally being overwhelmed and confused.

Grandma Hildegarde, sixty-nine, lives with the family for financial reasons. She expresses a generally cynical, pessimistic attitude and often dwells on "what a terrible life" she's had. She tends to interfere in Ozzie and Harriet's relationship and likes to tell them both what to do. She does love the children, especially Ricky, and likes to spend time with them. Her favorite pastime is watching daytime soap operas, especially "One Life to Live."

Hildegarde's perceptions of the family's problems include the following:

- Lack of money.
- Her social security check seems to get smaller every month.
- "Life is cruel."

Davida, fifteen, is Ozzie and Harriet's daughter. She is an outgoing, rebellious person to whom sarcasm comes easily. She is doing poorly in school, has flunked one grade, and has a truancy problem. She likes to stay out late with friends, especially older boys who are on probation. She was caught twice snorting coke in school. She is not one who likes to share how she really feels about things, especially her personal life and her family. She frequently fights with her parents.

The following are the problems as Davida perceives them:
- Lack of money.
- Frightened of being hit by her father when he's drunk (he's threatened her twice).
- Being sick and tired of fighting with her parents.
- Thinking that she's ugly.
- Wanting to go steady with one of the older guys she hangs out with.
- Being pretty depressed about life.
- Worry that she may be pregnant and not knowing what to do about it (she's not exactly certain who the father is).

Ricky, ten, has a shy, quiet personality. He doesn't have many friends. He maintains a C average in school. He doesn't like to do what his parents tell him to do (for example, going to bed when he's supposed to or doing the dishes). He has a close relationship with Grandma Hildegarde.
Ricky sees the problems as follows:
- Stopping his parents from constantly telling him what to do.
- Stopping his parents from fighting with each other all the time.
- Stopping his father from fighting with Grandma Hildegarde.
- Wanting more money, especially a greater weekly allowance.

Biff, thirteen, exhibits a "tough guy" attitude. He likes to be seen as the strong, mean, lean, killing machine, silent type. He doesn't say much but is usually sarcastic when he does. He's bored that he has to be involved in this interview. He doesn't feel very emotionally involved with the other members of his family except for Davida, over whom he tends to be protective. He spends most of his time with his gang, the Heavy Metals. He attends school irregularly, but has always managed to pass.
David's perception of the family's problems include the following:
- Wanting to "get out of here" and back to the Heavy Metals.
- Wondering how to make money almost any way he can.

3. The role-players should position themselves where the rest of the class can observe them clearly.
4. The role-play should last no longer than twenty-five minutes. Your instructor will tell you when it should stop. The workers should focus on implementing the suggestions for working with multiproblem families. The clients should portray their respective roles as best they can and elaborate details wherever they feel it's necessary.

5. Observers should note their reactions during the role-play on the role-play feedback from below.

Role-Play Feedback Form

a. What do you think are particularly *good techniques* used by the social workers? How did the *clients react* to these techniques? (Please be specific.)

b. Do you see any weaknesses or areas in which improvement would be helpful? (Specific suggestions for how to improve are beneficial.)

c. Do you have any additional thoughts or comments?

---

6. After the role-play is finished, your instructor will lead a class discussion for approximately fifteen minutes, focusing on the following questions:
    a. What feedback did you note on your forms?
    b. What were the strengths of the role-play?
    c. What were some of the critical points during the role-play?
    d. What techniques did the workers use that were exceptionally helpful?
    e. What weaknesses were evident in the role-play?
    f. What suggestions do you have for improvement? Please be specific.
    g. How did the worker feel about how the role-play progressed?
    h. How did the clients feel at the role play's critical points?
    i. What is your impression of multiproblem families?
    j. To what extent do you feel that the family portrayed in this role-play resembles multiproblem families in real life?
    k. To what extent did the workers achieve the goals noted above for working with multiproblem families?

Exercise 10.4: Practicing Specific Techniques

A. Brief description:
    Students are asked to volunteer for a family role-play where workers demonstrate the implementation of reframing or role-playing. Subsequently, the class evaluates the process.
B. Objectives:
    You will be able to:
    1. Describe reframing or role-playing.
    2. Demonstrate the technique within the context of a family role-play.
    3. Assess the implementation of the technique.

C.   Procedure:

    1.   Select reframing or role-playing and review the related explanatory material provided in the text.

    2.   Select one of the role-plays described in Exercises 1 through 3 above.

    3.   Volunteers are needed to portray the worker(s) and client(s) involved in the chosen role-play. The goal will be to utilize the chosen technique within that role-play context.

    4.   Continue the role-play for up to twenty minutes. By that time, the workers should have been able to implement the technique. The instructor may end the role-play earlier if the workers finish implementing the technique earlier.

    5.   With the entire class, discuss for about ten minutes the following questions and issues:

        a.   How was the chosen technique implemented in the role-play?

        b.   What suggestions do you have to improve implementation of the technique?

        c.   What did you learn about the technique from observing the role-play?

        d.   How did the workers feel about implementing the technique?

        e.   How did the clients feel about participating as the workers implemented the technique?

        f.   How useful do you think this technique might be in real practice situations?

I. **Introduction**

II. **The NASW *Code of Ethics***

    A. Six Core Values in the Preamble

        1. Service—The provision of help, resources, and benefits so that people may achieve their maximum potential

        2. Social justice—The idea that in a perfect world all citizens would have the same basic rights, protection, opportunities, obligations, and social benefits

        3. Dignity and worth of the person—Holding people in high esteem and appreciating individual value

        4. Importance of human relationships—Valuing the mutual emotional exchange; dynamic interaction; and affective, cognitive, and behavioral connections that exist between the social worker and the client to create the working and helping atmosphere

        5. Integrity—Trustworthiness and sound adherence to moral ideals

        6. Competence—Having the necessary skills and abilities to perform work with clients effectively

    B. Six Major Aims Identified in the "Purpose of NASW Code of Ethics"

        1. Identifying primary social work values

        2. Summarizing broad ethical principles as guidelines for practice

        3. Helping determine relevant considerations when addressing an ethical dilemma

        4. Providing broad ethical standards for the public in general to which it may hold the profession accountable

        5. Socializing new practitioners to the mission, goals, and ethics inherent in the profession

        6. Articulating specific standards that the profession may use to judge its members' conduct

    C. Ethical Principles—Based on the six core values, set forth standards to which all practitioners should strive

D.   *Highlight 11.1: A Summary of Ethical Standards in the NASW Code of Ethics*

E.   NASW Ethical Standards

     1.   Social workers' ethical responsibilities to clients

          a.   1.01   Commitment to clients—There will be times when other obligations will supersede loyalty to clients

          b.   1.02   Self-determination

                1)   Self-determination—Each individual's right to make his or her own decisions

                2)   *Critical Thinking Question 11.1*

          c.   1.03   Informed consent—Clients grant permission for the worker to undertake the intervention process after the worker clearly informs clients of all the facts, risks, and alternatives involved

          d.   1.04   Competence

                1)   *Critical Thinking Question 11.2*

          e.   1.05   Cultural competence and social diversity

                1)   Cultural competence

                    a)   Understanding the concept of culture

                    b)   Appreciating the strengths inherent in all diverse cultures

                    c)   Acquiring a continuously growing knowledge base about clients' cultures that can be applied to practice

                    d)   Being sensitive to and appreciative of cultural differences

                    e)   Seeking to understand the nature of oppression and social diversity as they apply to various groups

                2)   Social diversity—The configuration of elements characterizing various groups of people

          f.   1.06   Conflicts of interest

                1)   *Critical Thinking Question 11.3*

g.   1.07   Privacy and confidentiality

1)   Privacy—The condition of being free from unauthorized observation or intrusion

2)   Confidentiality—Workers should not share information provided by a client or about a client unless that worker has the client's explicit permission to do so

3)   *Critical Thinking Question 11.4*

h.   1.08   Access to records

1)   *Critical Thinking Question 11.5*

i.   1.09   Sexual relationships

1)   *Critical Thinking Question 11.6*

j.   1.10   Physical contact

1)   *Critical Thinking Question 11.7*

k.   1.11   Sexual harassment

1)   *Critical Thinking Question 11.8*

l.   1.12   Derogatory language

1)   *Critical Thinking Question 11.9*

m.   1.13   Payment for services

1)   *Critical Thinking Question 11.10*

n.   1.14   Clients who lack decision-making capacity

1)   *Critical Thinking Question 11.11*

o.   1.15   Interruption of services

1)   *Critical Thinking Question 11.12*

p.   1.16   Termination of services

1)   *Critical Thinking Question 11.13*

2.   Social workers' ethical responsibilities to colleagues

    a.   2.01   Respect

              1)   *Critical Thinking Question 11.14*

    b.   2.02   Confidentiality

    c.   2.03   Interdisciplinary collaboration

              1)   *Critical Thinking Question 11.15*

    d.   2.04   Disputes involving colleagues

              1)   *Critical Thinking Question 11.16*

    e.   2.05   Consultation

    f.   2.06   Referral for services

    g.   2.07   Sexual relationships

              1)   *Critical Thinking Question 11.17*

    h.   2.08   Sexual harassment

              1)   *Critical Thinking Question 11.18*

    i.   2.09   Impairment of colleagues

    j.   2.10   Incompetence of colleagues

    k.   2.11   Unethical conduct of colleagues

              1)   *Critical Thinking Question 11.19*

3.   Social workers' ethical responsibilities in practice settings

    a.   3.01   Supervision and consultation

    b.   3.02   Education and training

    c.   3.03   Performance evaluation

    d.   3.04   Client records

    e.   3.05   Billing

    f.   3.06   Client transfer

    g.   3.07   Administration

3.   Value 3: Service to humanity

4.   Value 4: Integrity in professional practice

5.   Value 5: Confidentiality in professional practice

6.   Value 6: Competence in professional practice

IV.   **Ethical Dilemmas**—Being faced with a situation where a decision must be made under circumstances where two or more ethical principles are in conflict

V.   **Conceptualizing and Addressing an Ethical Dilemma: Decision-Making Steps**

    A.   *Figure 11.1: Conceptualizing an Ethical Dilemma*

    B.   Step 1: Recognize the Problem

    C.   Step 2: Investigate the Variables Involved

    D.   Step 3: Get Feedback from Others

    E.   Step 4: Appraise What Values and Ethical Standards Apply to the Dilemma

    F.   Step 5: Evaluate the Dilemma on the Basis of Established Ethical Principles

    G.   Step 6: Identify and Think About Possible Alternatives to Pursue

    H.   Step 7: Weigh the Pros and Cons of Each Alternative

    I.   Step 8: Make Your Decision

VI.   **Ranking Ethical Principles: Dolgoff, Loewenberg, and Harrington's "Ethical Principles Screen"**

    A.   *Figure 11.2: A Hierarchy of Ethical Rights: ETHICS for U*

    B.   Principle #1: People Have the Right to **E**xist with Their Basic Needs Met

    C.   Principle #2: People Have the Right to **T**reatment That Is Fair and Equal

    D.   Principle #3: People Have the Right to **H**ave Free Choice and Freedom

    E.   Principle #4: People Have the Right to Experience **I**njury That Is Minimal or Nonexistent

    F.   Principle #5: People Have the Right to **C**ultivate a Good Quality of Life

    G.   Principle #6: People Have the Right to **S**ecure Their Privacy and Confidentiality

    H.   Principle #7: People Have the Right to **U**nderstand the Truth and All Available Information

    I.   Postscript

VII. **Discussion and Resolution of Ethical Dilemmas in Generalist Practice Contexts**

    A.   Confidentiality and Privileged Communication

        1.   Relative confidentiality—A more global concept intended to protect clients' privacy, yet permit some degree of disclosure, particularly to other agency staff who may need information to perform their part in the planned change process

        2.   Privilege—Refers to legal rights that what has transpired between worker and client is protected by law and cannot be revealed without that client's expressed permission

        3.   Court decisions and issues

            a.   *Tarasoff v. The Regents of the University of California* (1996)—First to recognize the duty of a psychotherapist to protect a third party from a foreseeable harm of a client

            b.   *Jaffe v. Redmond* (1996)—Clinical social workers and their clients have the right to privileged communication

        4.   Informed consent—In the event that information must be disclosed, a worker should inform the client of this fact and solicit from the client written permission to do so

        5.   Workers should discuss with clients limitations on confidentiality before situations arise that require disclosure

        6.   *Highlight 11.3: Ethics, Confidentiality, and "Netiquette" on the Internet*

    B.   Self-Determination and Paternalism

        1.   Self-determination—Deliberate action on behalf of a client or decision-making about what's best for a client with the intentional overriding of what the client wants to do or how the client prefers to be treated

        2.   Paternalism—Action that interferes with the client's wishes or freedom "for his own good"

        3.   *Highlight 11.4: Self-Determination and People with Physical Disabilities: An Empowerment Approach*

            a.   Adopt a consumer-oriented approach

            b.   Learn about services and resources

                1)   Self Determination Movement's primary principles

                    a)   Freedom

                    b)   Authority

           c)   Support

           d)   Responsibility

    c.   Advocate for clients with disabilities whenever possible

        1)   Americans with Disabilities Act of 1990 (ADA)

        2)   Discrimination is still widespread

4.   Informed consent—Workers should clearly inform clients about the purposes, risks, limitations, possible costs, alternatives, right of refusal, and time frames concerning the services provided

5.   Clients' decision-making capacity—Social workers may limit clients' right to self-determination when, in the social workers' professional judgment, clients' actions or potential actions pose a serious, foreseeable, and imminent risk to themselves or others. Also, to act on behalf of clients who lack the capacity to make informed decisions

6.   *Critical Thinking Question 11.20*

7.   *Critical Thinking Question 11.21*

C.   Dual Relationships—Where social workers engage in more than one relationship with a client, becoming social worker and friend, employer, teacher, business associate, or sex partner

1.   Boundaries—Invisible barriers that separate various roles and limit the types of interaction expected and considered ethically appropriate for each role

2.   Social workers' dual relationships with clients

    a.   *Critical Thinking Question 11.22*

    b.   *Critical Thinking Question 11.23*

    c.   *Critical Thinking Question 11.24*

    d.   Suggestions for handling potential dual-relationship problems

        1)   Think about boundary issues and establish clear professional boundaries from the beginning of involvement with a client

        2)   Consult with supervisors and professional colleagues about how to deal with potentially problematic dual relationships

        3)   Carefully scrutinize your own motivations, wants, and needs

4)   In the event that dual relationships occur involuntarily, discuss these issues frankly with clients, identify risks, and consider how to deal with such occurrences in the future

5)   If you feel attracted to a client and tempted to get sexually involved, address your feelings as early as possible. If you can no longer control your sexual feelings, terminate the professional relationship; however, make sure the client is referred to another practitioner so services will continue

3.   Social work educators' dual relationships with students

   a.   *Critical Thinking Question 11.25*

   b.   *Critical Thinking Question 11.26*

   c.   *Critical Thinking Question 11.27*

   d.   *Critical Thinking Question 11.28*

   e.   *Critical Thinking Question 11.29*

   f.   *Critical Thinking Question 11.30*

4.   *Highlight 11.5: Dual Relationships Between Supervisors and Supervisees*

   a.   Clearly define the nature of the dual relationship involved

   b.   Examine carefully the risk of exploitation and harm to the most vulnerable person

   c.   Anticipate possible consequences, positive and negative, of proceeding with a dual relationship

   d.   Discuss with colleagues and others the advisability of developing a dual relationship

   e.   Ascertain which other part of the code, in addition to the section on dual relationships, might help determine whether a dual relationship is inappropriate

   f.   Affirm the responsibility of the professional social worker to avoid even the possibility of exploiting the most vulnerable persons involved

   g.   *Critical Thinking Question 11.31*

D. Telling the Truth

    1. Social workers should not participate in, condone, or be associated with dishonesty, fraud, or deception

    2. Clients have a right to know what social workers record about their life circumstances, mental health symptoms, treatment plans, and progress

    3. *Critical Thinking Question 11.32*

    4. *Critical Thinking Question 11.33*

E. Laws, Policies, and Regulations

    1. *Critical Thinking Question 11.34*

    2. *Critical Thinking Question 11.35*

    3. *Critical Thinking Question 11.36*

F. Whistle-Blowing—The act of informing on another or making public an individual's, group's, or organization's corrupt, wrong, illegal, wasteful, or dangerous behavior

    1. Questions to consider before blowing the whistle:

        a. How great is the threat to the potential victims?

        b. How solid is your evidence?

        c. Are there less severe alternative measures to remedy the problem?

        d. Can you assume the burden of risk?

    2. Recommendations for whistle-blowers

        a. Clearly define the variables involved

        b. Know your rights

        c. Be prepared for the consequences

        d. Follow the chain of command

        e. Establish a clearly defined plan of action

G.   Distribution of Limited Resources

    1.   Variables to consider when distributing limited resources

        a.   Equality

        b.   Need

        c.   Client's ability to pay or contribute to his or her community in the future

H.   Personal and Professional Values

EXPERIENTIAL EXERCISES AND SIMULATIONS

Four exercises in this chapter cover various aspects of ethical decision making. The first exercise presents an ethical dilemma experienced by a social worker with a B.S.W. degree in a typical human service agency. The second exercise confronts a worker with an ethical challenge arising from the actions of a professional colleague. The client's rights conflict with the professional judgment of the worker in the third exercise. In each of these exercises you will be asked several questions and invited to give your reactions to the situation. In exercise 4, you will be participating in a debate about several naturally occurring ethical dilemmas. Exercises 5 through 9 address various aspects of dual relationships.

Exercise 11.1: Mike Howard's Dilemma

A.   Brief description:
In this exercise, you will encounter an ethical dilemma faced by a social worker in a human service agency. After discussing the dilemma in a group, you will report your decision to the entire class.

B.   Objectives
You will be able to:
    1.   Recognize ethical dilemmas when they arise in your work with clients or other systems.
    2.   Use the NASW *Code of Ethics* as a guide for your professional behavior.

C.   Procedure:
    1.   Review the NASW *Code of Ethics* cited and discussed in the text which governs the professional behavior of social workers.
    2.   The instructor will divide class members into groups of four or six students, with one member identified as the recorder.
    3.   The instructor will read the case illustration noted below and answer any questions about the activity.

4.   Within your groups, take about ten minutes to identify the ethical dilemma(s).

5.   Refer to the NASW *Code of Ethics* and appraise what professional values apply.

6.   Review the hierarchy of ethical principles, ETHICS for U, and determine which levels apply to this situation. Establish a group consensus regarding what you would do in this situation.

7.   Report your decision to the entire class.

8.   The instructor will lead a class discussion focusing on the following questions:

   a.   What made this an ethical dilemma for Mike?

   b.   What professional values supported by the NASW *Code of Ethics* apply to this case?

   c.   What principles in the hierarchy of ethical principles, ETHICS for U, apply?

   d.   What is your duty to your client and to society in this case?

   e.   Consider Mike's options. How might each of his choices affect his relationship with the client and his friend?

   f.   To which person is his obligation greater? Why?

   g.   Should Mike consult his supervisor before making a decision? Why or why not?

Exercise 11.2: The Case of the Missing Experience

A.   Brief description:

A situation is presented where one of your close colleagues has misrepresented her qualifications on an employment form. You are faced with making an ethical decision regarding what to do about it.

B.   Objectives:

You will be able to:

   1.   Use the NASW *Code of Ethics* and the hierarchy of ethical principles, ETHICS for U, to help resolve an ethical dilemma.

   2.   Make an ethically correct decision about a difficult situation.

C.   Procedure:

   1.   Review the NASW *Code of Ethics* and ETHICS for U as guides for helping you make ethical decisions.

   2.   The instructor will review the case situation described below for the entire class.

   3.   In the space provided, write down your answers to each of the questions listed below the case description. Take about ten minutes.

   4.   Your instructor will lead a class discussion about each of the questions. Be prepared to share your answers with the rest of the class.

Case Situation

Gemma Howser is a social worker with the Piedmont City Health Department. She is primarily responsible for doing HIV counseling with clients who have tested positive, and case management with those receiving longer-term care. Her agency is in the process of expanding services and will be hiring a new social worker. Gemma's supervisor asks her to look at the job applications as they arrive.

As Gemma reviews the job applications and résumés received for the position, she notices one from a colleague from another agency in the community. Gemma has known Zena Carson for many years and is very familiar with her education and background. What is surprising is that Zena says in her application that she has a minimum of two thousand hours in clinical work with clients, one of the job requirements for this new position. However, Gemma knows that this is not the case since none of Zena's positions since graduation has involved this type of clinical work. Moreover, a review of her résumé does not show any evidence of this experience. Gemma is troubled. She considers the following options:

1. Call Zena and ask her about the obviously inaccurate job application.
2. Tell her supervisor that Zena does not have the required two thousand hours and quietly have them pass over her application.
3. File a complaint with the NASW Commission on Inquiry stating that an NASW member has misrepresented her qualifications.

Questions to be considered:

1. What professional values cited in the NASW *Code of Ethics* apply to this case?
2. What ethical principles in the hierarchy ETHICS for U apply here?
3. Are there other options which Gemma should consider?
4. What are the advantages and disadvantages of each of these options?
5. What are the most important issues at stake in this scenario?
6. If you were Gemma, what would you do and why?

Exercise 11.3: The Client's Choice

A. Brief description:

This exercise highlights conflict between client and worker over the best intervention for an identified problem. As the worker, your recommendation is based upon sound research and the most up-to-date information available. The client's decision is based upon questionable judgment and inaccurate information. As in the other exercises, your opinion of what should be done will need to be guided by the *Code of Ethics* and the ethical principles screen ETHICS for U.

B. Objectives:

You will be able to:

1. Recognize the potential conflicts which can occur between a social worker's professional knowledge and the client's rights.
2. Make a decision in cases which involve these two competing issues.

C. Procedure:

1. The instructor will divide you into groups of six to seven people. Select one person in each group to serve as the recorder.
2. Review the case situation presented below. By yourself, without group input, answer the questions listed after the case situation.
3. Discuss the case situation within your group and come to a consensus on the best answers to each of the questions.
4. The instructor will ask each group to report its answers to the larger class.

Case Situation

Judy Allison has a severe eating disorder, known as bulimia nervosa, which can be life threatening. This condition is one "in which a pathologically excessive appetite with episodic eating binges is sometimes following by purging. The purging may occur through such means as self-induced vomiting, or the abuse of laxatives, diet pills, or diuretics. Bulimia usually starts as a means of dieting."[1] She was admitted to the hospital two days ago after her sister found her unconscious in the bathroom of the home they share. As a hospital social worker, you have interviewed Judy at the request of the physician who has been treating her during her hospital stay.

Judy acknowledges she has a serious problem, but says a friend told her that it can be cured by a diet of fruits and vegetables. You are unaware of any current research for treating this illness that involves the diet she describes. Instead, you are aware of two treatment programs which have been very successful in treating this disorder. Both are multidisciplinary programs offering inpatient and outpatient treatment, individual and group therapy, and follow-up. You recommend that Judy consider entering one of these programs and offer to have a representative of the program contact her. Judy says she'd rather try the new diet her friend told her about first. She refuses further treatment.

Questions to be considered:

1. If you are the worker, what is your obligation, if any, to encourage and convince Judy to pursue effective treatment?
2. What professional values and ethical principles conflict in this situation?
3. At what point (if any) does a professional have an obligation or duty to ignore the client's expressed choice?
4. If you determined (after proper consultation) that Judy's new diet could be life-threatening, what would you do?

Exercise 11.4: What Is the Ethical Thing to Do?

A. Brief description:
    Students are divided into small groups. Each group is presented with an ethical dilemma. They discuss the case and come to a decision about what to do, after which the group shares findings with the entire class.
B. Objectives:
    You will be able to:
    1. Examine a range of ethical dilemmas occurring in practice.
    2. Propose resolutions and identify the professional values and ethical principles upon which that resolution is based.
C. Procedure:
    1. Review the material on ethical standards proposed by the NASW *Code of Ethics* and on the hierarchy of ethical principles ETHICS for U.
    2. The instructor will divide the class into groups of four or five students. Each group will be assigned one of the ethical dilemmas identified below. Students will be allowed approximately fifteen minutes to discuss the dilemma, evaluate professional values and ethical principles, and come to a decision about what to do.[2]

---

[1] R. Barker, *The Social Work Dictionary* (Silver Spring, MD: The National Association of Social Workers, 1995) p. 43.

[2] Instructors should note that these exercises may be addressed in a variety of ways depending on class size. Students may individually be assigned a dilemma to address and subsequently present their findings to the class.

Ethical Dilemma #1

Yvonne is a child protective services worker. After receiving a referral, she or other assigned workers will "investigate reports of child abuse and neglect, assess the degree of harm and the ongoing risk of harm to the child, determine whether the child can remain safely in the home or should be placed in the custody of the state, and work closely with the family or juvenile court regarding appropriate plans for the child's safety and well-being"(Liederman, 1995, p. 425).

Yvonne has a client, Lolita, four, who was allegedly abused by both parents. Lolita currently resides with her mother, Reza, while Reza is receiving counseling and other services including job training. Bill, Lolita's father, no longer lives in the home but has told Yvonne he would like to seek custody of Lolita. Bill calls Yvonne to complain about Reza's treatment of Lolita. He states that Lolita often wets her bed at night and Reza simply ignores it. Reza subsequently allows Lolita to sleep in her wet bed. Then, even worse, the next day or night Reza does not change the sheets for Lolita. Yvonne notes carefully what Bill tells her in Lolita's case record.

The next day, Reza calls Yvonne in a panic. She cries that Bill is threatening to take Lolita away from her. Reza says Bill told her he called Yvonne to complain about Reza's treatment of Lolita. Reza stresses that she does not want to lose her little girl. She demands to see Yvonne's records.

What should Yvonne do: Show Reza the incriminating records, or not?

Ethical Dilemma #2

Herman is a substance abuse counselor. He is currently seeing an alcoholic client, Anne, age thirty-seven. Herman views Anne as a timid, needy woman who is working on increasing her self-esteem, problem solving skills, and assertiveness in the context of addressing her alcoholism problem. Treatment is going exceptionally well. Anne has not been drinking for months and has been attending Alcoholics Anonymous meetings regularly. Anne is very grateful to Herman for all she feels he has done for her. One day at the end of the counseling session, Anne walks up to Herman and says, "I really need a hug!" What should Herman do? On the one hand, Anne is needy of approval and affection. She wishes to convey her gratitude to Herman. On the other, he does not want to convey inappropriate feelings that do not exist.

Should he allow her to hug him or not?

Ethical Dilemma #3

Sue married Jim two years after the biological father of her daughter Andrea disappeared seemingly from the face of the earth. They have now been married for seven years. Andrea, eight, and Jim have become very close. Jim feels just like Andrea is his biological daughter. Jim and Sue pursue the possibility of Jim adopting Andrea. Mary Ellen is the adoptions worker assigned to the case. She helps with the relatively complex process of having the biological father relinquish his parental rights for Andrea when he is nowhere to be found. Mary Ellen has completed a number of stepparent adoptions and has become quite competent in their successful completion. Jim and Sue are very thankful. They give Mary Ellen a $50 gift certificate for a popular local restaurant.

Is this appropriate or not? Should Mary Ellen keep the gift or return it? What is the ethical and tactful thing to do?

Groups may be assigned more than one dilemma. Dilemmas may be read out loud to the class, after which students may participate in a large group discussion.

Ethical Dilemma #4

Lloyd is a social worker at a group home for people who are cognitively challenged or have cognitive disabilities (the former, more negative term is mentally retarded).[3] Ellie, thirty-five, has been a resident at the group home for eight years. She has relatively high adaptive functioning in terms of daily living skills, can read at the fourth grade level, and has successfully worked at a sheltered workshop since entering the group home. She has no known relatives. The court has designated a lawyer as her guardian *ad litem* (that is, a court appointee whose responsibility is to "preserve and manage the affairs of another person who is considered incapable of managing his or her own affairs," especially when court actions are involved) (Barker, 1995, p. 158).

Without warning, Ellie cheerfully approaches Lloyd one day and informs him that she has saved enough money to go to Disney World, her dream of a lifetime. She chatters on about getting the tickets and taking her first airplane ride. Lloyd is familiar with Ellie's capabilities and strongly feels this endeavor is far beyond her capabilities.

What should he do?

Ethical Dilemma #5

Ricardo is a social services worker who specializes in teaching parents effective child management skills. Over the past six months, he has been working with Irma, a former crack user, to gain control of her four children's behavior. Although it was very difficult at first for Irma to trust Ricardo, they now have established a trusting relationship in which Irma feels free to discuss difficult issues with Ricardo. Ideally, Ricardo would like to continue work with Irma for the next several months. However, he has been transferred to another unit's position with a higher salary. Irma has achieved many of the major goals, but still could make significant improvements in how she treats her children. Ricardo feels it would be very difficult for Irma to become accustomed to and work with another worker.

What should he do?

Ethical Dilemma #6

Nick is a counselor for teenagers with severe emotional and behavioral problems who reside in a residential treatment center. He sees himself as a shy person who finds it difficult to confront issues in conflictual situations. As a member of an interdisciplinary team, he attends a staffing for one of his clients at which progress is reviewed and future plans established. Dr. Schmaltz, the psychiatrist attending the meeting, is a powerful, authoritarian man who makes strong points completely in opposition to what Nick is proposing for the client being reviewed. Dr. Schmaltz commands much authority and respect among other staff.

What should Nick do?

---

[3] *Cognitively challenged* is an alternative term referring to mental retardation. *Mental retardation* is "significantly below-average intellectual functioning and potential, with onset before age 18, resulting in limitation in communication, self-care and self-direction, home living, social and interpersonal skills, use of community resources, academic skills, work, leisure, health, and safety" (Barker, 1995, p. 232). Many professionals feel that referring to such individuals as being cognitively challenged is far more positive than using the term mentally retarded (DeWeaver, 1995).

Ethical Dilemma #7

Chuck is a youth counselor at an urban YMCA.[4] He is in his early twenties, good at sports, familiar with young people's jargon, and, thus, extremely popular with his teenage clientele. Emilio is another youth counselor at the same agency. One night after work, Emilio accidentally observes Chuck smoking a joint with two of his clients in the shadows of an alley. After serious thought, the next day Emilio confronts Chuck about his behavior. Chuck responds that it was only marijuana and it provided a way for him to "join with" and be accepted by some of his clients. Chuck rationalizes that smoking joints prevents many young people from using harder, more dangerous drugs. Chuck implies that Emilio is just jealous of Chuck's good rapport with the clientele.

What should Emilio do now?

Ethical Dilemma #8

Willie Lee, twenty-three, is a resident in a center for people who have cognitive disabilities. Willie Lee can eat by himself and take care of most of his daily hygiene needs. His vocabulary is small, but he usually understands much more than he can express. Willie Lee is a very friendly person who socializes well with peers and is generally respectful of staff. He looks forward to his father's rare visits, sometimes only once or twice a year. His mother died at his birth.

Willie Lee's father, Horace, has recently remarried and is moving across the continent. He has hired an attorney and wants to terminate his guardianship and responsibility for Willie Lee. Horace has always found Willie Lee to be a burden and has been embarrassed by his disability. Horace feels this is his chance to abandon the whole problem and not think about it anymore. Although Willie Lee is always happy when Horace visits, he never asks about him. This may be partially due to Willie Lee's communication difficulties.

Horace succeeds in terminating his rights and moves away. He informs the center that he plans on having no further contact with Willie Lee.

Should the center social worker inform Willie Lee of this turn of events? Does Willie Lee have the right to know about his father's status?

Ethical Dilemma #9

Ling, eighty-six, is a bed-bound resident in a nursing home. Although she has numerous physical difficulties, she has maintained fairly strong mental faculties. She enjoys the company of her two daughters who visit regularly. Ling's physician has just discovered that Ling has developed a lethal form of intestinal cancer and has only weeks, possibly a few months, to live. Ling's daughters beg the nursing home social worker not to tell Ling of her condition. They plan to visit Ling daily and want her to enjoy her time as best she can. They feel that informing her about the cancer would only ruin her last days.

What should the social worker do? Should she inform Ling of her condition? What are the pros and cons of informing or not informing?

---

[4] *YMCA* refers to the Young Men's Christian Association. They are a "worldwide group of organizations devoted to the physical, intellectual, social, and spiritual well-being of young men" (Barker, 1995, p. 413). One should note that they no longer restrict themselves to Christians.

Ethical Dilemma #10

Sissy is a financial assistance worker. Agency policy requires her to report any extra income clients may earn. The exact amount of such income is then deducted from their financial assistance checks. An excited client, Bertha, with four children, burst out, "I'm so happy! My neighbor is going to pay me to take care of her two children while she works. This will do wonders for my grocery bill."

As her worker, what should Sissy do? Should she report the additional income and thereby decrease her financial assistance check? If so, should she tell Bertha what she plans to do? What might Bertha's reaction be? Or should Sissy keep her statement confidential, thereby disobeying agency policy? What is the ethical thing to do?

Ethical Dilemma #11

Chuck works for a social services agency serving almost all Hispanic and African American clients. All the social workers and administrators are white. None of the professional staff speak Spanish.[5] Chuck is very concerned about this situation, but hesitates to make waves. It is such a major problem. He feels too insignificant to take it on himself. Yet, he can't keep it from bothering him.

How might clients be better served? What are the agency's needs? What options might Chuck consider pursuing? What is the ethical thing to do?

Ethical Dilemma #12

Lai is a social worker at a shelter and treatment center for runaways. The center typically uses volunteers to serve many of its functions, including counseling youth and families. Although volunteers receive twenty hours of training, Lai feel this does not make them competent to counsel young people and their families.

What, if anything, is wrong with this agency's volunteer policy? What might Lai do to make changes? What might those changes be? What is the ethical thing to do?

3. After approximately fifteen minutes, the instructor will call the groups back to join the entire class. Representatives from each group will first read the vignette depicting their assigned dilemma, and then describe their decision about what to do.

4. The entire class then discusses the group's decision and debates its merit. Alternative solutions may be proposed.

Exercise 11.5: What Would You Say and Why?

A. Brief Description:
    You are broken down into pairs and asked to role play social workers and clients addressing a potential dual relationship issue. A discussion concerning boundaries follows.

B. Objectives:
    You will be able to:

    1. Dramatize and examine the dynamics involved in a dual relationship between a professional social worker and client.

    2. Discuss some of the issues involved in dual relationships and propose the most ethical means of dealing with such a situation.

---

[5] This vignette is adapted from one presented in B. Cournoyer, *The Social Work Skills Workbook*, 2nd ed. (Pacific Grove, CA: Brooks/Cole, 1996) p. 72.

C.   Procedure:
1.   Review material on dual relationships.
2.   One at a time, your instructor will read each role play to the class. You will be asked to think about what you would do if you were the worker, but not to discuss your feelings yet.
3.   The instructor will break the class down into pairs and ask one in each dyad to play the worker and the other the client in each of the scenarios. Process each scenario separately. For each, you should begin the role play with the client making the comments or asking the worker designated questions as indicated in the scenario. Your instructor will allow about five minutes to conduct the role play.
4.   Your instructor will lead a full class discussion on the following questions.
> What were the boundary issues involved?
> How did the worker feel during the role play?
> What did the worker decide to do?
> What was the ethical thing to do and why?
> How did the client feel at the end of the role play?
> What have you learned from this role play about dual relationships?

SCENARIO #1

Harriett, the Worker: You're a worker at a nursing home who has spent significant amounts of time with Polly, a delightful 83-year-old. She sincerely appreciates your time and maintains a good sense of humor despite her increasingly failing health. You've helped link her to a variety of resources, arranged for her to participate in a number of the home's activities including outings, and have helped her work out some personal issues with her daughter Pru. You genuinely like and respect Polly who maintains such a positive attitude despite her health problems.

Polly, the Client: You've always seen yourself as a positive person who enjoys and appreciates the other people around you. At 83 you continue striving to appreciate the positive elements in life. You are finding it increasingly difficult to get around easily, even using your walker, and are suffering from increasing pain caused by a number of gastrointestinal and other difficulties. You really like Harriett who always seems to have time for you and has helped you work out some difficult issues. You'd love to have her join you at your 84th birthday party over at Pru's next Saturday. You don't know how many more special occasions, if any, you have left. You're going to invite Harriett, that's all that's to it.

SCENARIO #2

Ashanti, the Worker: You are a social worker at a shelter for battered women. You've been working closely with Fola, one of your clients, for over six months now. With her two small children, she has left her abusive spouse, found an apartment, and started a new job training program. You've helped her get the appropriate financial assistance to get her started on the road to independence. You genuinely like her and respect her for her courage in getting through the rough times she's had. Occasionally, you think you might have become friends in some other non-professional context.

> **Fola, the Client:** You have finally gotten your act together and are on your way to a strong and independent future with your children. The only bad thing is that you will sincerely miss Ashanti, who has helped you work out many aspects of your life. In another two weeks, she will no longer be formally involved as your worker. You feel you have developed a meaningful friendship with her and would like to keep in touch. You're going to ask her to continue to be her friend. At least you could keep in touch by phone and occasionally go out to lunch or to a movie together.

SCENARIO #3[1]

> **Carlton, the Worker:** Carlton is a substance abuse counselor working for a private social services agency. Bob, a car mechanic, has been one of his clients for almost a year. Carlton has assisted Bob in making many life changes and establishing a life of sobriety. Carlton feels they have a good and productive relationship. This is despite the fact that sometimes Bob has missed his payments due to the financial problems resulting from prior years of substance abuse. Bob always eventually pays his bills when he can.
>
> One day Carlton has unexpected car trouble and so is forced to cancel an appointment with Bob. Carlton calls the agency and an administrative assistant calls Bob about the cancellation, briefly explaining the reason. During their informal initial greeting right before their next counseling session, Bob asks Carlton what was wrong with his car and Carlton briefly explains.
>
> **Bob, the Client:** Bob thinks very highly of Carlton who has helped him get through some very rough times. Bob considers himself an excellent mechanic who works for a local gas station and garage that does a good business in auto repair. When he hears about Carlton's car problems, he eagerly volunteers to give the car a good check-up and make certain the repairs would be done right. All Carlton needs to do is to bring the car in. He feels this would be a way to repay Carlton a little in a personal way for all the help Carlton's given. Bob thinks silently to himself that he might even be able to do this for free on his own time or, at least, give Carlton a greatly cut rate. Bob makes the suggestion to Carlton.

Exercise 11.6: A Dual Relationship Questionnaire—Clients and Supervisors

A. Brief Description:

You are administered a questionnaire focusing on various aspects of dual relationships with current and former clients, and current and former supervisors. Discussion follows.

B. Objectives:

You will be able to:

1. Examine some of the dual relationship issues involving current and former clients and current and former supervisors.
2. Propose ethical alternatives for determining appropriate behavior for a range of dual relationship scenarios.

---

[1] This scenario is loosely based on one discussed *Social Work Values and Ethics* by E. P. Congress (Chicago: Nelson-Hall, 1996, p. 111).

C. Procedure:
1. Fill out the following questionnaire. Note that it involves opinions about dual relationships with current clients, former clients, current supervisors, and former supervisors. Circle from 1 to 4 what you consider the best answer for each question. This will take about 10 minutes.
2. When you've finished, add up your scores for each section and divide that total by 6. The result is an average score indicating how much you feel dual relationships with clients or supervisors are appropriate or inappropriate, 1 being never appropriate and 4 being always appropriate.
3. Your instructor will then lead the class in a discussion addressing the following questions:
    ➤ What were your average scores for each section?
    ➤ What were the differences among current and former clients, and current and former supervisors?
    ➤ What were the reasons for these differences?
    ➤ What questions, if any, did you find particularly difficult to answer? Explain why.
    ➤ What did you learn from this questionnaire about issues you might encounter in practice?

DUAL RELATIONSHIP QUESTIONNAIRE

CURRENT CLIENTS:
1. Is it appropriate and ethical for a professional social worker to become friends with a client while working with that client?

1	2	3	4
Never	Infrequently	Sometimes	Always

2. Is it appropriate and ethical for a social worker to accept an invitation to a special event (e.g., wedding or graduation) from a current client?

1	2	3	4
Never	Infrequently	Sometimes	Always

3. Is it appropriate and ethical to accept a gift from a client (e.g., as a thank you or for Christmas or birthday)?

1	2	3	4
Never	Infrequently	Sometimes	Always

4. Is it appropriate and ethical for a social worker to go out to lunch or dinner with a current client after a counseling session?

1	2	3	4
Never	Infrequently	Sometimes	Always

5. Is it appropriate and ethical for a social worker to invite a current client to a personal party or social event?

1	2	3	4
Never	Infrequently	Sometimes	Always

6. Is it appropriate and ethical for a social worker to invite current clients to an agency function such as an open house?

1	2	3	4
Never	Infrequently	Sometimes	Always

Total _____ /6=_____

FORMER CLIENTS:

7. Is it appropriate and ethical for a social worker to become friends with a client after their professional relationship has ended?

1	2	3	4
Never	Infrequently	Sometimes	Always

8. Is it appropriate and ethical for a social worker to accept an invitation to a special event (e.g., wedding or graduation) from a former client?

1	2	3	4
Never	Infrequently	Sometimes	Always

9. Is it appropriate and ethical to accept a gift from a former client (e.g., as a thank you or for Christmas or birthday)?

1	2	3	4
Never	Infrequently	Sometimes	Always

10. Is it appropriate and ethical for a social worker to invite a former client to a personal party or social event?

1	2	3	4
Never	Infrequently	Sometimes	Always

11. Is it appropriate and ethical for a social worker to go out to lunch or dinner with a former client?

1	2	3	4
Never	Infrequently	Sometimes	Always

12. Is it appropriate and ethical for a social worker to become involved in a sexual relationship with a former client?

1	2	3	4
Never	Infrequently	Sometimes	Always

Total _____ /6=_____

CURRENT SUPERVISORS:

13. Is it appropriate and ethical for a worker to become friends with her current supervisor?

1	2	3	4
Never	Infrequently	Sometimes	Always

14. Is it appropriate and ethical for a social worker to accept an invitation to a special event (e.g., wedding or graduation) from a current supervisor?

1	2	3	4
Never	Infrequently	Sometimes	Always

15. Is it appropriate and ethical to accept a gift from or give one to a current supervisor (e.g., as a thank you or for Christmas or birthday)?

1	2	3	4
Never	Infrequently	Sometimes	Always

16. Is it appropriate and ethical for a social worker to go out to lunch or dinner with a current supervisor?

1	2	3	4
Never	Infrequently	Sometimes	Always

17. Is it appropriate and ethical for a social worker to invite a current supervisor to a personal party or social event?

1	2	3	4
Never	Infrequently	Sometimes	Always

18. Is it appropriate and ethical for a social worker to become involved in a sexual relationship with a current supervisor?

1	2	3	4
Never	Infrequently	Sometimes	Always

Total _____ /6= _____

FORMER SUPERVISORS:

19. Is it appropriate and ethical for a worker to become friends with a former supervisor?

1	2	3	4
Never	Infrequently	Sometimes	Always

20. Is it appropriate and ethical for a social worker to accept an invitation to a special event (e.g., wedding or graduation) from a former supervisor?

1	2	3	4
Never	Infrequently	Sometimes	Always

21. Is it appropriate and ethical to accept a gift from or give one to a former supervisor (e.g., as a thank you or for Christmas or birthday)?

1	2	3	4
Never	Infrequently	Sometimes	Always

22. Is it appropriate and ethical for a social worker to go out to lunch or dinner with a former supervisor?

1	2	3	4
Never	Infrequently	Sometimes	Always

23. Is it appropriate and ethical for a social worker to invite a former supervisor to a personal party or social event?

1	2	3	4
Never	Infrequently	Sometimes	Always

24. Is it appropriate and ethical for a social worker to become involved in a sexual relationship with a former supervisor after their professional relationship has ended?

1	2	3	4
Never	Infrequently	Sometimes	Always

Total _____ /6= _____

Exercise 11.7: Dual Relationships Involving Students and Instructors

A. Brief Description:

The class is broken down into small groups and given a series of vignettes involving dual relationships between instructors and students. You then examine the extent to which the behavior depicted is ethical.

B. Objectives:

You will be able to:

1. Identify ethical issues and dilemmas.
2. Evaluate the appropriateness of behavior involved.
3. Propose ethical alternatives where appropriate.

C. Procedure:

1. Divide up into small groups of 4 to 6.
2. Read the following vignettes.
3. Discuss the following questions for each vignette:
   - ➤ To what extent is the behavior portrayed in each scenario ethical?
   - ➤ What are the potential positive and negative consequences of the behaviors involved?
   - ➤ What should the professional social worker(s) involved have or have not done?
4. After about 20 minutes your instructor will bring you back for a full class discussion regarding your findings.

Vignette #1

"A male social work student presented a dozen red roses to his female field instructor on the last day of supervision and one month later they were engaged. At the risk of being unromantic, one can question the quality of her social work supervision throughout the year if there had been a growing personal relationship" (Congress, 1996, p. 334).

Vignette #2

A single male professor dated students for years, one student at a time. Sometimes, the student was taking the course he was teaching, sometimes not. Eventually, he married one of them.

Vignette #3

A male professor in his mid-50s had been in social work education for over two decades. He lost his wife whom he dearly loved and to whom he was earnestly devoted to cancer ten years earlier. Since then he dated occasionally, but found no one whom he felt was right for him. A returning student of about his age entered his social work program and took a course he taught. They immediately hit it off, being quite attracted to each other. As soon as the course was over, they began discreetly dating. They were married shortly after she graduated from the program.

Vignette #4

A Social Work Club holds annual banquets for its members and invites faculty, who usually attend. Often, faculty and students meet in the bar for cocktails and cokes before the banquet begins. Conversations are informal and mildly personal in terms of focusing on non-academic topics.

Vignette #5

Petula, a female professor, was Burt's advisor throughout his four years of college in addition to being his instructor for several courses. Upon meeting they immediately developed a good rapport. They came from the same town and both had a straightforward, "say it like it is" personal communication style. Throughout his college career, they addressed various academic issues in addition to discussing some personal problems. He had cerebral palsy which sometimes limited his ready access to campus resources and made dating more difficult because of discrimination.

Burt graduated with his BSW and immediately went on for his MSW. Upon completion Burt called Petula and volunteered to serve as a speaker in one of her courses. She invited him, and he did a nice job. Afterwards, she invited him to lunch which she did with all her speakers. Over the next ten years, Petula invited him to speak each semester. Over time they became good friends, comfortable in discussing many topics ranging from family problems to vacation plans to financial worries to professional issues. Petula occasionally invited Burt to social events at her home.

Vignette #6

Alicia, 32, originally from Ecuador, was bilingual. She consistently expressed feelings of inferiority and felt her peers were exceptionally critical of her due to her accent. Chantrell, one of her instructors, met several times with Alicia over the course of the two semesters at Alicia's request. They focused on Alicia's many strengths and helping her develop ways to deal with her classmates. Alicia made two trips back to her home in Ecuador during this period. Each time she brought Chantrell some small gifts of coffee or local handicrafts which Chantrell accepted.

Vignette #7

Earl, a county social services supervisor, took his supervisee Carla, a relatively new MSW with one year's experience, under his wing. Earl genuinely liked Carla, her enthusiasm, and her serious desire to do the best job possible. He took her on home visits to provide a role model for how these should be done. At her request, he helped her develop counseling techniques and write efficient, effective reports. In some ways, he assumed the role of friend with her. For example, when he held a party for all his supervisees and co-workers, he asked her to help him with the arrangements, which she gladly did. Carla respected and admired Earl. At one point, she felt she was even falling in love with him, although Earl never felt any reciprocal romantic feelings toward her (they were both single). Eventually, Earl left the agency for another position. Twenty-five years later Carla still thinks fondly of Earl and appreciates all he taught her. Carla, by the way, is happily married to somebody else.

Exercise 11.8: Dual Relationships Involving Clients

A.   Brief Description:
You are given a series of scenarios involving dual relationships with clients. A full class discussion will respond to the questions posed below.

B.   Objectives:
You will be able to:
1.   Examine several scenarios concerning dual relationships.
2.   Identify various potential courses of action and discuss the pros and cons of each.
3.   Evaluate the ethical implications involved.
4.   Recommend the most appropriate and ethical course of action.

C.   Procedure:
1.   Read each of the following scenarios.
2.   Respond to the following questions for each of the ethical dilemmas posed below:
➢ What is the worker's professional role and what are the boundary issues involved?
➢ What emotions, wants, and needs might characterize the worker involved in the scenario?
➢ What alternatives are available for the worker to take?
➢ What are the potential positive and negative consequences for each alternative?
➢ How might each alternative affect the client and the worker/client relationship?
➢ What course of action should the worker take that is the most ethical and appropriate for both worker and client? Explain why.

Ethical Dilemma #1: Fernando is a substance abuse counselor who had been working with his client Trixie for several years. Trixie attributes much of her success in maintaining sobriety to Fernando's help and efforts. Fernando receives an invitation to Trixie's wedding with a note saying how much it would mean to Trixie for him to attend.

Ethical Dilemma #2: Kasinda, a hospice social worker, visits her 72-year-old hospice client Leona weekly to provide supportive counseling and link her with needed resources. One week Leona invites Kasinda to have lunch with her.

Ethical Dilemma #3: Darwin, a private practitioner in a rural area, provides counseling on a range of issues. Gilbert, his client for two years, addressed serious self-esteem issues during the course of counseling. Partially as a result of the counseling Gilbert went back to school and earned a BSW and MSW. Six years after his counseling ended, Gilbert approaches Darwin and asks him to provide clinical supervision. Gilbert expresses how much he respects Darwin and how no other MSWs are available in the area.

Ethical Dilemma #4: Freddy, 55, has a cognitive disability, an IQ within the borderline range, and a serious speech impediment. He can live by himself in a small Midwestern town with regular support from the local Center for People with Cognitive Disabilities. His sister Farrah and her family are also very involved with his life, although they live four hours away.

Freddy has lived in this small town all his life and does not want to leave and live elsewhere even to join his family. Shirley, his assigned social worker at the center, has been very helpful by making regular home visits to make sure things were going smoothly, setting up appropriate vocational testing, helping Freddy get involved in regular social and recreational activities at the center, and getting him a part-time job at Don's Dinky Diner, a local restaurant.

Freddy's family is very thankful to Shirley for her help. It would be very difficult for Farrah and other family members to visit Freddy on a weekly basis as Shirley does. Farrah gives Shirley a $30.00 gift certificate to the local All-Mart store as an appreciation gift before the Christmas holidays.

Ethical Dilemma #5: Jennifer, 23, is a student working at a halfway house for men on parole who are also substance abusers. This is part of her final 480 hour field internship. Jennifer is very attracted to Sly, a 26-year-old, handsome client who is also quite charming. She finds it very difficult to avoid responding to his flattering, flirtatious advances. She is halfway through her placement and is finding it extremely difficult not to respond to Sly and secretly date him. The agency has a strict policy that no worker should date a client within six months after either have left the agency. Jennifer finds herself preoccupied thinking about him much of the time. She feels that she's losing control.

Exercise 11.9: HELP! The NASW Code of Ethics

A. Brief Description:
    You are directed to several parts of the NASW Code of Ethics that address dual relationships. You then discuss the application of relevant passages to scenarios described in earlier exercises.
B. Objectives:
    You will be able to:
    1. Discuss the application of relevant portions of the NASW Code of Ethics to various scenarios.
    2. Evaluate the extent to which individual professional discretion is required.
C. Procedure:
    1. Read the following citations from the NASW Code of Ethics.
    2. Evaluate how each section relates to the scenarios described earlier in Exercise 8 by responding to the questions provided below.

WORKERS AND CLIENTS

The NASW Code of Ethics (NASW, 1996) states:

"Social workers should not engage in dual or multiple relationships with clients or former clients in which there is a risk of exploitation or potential harm to the client. In instances when dual or multiple relationships are unavoidable, social workers should take steps to protect clients and are responsible for setting clear, appropriate, and culturally sensitive boundaries. (Dual or multiple relationships occur when social workers relate to clients in more than one relationship, whether professional, social, or business. Dual or multiple relationships can occur simultaneously or consecutively.)"(1.06c).

"Social workers should under no circumstances engage in sexual activities or sexual contact with current clients, whether such contact is consensual or forced" (1.09a).

Review the ethical dilemmas cited above in Exercise 4 above and discuss the following questions:
- To what extent does the Code provide clear direction regarding what workers should do in each vignette?
- For what aspects of each dilemma must workers use their own discretion regarding what behavior is ethical and what is not?
- According to the Code, what do you think the worker should do?

INSTRUCTORS AND STUDENTS

The NASW Code of Ethics states:

"Social workers who function as educators or field instructors for students should not engage in any dual or multiple relationships with students in which there is a risk of exploitation or potential harm to the student. Social work educators and field instructors are responsible for setting clear, appropriate, and culturally sensitive boundaries" (3.02d).

Review the ethical dilemmas cited in Exercise 3 above and discuss the following questions:
- To what extent does the Code provide clear direction regarding what supervisors and workers should do in each vignette?
- For what aspects of each dilemma must supervisors and workers use their own discretion regarding what behavior is ethical and what is not?
- According to the Code, what do you think the supervisor and worker should do?

Chapter 12
Culturally Competent Social Work Practice

I. **Introduction**

    A.   The United States is a pluralistic nation

        1.   Over 38 million people are of African American heritage

        2.   13.8 million people are from Asian American or Pacific Islander backgrounds

        3.   44.3 million people are of Hispanic or Latino extraction

        4.   2.9 Million people are First Nations People

II. **Diversity in the United States**

    A.   Race and Ethnicity

    B.   *Highlight 12.1: Common Terminology*

        1.   Ableism—Assumes the superiority of the person who is nondisabled and views persons with disabilities who have different physical and mental characteristics as somehow inferior

        2.   Cultural competence—The ability to apply knowledge and skills to social work practice with diverse groups

        3.   Ethnocentrism—An orientation or set of beliefs that holds that one's own culture, racial, or ethnic group or nation is inherently superior to others

        4.   Individual racism—Racism is the cognitive belief that one ethnic group is superior to and dominant over another inferior and subjugated group, supposedly because of genetic composition, intelligence, skin color, character, or related rationale

        5.   Institutional racism—Those policies, practices, or procedures embedded in bureaucratic structures that systematically lead to unequal outcomes for people of color

        6.   Minority—A term referring to any group or person lacking power or resources when compared to the dominant majority in a community or society

        7.   People of color—People whose skin color differs from that of the community's predominant group

C.   Disabilities

1.   American with Disabilities Act 1990 (ADA) defines disabilities as a physical or mental impairment that substantially limits one or more of the major life events of such an individual

2.   Almost 50 million people over age 5 suffer from disabilities

D.   Historic and Current Discrimination

1.   Discrimination based on culture

   a.   Institutional racism within education was the law of the land until 1954. De facto segregation of school systems still exists

   b.   The right to vote was not extended to Native Americans until passage of the Indian Citizenship Act (1924)

   c.   1960s, 70s, and 80s—continued efforts were made to improve economic opportunities for people of color

   d.   1980s—conservative, antigovernment political administrations systematically eliminated or reduced the role of federal government in helping assure equality and economic justice to multicultural groups

   e.   The picture for people of color in the first decade of the millennium remains problematic

2.   Discrimination based on ability

   a.   National Defense Act (1916)—created to help disabled soldiers find employment when they returned to civilian life

   b.   National Rehabilitation Act (1920)—provided funds so ordinary citizens could get job training and employment assistance, in addition to prosthetics

   c.   Social Security Act (1935)—provided public funds for blind persons and children with disabilities. (1956)—expanded coverage to anyone with a disability

   d.   Supplemental Security Income program (SSI) (1974)—guaranteed a basic income for people with disabilities using federal funds

   e.   Rehabilitation Act (1973)—ensured priority services and creation of an individual rehabilitation program. Also began a process of eliminating physical barriers in public buildings

   f.   Equal Education for All Handicapped Children Act (1975)—mandated that education for children between the ages of 3 and 21 be provided in the least restrictive or most normal environment

g.   Americans with Disabilities Act (1990)—defined disability and required employers and others to provide reasonable accommodations to assist those with disabilities to attain and maintain employment

h.   Those with disabilities still face major obstacles to gainful employment

III.   Barriers to Effective Culturally Competent Social Work

A.   Continued acceptance of the myth of the melting pot

B.   The assumption that all who come to our country will be overjoyed to be here

C.   The tendency to explain people's behavior by reference to their culture or disability

D.   An attempt to be color-blind—occurs when a person decides to treat everybody alike and pretends that culture and experience have no role in determining behavior

E.   Assumption that words mean the same thing to everyone

F.   Assumption that clients think as you do

G.   Expectation that clients will understand the social worker's role

H.   Lack of understanding of your own culture

I.   Absence of a repertoire of effective, multicultural intervention techniques

J.   Lack of knowledge of the culture and experiences of specific groups with whom you are likely to work

K.   *Critical Thinking Question 12.1*

IV.   Integrating Cultural Competence in the Generalist Intervention Model

A.   Engagement

1.   Approach clients from multicultural groups with a clear understanding of their own view of the world and how it differs from that of others

a.   Individuals who have routinely experienced discrimination and oppression may approach the process with trepidation, anger, or distrust

b.   Recent immigrants may not be familiar with American norms

c.   Stigma associated with mental health problems may be a barrier

d.   Platicando—Informal and leisurely chatting that contributes to the warm atmosphere

e.   Eye-contact interpretation

B.   Assessment

       1.   Client is operating in dual environments—the dominant one and the one associated with their ethnic or racial background

       2.   Recognize the client system strengths

       3.   Recognize that different approaches to understanding and treating physical or emotional illness reflect group traditions

       4.   Be aware of your own way of thinking about a client's situation

       5.   Concern of client's cultural and racial identity

       6.   Responsiveness of agencies to the needs of multicultural groups

C.   Planning

       1.   Confront community social problems that can be influenced by differences among multicultural groups

       2.   Possibly consider the family as the client instead of the individual when working with Asian or African American clients

       3.   Possibly include the elderly in Hispanic and Asian families in the planning process

D.   Implementation

       1.   Short stories or analogies may be more effective in approaching a topic with Hispanic and Asian clients to alleviate feeling threatened

       2.   Nonverbal communication may have greater importance than spoken words

       3.   Workers may need to self-disclose more than usual

E.   Evaluation

       1.   Recognize that much of the research reported in literature has limited generalizability

       2.   Involve the client directly in the evaluation process

       3.   Consider whether or not the method needs to be adapted to multicultural groups

       4.   Instruments that were normed on Anglo Americans cannot be used with equal validity on other groups

F.   Termination and Follow-Up

    1.   Take time to discuss diversity issues that were dealt with in prior stages

    2.   If termination occurs prematurely, offer client the opportunity to come back at any time

V.   Practical Knowledge and Skills

A.   Acculturation—An ethnic person's adoption of the dominant culture in which he or she is immersed

B.   Native Americans/First Nations Peoples

    1.   First Nations People reinforces the fact that Native Americans were an intact nation prior to the arrival of the Europeans

    2.   Understand the unique differences

        a.   Resided here first

        b.   Range from highly sophisticated social system to more simple organization

        c.   Massive efforts to teach "white man's ways" have deprived many children from learning the traditional child-rearing approaches

        d.   Child abuse was relatively unknown until recently because corporal punishment was rare

        e.   Many of the poor parenting skills today can be traced to Bureau of Indian Affairs boarding schools treatment

        f.   Traditional cultural styles are significantly different from most European cultures

    3.   The value of time—First Nations People do not share the near obsession with time that white Americans have (less rigid with appointment times)

    4.   First Nations noninterference

        a.   Noninterference could be considered a logical extension of social work's value of client self-determination

        b.   Intrusive, aggressive styles of probing for information are likely to be ineffective. Participatory, self-directed relationships have greater value

        c.   Silence and lack of peer pressure are common

5. Communication patterns

    a. More nonverbal

    b. Not a loud culture

    c. Deference to authority and individual dignity

    d. Do not self-disclose readily

    e. Family loyalty important

    f. Less likely to brag

    g. Praise in front of others may be embarrassing

6. Fatalism—The attitude that one has relatively little control over events in one's life and that attempting to change is fruitless because such efforts cannot alter predetermined outcomes [what will be, will be]

7. Sharing and Acquiring

    a. Sharing is typically more important than acquiring

    b. This value is not universal within First Nations culture

    c. It is commonplace for many children from the extended family to share a small space in the family dwelling or outbuildings or tents during the summer

8. Attending skills

    a. Leaning forward may be seen as intruding into the life space of another

    b. Sustained eye contact is considered rude

9. Intervention styles

    a. Restatement, clarification, summarization, reflection, and empathy can be useful

    b. Client-centered strategies are less likely to work

    c. Network therapy may be helpful

    d. Involvement in other aspects of the client's life may increase trust

10. A cautionary note

    a. There are over 560 federally recognized American Indian tribes in the United States, and their histories and tribal experiences are often quite different

    b. Consider First Nations People on a continuum of lifestyles ranging from traditional, marginal, middle class to Pan-Indian

    c. Pan-Indians have a multitribe perspective and adopt lifestyles that are in concert with traditional First Nations values, though not those necessarily of a particular tribal group

    d. *Highlight 12.2: On-Line Resources*

C. Hispanics/Latinos

1. Hispanics are one of the fastest growing multicultural groups in the United States

2. The term Hispanic covers people from 26 countries including Puerto Rico, Cuba, Mexico, and Central and South America

3. While the term Hispanic is used frequently, Latino is preferred by many others. Chicano, a term used on the West Coast, refers to Mexican-Americans and persons of Mexican lineage born in the Unites States

4. Family centering

    a. "Family" may be both nuclear and extended relatives as well as friends and neighbors

    b. Father is primary authority figure

    c. Children owe respect and debt to their parents

    d. Individualism must occur within the context of the family and traditional Hispanic values

    e. Familismo emphasizes interdependence over independence, affiliation over confrontation, and cooperation over competition

5. Parental roles

    a. Father less likely to express emotional support, he may not consult the mother in making decisions, yet he expects to be obeyed

    b. The mother's role typically is to balance the father's

    c. When intervening in Hispanic families, including other family members who play crucial roles in the family constellation may be necessary

6. Communication patterns

    a. Hispanic communication patterns have a strong nonverbal tradition

    b. Interviews should typically begin with a period of small talk reflecting the informality values by Hispanics

    c. Hispanic culture emphasizes being personal and informal in contrast to the Anglo focus on efficiency and impersonality

7. Fatalism

    a. Plays major role in outlook on the future

    b. Future-oriented approaches may be of less importance than concrete services offered right now

8. Bilingualism

    a. Shortage of bilingual workers will stymie efforts to serve large groups of Hispanics

    b. Children having to learn two languages may be a source of stress for them

9. Intervention styles

    a. The usual approaches associated with good interpersonal interventions will be effective with many Hispanic clients

    b. A more directive approach using fewer reflective techniques may be useful

    c. Using group and family interventions may also be appropriate because of the strong sense of connectedness in Hispanic families

    d. Recommendations when working with Hispanic clients

        1) Ask where the client is from

        2) Ask if the client is a member of an ethnic group within that nationality

        3) Become familiar with the group history and the history of the group's migration

        4) Identify formal or informal providers of services directed toward members of this national group

10. A cautionary note—Never assume a client is controlled by cultural, ethnic, or racial experience

D.   African Americans

1.   African Americans are the only ethnic and racial group that came here as slaves

2.   African Americans have a substantially lower per-capita income, despite their level of education

3.   Almost 24 percent of African American families live in poverty

4.   African Americans have a higher prevalence of mental disorders, are under-represented in some private outpatient populations, over-represented in inpatient populations, and more likely than whites to use the emergency room for mental health treatment

5.   Instead of having fewer people in poverty, a trend that began in the 1960s and continued into the 1970s, we have stagnated

6.   In 2002, we had a larger percentage of people in poverty (12.1 percent) than was true in 1973 (11.1 percent)

7.   Conservative attempts to gut affirmative action programs have similarly hurt African Americans and other minorities

8.   Communication patterns

   a.   Ebonics (Black English)—The language patterns of many African Americans follow a set of rules as complex and understandable as standard English

   b.   Do not try to adopt a language you are not comfortable with; if you don't understand, ask for clarification

   c.   Be aware how past interactions with social systems have reinforced or extinguished certain behaviors

9.   Family experiences

   a.   Religion plays an important role in the family lives of most African American and other people of color

   b.   Attention should be paid to extended family members who may play an important role in family decisions

   c.   African American families have a rich tradition of kinship care in which members of the extended family provide temporary caregiving for children of relatives

10. Intervention styles

    a. Show respect by using their formal names and titles; do not use nicknames, and so on, unless invited to do so

    b. Study African American literature, music, and newspapers

    c. Brokering is very effective

    d. Provide concrete services and avoid vague discussions about what might be done and concentrate on achievements that show your commitment to helping solve the client's problems

    e. To the greatest extent possible, our interventions should be based on a goal of empowering our clients

    f. Afrocentricity—Does not consider either thoughts or feelings as occurring independently. Rather, they are coequal with neither being more important than the other. Rationality and emotionality are two sides of the same coin

    g. Assess if race or ethnicity is a factor within the institutional or organizational environment

11. Macro-level approaches to intervention

12. A cautionary note—Remember that people's behaviors or problems cannot be explained solely by their ethnicity or culture

E. Asian American and Pacific Islanders

1. General information

    a. Asians and Pacific Islanders are not homogeneous

    b. Between-group differences

    c. Within-group differences

    d. *Highlight 12.3: Within-Group Differences*

        1) Migrational experiences

        2) Location of residence

        3) Degree of assimilation/acculturation

        4) Degree of fluency with one's native language

        5) Degree of fluency with English

6)   Extent of identification with one's country or region of origin

7)   Level and location of education

8)   Age

9)   Composition and degree of intactness of one's family

10)   Level of integration into formal and informal networks

11)   Religious/spiritual beliefs and values

12)   Financial resources

13)   Whether both parents are from the same nation

e.   Filial piety—Devotion to and compliance with parental and familial authority, to the point of sacrificing individual desires and ambitions

f.   May have sense of guilt or shame in seeking social services

g.   "Losing face"—Generally speaking, losing face is equated with being embarrassed, challenged, contradicted, or made to look bad in public

2.   Family centering

a.   Clients reluctant to discuss problems with nonfamily members

b.   Father is head of family—whenever possible, work through father when planning interventions

c.   Recent and older immigrants may request specific services—advocacy and brokering

d.   American-born Asians are more likely to accept counseling and interpersonal interventions

e.   Refugees who left their homeland suffering enormously in the process will be quite different from other Asian immigrants

f.   Asian Americans and Pacific Islanders are less likely to show much feeling in interactions with their children, especially in the presence of strangers

3.   Communication patterns

a.   Many cultures, including Asian American, employ nonverbal communication to a much greater extent than verbal communication, and some gestures may be confusing to the novice

b.   Do not confuse respect for authority with passiveness or refusal to express feelings

c.   Showing respect by learning the client's name is important. The first word is the family name, the second is the middle name, and the third is a given name. Respect the client by using the formal title of Mr. or Mrs., etc.

4.   Attending skills

      a.   Avoidance of eye contact is typical among some Asians

      b.   Within traditional Vietnamese culture it is an insult for an adult male to shake the hand of, or touch, adult females. Also avoiding being in a closed room with females over 12 years of age is important

      c.   The degree of adaptation to the new culture will differ from one generation to another and over time within the same generation

5.   Intervention skills

      a.   Direct, goal-oriented approach is often preferable

      b.   Reliability and dependability are virtues in the Asian culture

      c.   Paraphrasing is a skill that probably should be used less than in most practice situations because it may seem unnatural to the client

      d.   Questioning should be used carefully and sparingly

      e.   View time as elastic, not static

      f.   Community-based services are more likely to be accepted and used

      g.   Asian Americans and Pacific Islanders are more group-oriented than self-oriented

      h.   Cognitive approaches are more useful

      i.   Recognize the values of indigenous healing approaches

      j.   Adopt empowerment approaches accordingly

      k.   Children should never be used as translators

      l.   Focusing efforts on providing concrete services such as referrals, housing resources, and economic assistance in an atmosphere of respect for the client and his or her values is appropriate

6.   A cautionary note—Asian Americans and Pacific Islanders are an extremely diverse group

7.   *Critical Thinking Question 12.2*

F.   People with Disabilities

      1.   Language and communication

          a.   *Highlight 12.4: Talking About Disabilities—Some Dos and Don'ts*

      2.   Social work roles

          a.   People with hearing impairments

          b.   People with psychiatric disabilities

      3.   General intervention principles

          a.   Always assume people are capable or potentially capable

          b.   Refuse to accept interventions or approaches that target the problem as being the individual who in turn must be "fixed"

          c.   At least at one level, intervention is a political activity that recognizes how the access to societal rewards and benefits affects persons with disabilities

          d.   Disability has both a history and a culture

          e.   There is also the possibility of joy to be found in disability

          f.   People with disabilities have the right to manage their own lives

VI.   Developing Culturally Competent Interventions

A.   *Highlight 12.5: Strategies for Cultural Competence*

      1.   Consider clients first as individuals

      2.   Do not assume that ethnic identity tells you anything about a person's values or behavior

      3.   Treat "facts" you have learned about cultural values and traits as hypotheses, and subject them to testing with each new client

      4.   Remember that multicultural groups are at least bicultural

      5.   Allow clients to tell you which portions of their cultural history, values, and lifestyle are relevant to your work with them

      6.   Identify strengths in the client's cultural orientation that you can build upon

      7.   Be aware of your own attitude about cultural pluralism

8. Engage your client actively in the process of learning what cultural content should be considered by asking clearly about the client's experiences, beliefs, and values

9. Keep in mind that there are no substitutes for good clinical skills, empathy, caring, and a sense of humor

10. Demonstrate interest in a client's traditions and customs

11. Consult traditional healers and spiritual leaders

12. Respect and courtesy are always culturally appropriate

B. *Table 12.1: A Brief Summary of Cross-Cultural Differences*

C. Recommendations for Effective Cross-Cultural Intervention

1. Nonverbal communication probably constitutes more of the communication in a counseling relationship with people of color than does the verbal component

2. Eye contact can be a problem for many ethnic groups

3. Use both open-ended and close-ended questions

4. Reflection of feelings works with many cultures, but not with all

5. Paraphrasing generally is an acceptable technique in most cultures

6. Utilize self-disclosure judiciously

7. Give interpretations and advice in cultures expecting a directive helper

8. Summarize from time to time

9. Use confrontation appropriately and carefully with certain racial groups

10. Remember that openness, authenticity, and genuineness are respected in all cultures

D. *Critical Thinking Question 12.3*

EXPERIENTIAL EXERCISES AND SIMULATIONS

The exercises in this chapter are designed to help students expand their awareness of and sensitivity to cultural differences. The first exercise is essentially a library research project for individual students combined with a classroom activity. The second asks students to look at their own ethnic heritage and how it has influenced their lives. The third exercise asks students to apply their knowledge of cultural differences and deal with their own values as they make decisions in a series of case situations. Finally, the last exercise offers students out-of-class activities that can be combined with in-class discussion, if desired.

Exercise 12.1: Ethnic-Sensitive Strategies

A. Brief description:
    Using social work literature, you will locate one source which describes an ethnically and/or racially sensitive intervention strategy and report on this approach in class.

B. Objectives:
    You will be able to:
    1. List and describe at least one ethnically and/or racially sensitive approach to working with culturally diverse people.
    2. Use social work literature to identify techniques and strategies supported by research.

C. Procedure:
    1. Locate one journal article, book, or professional paper which describes some aspect of social work practice with people of color. You might begin by looking at the bibliography for your text. In addition, you might wish to consult *Social Work Research and Abstracts*, *Psychlit*, or any computerized database available in your library.
    2. Read the article and identify one technique or strategy which the author(s) suggest will be helpful in working with people of color.
    3. Prepare a brief (one page) written summary of the technique and a critique of the author's research. In your review, answer these questions:
        a. Describe the approach suggested by the author(s).
        b. Does the author cite any research or study which supports his or her suggestions?
        c. Does the author mention the work of any other writers in her or his material?
        d. With which group(s) would this approach be most successful, according to the author(s)?
        e. Would you be comfortable using this approach? Why or why not?
    4. Briefly report on your findings in class. Be prepared to answer any questions from the instructor or other students.
    5. Turn your one-page paper in at the end of the class.

Exercise 12.2: Ethnic Heritage

A. Brief description:
    Using your life experiences, you will begin to recognize the ways in which your life and behavior have been influenced by ethnic heritage.

B. Objectives:
    You will be able to:
    1. Identify several ways in which your life has been influenced by your cultural and ethnic heritage.
    2. Understand the importance of ethnic heritage in shaping behavior, beliefs, and perceptions.

C. Procedure:
    1. List the ethnic groups with which you most identify. This might include German, Polish, Nigerian, Japanese, etc.
    2. Identify the country(ies) from which your grandparents or great-grandparents came.
    3. Record any religious orientation held by your great-grandparents, grandparents, parents, and you.
    4. Look at the list you have produced. Which groups (ethnic, cultural, religious, and so on) have affected your development? Think about the messages which you have received from each of these groups. What are the behaviors, attitudes, beliefs, and values transmitted by these groups? To what extent are you in agreement with these? Which

have you rejected and why? What advantages or benefits have you experienced because of your background? What disadvantages, if any, have you experienced?

5.   In what ways might your own cultural heritage affect your work as a social worker? Is being aware of your heritage likely to enhance or detract from your ability to work with people from different groups? Why?

6.   The instructor will go around the class asking each member to identify his or her primary ethnic groups, one behavior, belief, value, or attitude which he or she carries forward from this heritage, and one which has been rejected or not accepted. She or he will then lead a general discussion around the questions posed in procedure 5 above.

Exercise 12.3: Tough Decisions

A.   Brief description:

You will be presented with several brief case situations and asked to discuss the actions you would take in each. You will complete this exercise in a group.

B.   Objectives:

You will be able to:

1.   Recognize a series of typical situations involving people of color and consider various strategies for handling each.

2.   Develop sensitivity to unanticipated consequences of initially positive activities.

C.   Procedure:

1.   The instructor will divide the class into groups of four to six students. Each group will be asked to read the case situation and decide how to answer the questions which follow. A group may have a majority answer and a minority answer if it cannot come to consensus on a particular question.

Case Situation #1

Mary Wong and Mary Perez have both applied for the Social Worker I position in your agency. Both have similar educational backgrounds, and neither has experience since they just graduated from the same B.S.W. program. Mary Wong, who is Chinese, and Mary Perez, who is Mexican-American, are both qualified for the position. If you were in a position to hire one of them, what further information would you need or like to have? If both are equally qualified, upon what would you base your decision?

Case Situation #2

Assume that Mary Wong is not Chinese, but is married to Richard Wong, who is. Does this change your decision-making process in any way? Why or why not?

Case Situation #3

Roberto and Ernesto Rivas have been picked up by the police for shoplifting. You are the social worker responsible for doing an initial assessment and either recommending information (non-court) intervention or referring them to juvenile court for a finding of delinquency. What information would you need before making a decision? Does the ethnic or cultural background of the clients make any difference in what you might do? Why or why not?

Case Situation #4

You are a school social worker. The teacher has referred to you a young Native American boy who she says is "too quiet" in class. According to the teacher, he speaks only when spoken to and rarely makes eye contact with her. She is concerned that he is having a problem relating to her and is afraid that his quietness will cause him academic problems eventually. What will you say to the teacher? To the boy? Why?

Exercise 12.4: Understanding Culturally Sanctioned Behavior

A.   Brief description:
You will be given three case situations involving behavior deemed inappropriate or problematic by others. Your task will be to identify which aspects of the behavior appear to be culturally sanctioned (approved).

B.   Objectives:
You will be able to:
1.   Recognize culturally sanctioned behavior.
2.   Suggest strategies for working with people from different cultures.

C.   Procedure:
1.   On your own, read each case situation below and answer the questions.

Case Situation #1

Alice is a twenty-seven-year-old Native American woman who lives with her two children. She is unmarried and currently lives on welfare. She works a part-time job, but the combination of welfare and the job still leaves her strapped for money. Her nineteen-year-old sister moved in with Alice about a month ago, though she has no income, no job, and few employment-related skills. Alice is now helping to support her sister as well as her own children. However, when asked about this, Alice sees nothing wrong with the arrangement and can't understand why anyone would find it odd.

    a.   Is Alice's behavior culturally sanctioned?
    b.   Why do you think this behavior is or is not culturally sanctioned?
    c.   If you were Alice's social worker, what would you do in this situation and why?

Case Situation #2

Juanita Villa is seventeen years old and a senior in high school. She mentions to her teacher that she must get home right after school and cannot attend the school dance. She explains that her father does not want her spending time with young men and that she is not yet able to date. Juanita is not really complaining, but the teacher senses that she would really like to attend the dance. The teacher mentions this case to you over lunch and asks your opinion.

    a.   Is Juanita's father behaving in a culturally sanctioned manner?
    b.   Why do you think this behavior is or is not culturally sanctioned?
    c.   What would you suggest to the teacher and why?

Case Situation #3
Roseanna, fifteen, is the daughter of a Chinese-American family, all of whom are college educated. She tells her friends that she is not interested in going to college but that her parents expect her to. She feels enormous pressure to do well in high school and to get into a good college. Some of her friends encourage her to talk with the school social worker, which is how you came to know Roseanna.

    a.   Is Roseanna's family behaving in a culturally sanctioned manner by expecting her to do well in school and to go to college?
    b.   Why do you think this behavior is or is not culturally sanctioned?
    c.   As the school social worker, what, if anything, would you do?

2.   The instructor will begin a discussion by asking for volunteers to give their answers to each of these cases. Once each case has been reviewed and several students have shared their opinions, the following questions will be open for discussion:
    a.   When a behavior is culturally sanctioned, when might a social worker choose to intervene?
    b.   When culturally sanctioned behaviors clash with values of the larger society, which have precedence? Why?
    c.   When cultural and larger society values conflict, what values of the social work profession come into play?
    d.   Are there any attending skills which might be especially important in working with the individuals and families described in the above cases?

Exercise 12.5: Out-of-Class Experiences

A.   Brief description:
A series of exercises and activities is presented for use outside of the classroom. By your involvement in these activities, you will be exposed to various experiences not replicable in the classroom.

B.   Objectives:
You will be able to:
    1.   Recognize common experiences of people from different cultures.
    2.   Develop increased understanding of human behavior as it is shaped by cultural experiences.

C.   Procedure:
    1.   Select one of the following activities and follow the instructions.

Activity #1
Make a visit to an ethnic neighborhood in your community or in a nearby city. Participate in one or more activities within that community. Examples include:
    a.   Attend a church service.
    b.   Shop at rummage or garage sales.
    c.   Eat lunch or dinner in an ethnic restaurant.
    d.   Purchase food in a neighborhood grocery.
    e.   Attend an after-school sporting event or play.
Keep a log of what you learn. Each log should contain a description of what you did, what thoughts you had about the experience, what your feelings were, and what you learned about the ethnic group or culture which you observed.

Activity #2

Develop a set of questions about the ethnic experiences of members of a particular people of color, e.g., African Americans. You might wish to ask about any discrimination they have experienced while attending your college or university. Similarly, you might ask what values were most stressed by their families or what messages they received about the value of education. Type these questions on a single sheet of paper. Prepare two copies of this questionnaire.

Interview two students of color on your campus. Explain that the assignment is part of a learning activity for a social work course. Write down your interviewee's answers on your questionnaire.

Summarize your findings in a short (two- to three-page) paper. In the paper explain why you selected certain questions and indicate the answers you received to those questions. Do the answers on the questionnaire diverge from what you know about the cultural group being interviewed? What might explain the divergence?

Activity #3

Attend a Native American powwow or other ethnic celebration and participate in as many activities as possible. Observe both verbal and nonverbal behavior of other participants. Note these in a notebook along with your immediate reaction to the behavior.

Later, review your observations. Classify those that appear to be consistent with your knowledge of a particular culture and those which are equally common in the general society. Were there some behaviors which you could not classify? If so, list those. Look at your reactions which you recorded at the time the behavior occurred. In retrospect, do any of them appear to be culturally insensitive or biased by the viewpoint of your own culture (ethnocentric)?

2.   Turn your paper or log in to your instructor.

Chapter 13
Gender Sensitive Social Work Practice

I. **Introduction**

II. **Gender Sensitivity**

    A.   Sexism—Prejudice or discrimination based on sex, especially discrimination against women

    B.   Sex (or Gender) Role Stereotypes—Expectations about how people should behave based upon their gender

    C.   Oppression—The act and result of putting extreme limitations and constraints on some person, group, or larger system because the involved targets fit into some common category or have some common set of characteristics

    D.   Sex Discrimination—Differential treatment of people based solely on their gender

    E.   Facts

        1.   Over 59 percent of all women over age 16 work outside of the home. Sixty-six percent of single mothers and almost 61 percent of married mothers are employed outside of the home

        2.   White women earn about 75 percent of what men earn

        3.   For all races, women earn significantly less than men do at every educational level

        4.   Women are significantly more likely to be poor than men

        5.   Even with a college education, women are far less likely than men to get to the top of their professions or corporations

        6.   African American and Hispanic women are more than twice as likely to be poor than white women

        7.   Women are clustered in low-paying supportive occupations, such as clerical workers, teachers, and service workers, while men tend to assume higher paying occupations such as managers, professionals, and construction workers

        8.   Women earn significantly less than men in the same job category doing the same work

        9.   Every five minutes a woman reports being raped

        10.   Only a small percentage of all rapes are ever reported

11. According to various studies, women have between a 15 and 25 percent chance of being raped sometime in their lives

12. As many as 4 million women are battered by their male partners each year; they account for 37 percent of all women's visits to hospital emergency rooms

III. **Women and the Generalist Intervention Model**

A. Engagement

B. Assessment

C. Planning

D. Implementation

E. Evaluation

F. Termination

G. Follow-Up

IV. **Feminist Perspectives on Micro, Mezzo, and Macro Aspects of Generalist Practice**

A. Feminism—The philosophy of legal, social, educational, and economic equality between women and men

B. *Highlight 13.1: Are You a Feminist?*

C. A feminist perspective on micro practice with women targets women's inner feelings and access to personal power

D. A feminist perspective on mezzo practice focuses on women's relationships with others around them. The micro and mezzo levels of a feminist practice perspective are intimately intertwined

E. A feminist perspective on macro practice looks at the social policies and political structures that hamper women in leading free and productive lives

F. A Definition of Feminism for Practitioners—The philosophy of equality between women and men that involves both attitudes and actions, that infiltrates virtually all aspects of life, that often necessitates providing education and advocacy on behalf of women, and that appreciates the existence of individual differences and personal accomplishments regardless of gender

G. *Highlight 13.2: Principles of Feminist Counseling*

1. A client's problems should be viewed "within a sociopolitical framework"

2. Clients need encouragement to free themselves from traditional gender role bonds

3.   Intervention should focus on the identification and enhancement of clients' strengths rather than on pathologies

4.   Women should be encouraged to develop "an independent identity that is not defined by one's relationships with others"

5.   Other women are considered valuable and important in a society that devalues women in general, seeing other women as being insignificant is easy even for women

6.   Feminist intervention emphasizes finding a balance between work and personal relationships

7.   Whenever possible, the personal power between practitioner and client approaches equality

8.   *Critical Thinking Question 13.1*

V.   Micro Practice with Women: Common Problems

A.   Stressful Life Events

    1.   Happenings in women's personal lives

    2.   Work and financial status

B.   Lack of Self-Esteem and a Sense of Powerlessness

    1.   Women who have been taught to be deferent and dependent often do not feel they can take control of their lives

    2.   Women who have devoted themselves to nurturing and caring for others may feel their own identity is lost

    3.   If a woman has low self-esteem and little experience in independent action, she may have difficulty trusting her own judgment

VI.   Empowering Women in Micro Practice

A.   Enhance Self- Esteem

    1.   Help your client explore how she feels about herself

    2.   Give your client feedback about her responses

    3.   Help your client look more realistically at those areas where she is experiencing guilt

    4.   Help your client accept the fact that most aspects of life have both positive and negative sides

5. Help clients target those areas in which they want to see improvements

6. Encourage a female client to take care of herself

B. Increase Assertiveness

    1. The meaning of assertiveness

        a. Assertiveness can be perceived as the center of a continuum ranging from aggression to passivity

            1) A martyr is a nonassertive, passive person whose primary aim is to keep others happy

            2) The persecutor thinks of only herself as being important

            3) The balancer has appropriate assertiveness and balances both her needs and the needs of others

        b. Assertiveness training

            1) Help your client scrutinize her own actions

            2) Ask your client to make a record of those situations where she feels she lacked assertiveness

            3) Help your client select and focus on some specific instance where she feels she could have been more assertive

            4) Help your client analyze how she reacted. Monitor the following aspects of behavior

                a) Eye contact

                b) Body posture

                c) Gestures

                d) Facial expressions

                e) Voice tone, inflection, and volume

                f) Timing

                g) Content

            5) Help your client identify a role model and examine how that person handled a situation requiring assertiveness

            6) Assist your client in identifying a range of other new responses for situations where she lacks assertiveness

7)   Ask your client to picture herself in the identified problematic situation

8)   Help your client practice the way she has envisioned herself being more assertive

9)   Once again, review her new assertive responses

10)   Continue practicing steps seven, eight, and nine until her newly developed assertive approach feels comfortable and natural to her

11)   Direct your client to try out her new assertiveness approach in a real-life situation

12)   Encourage your client to continue to expand her assertiveness repertoire until such behavior becomes part of her personal interactive style

13)   Reinforce your client for her achievements in becoming more assertive

2.   *Highlight 13.3: Each of Us Has Certain Assertive Rights*

     a.   The right to express your ideas and opinions openly and honestly

     b.   The right to be wrong

     c.   The right to direct and govern your own life

     d.   The right to stand up for yourself without unwarranted anxiety and to make choices that are good for you

     e.   The right *not* to be liked by everyone

     f.   The right to ask for information if you need it

     g.   The right to decide not to exercise your assertive rights

3.   *Critical Thinking Question 13.2*

C.   Expand Options

D.   Change Old Rules and Expectations

E.   Macro-Level Empowerment: Help Women Work Together

VII.   **Common Circumstances Facing Women**

    A.   *Highlight 13.4: A Feminist Approach to Macro Practice*

        1.   Four aspects of the feminist approach that can be applied to macro practice

            a.   Values the process of how things are accomplished as much as the final result of the process

            b.   Adopts a "win-win" rather than a "win-lose" philosophy

            c.   Emphasizes the importance of interpersonal relationships

            d.   Places a high value on human diversity

        2.   How the principles apply to the actual practice of generalist social work

            a.   The emphasis on diversity helps to sensitize feminist practitioners to the existence of inequality and oppression

            b.   The high value placed on the process of how things are accomplished orients practitioners to focus on policy

            c.   The feminist's concern with equality and collaborative decision making fits well with the idea of getting as many community people involved as possible

            d.   Feminists emphasize the value of employee input

VIII.   **Women as Survivors of Sexual Assault**

    A.   Rape Statistics

        1.   It is estimated that 2,000 rapes (or about one every 5 minutes) are committed in the United States every day

        2.   One study found that 20 percent of women college students said they had been forced to have sexual intercourse, most often by someone known to them

        3.   Almost 70 percent of college women reported experiencing some type of forced sexual interaction since age 14

        4.   A woman has a 15 to 25 percent chance of being raped sometime in her lifetime

        5.   It is estimated that the number of rapes being reported is only 12 to 28 percent of those actually committed

B.   Definitions

    1.   Sexual assault—Any unwanted sexual contact where verbal or physical force is used

    2.   Rape—Definitions commonly include three elements: penetration of the vagina, mouth, or anus; force or threat of force; and nonconsent of the victim

C.   The Feminist Perspective on Sexual Assault

    1.   A prevalent rape myth is that sexual aggression is a part of normal human behavior

    2.   The term *victim* implies weakness and powerlessness; in contrast, the term rape *survivor* implies strength and is oriented toward the future

D.   Reactions to Rape

    1.   Rape trauma syndrome—Women can experience serious psychological effects that can persist for a half-year or more following a rape. Now considered a specific aspect of posttraumatic stress disorder

        a.   The acute phase—Two primary emotions experienced during this phase are fear and self-blame

        b.   The long-term reorganization phase—The emotional changes and reactions may linger on for years

E.   Counseling Survivors of Sexual Assaults

    1.   Emotional issues

        a.   Provide warmth and support

        b.   Elicit support from others

        c.   Rebuild survivor's trust in herself, her environment, and other personal relationships

    2.   Reporting to the police—Reporting should be done as soon as possible after the assault

    3.   Medical status of the survivor

F.   Macro Perspectives on Sexual Assault

    1.   General societal responses

2. Current services

    a.   Continuance of 24-hour hot lines, as well as support and advocacy assistance

    b.   Short-term counseling for victims in either individual or group situations

    c.   Long-term work with victims (one year or more after the assault)

    d.   Couples and group work with victims and significant others

    e.   Group work with families, especially around an assault situation within the family

    f.   Special focus on adolescent victims

    g.   Counseling for mothers of children who are victims

    h.   Individual and group counseling with women who were victims of rape or incest in the past

IX. Battered Women

A. Myths about battered women

1. Battered women are not really hurt that badly

2. Beating and other abuses just happen; they are not a regular occurrence

3. Women who stay in such homes must really enjoy the beatings they get; otherwise they would leave

4. Wife-battering only occurs in lower-class families

B. A Profile of Battered Women

1. Women are five to eight times more likely than men to be victimized by an intimate partner

2. Approximately 324,000 women in one year experienced intimate partner violence during their pregnancy

3. More than three women die daily in the United States from intimate partner violence, accounting for over a third of all murders of women. Only four percent of homicides caused by intimate partner violence involved male victims

C. Survivors Versus Victims—A Strengths Perspective

D.   The Abusive Perpetrator

   1.   Many tend to adhere to common masculine gender role stereotypes

   2.   Alcohol or substance abuse, a history of trauma, limited support systems, emotional dependency and jealousy, and male unemployment are additional factors

   3.   Some men rationalize their violent acts as having been provoked by their wives or partners

E.   Cultural Influences and Battered Women

   1.   Cultures that emphasize honor and portray females as passive, and emphasize loyalty and sacrifice for the family, may also contribute to tolerating abuse

   2.   If the social worker establishes that a patient has a history of victimization, the client should be reassured that help is available

   3.   *Critical Thinking Question 13.3*

F.   The Battering Cycle

   1.   Buildup of stress and tension

   2.   Explosion

   3.   Making up

G.   Why Does She Stay?

   1.   Economic dependence

   2.   Lack of self-confidence

   3.   Lack of power

   4.   Fear of the abuser

   5.   Guilt

   6.   Feeling isolated with nowhere to go

   7.   Fear for her children

   8.   Love

H.   Empowering Battered Women

    1.   Shelters for battered women

          a.   Crisis intervention hotlines

          b.   Individual counseling and support groups

          c.   Public education

          d.   Legal advocacy

          e.   Batterers' intervention programs

          f.   *Critical Thinking Question 13.4*

    2.   Counseling strategies

          a.   Offer support

          b.   Emphasize strengths

               1)   Believe the client

               2)   Discover what the client wants

               3)   Move the assessment towards personal and environmental strengths

          c.   Review alternatives

          d.   Furnish information

          e.   Advocate

          f.   The initial interview

               1.   Try to make the woman as comfortable as possible and emphasize that she does not have to talk about anything if she does not want to

               2.   Put your personal feelings aside and do not pressure the battered woman into any particular course of action

               3.   Assure her that no information will be given to anyone unless she wants it to

               4.   Make efforts to dispel any embarrassment by emphasizing that she is not the perpetrator

          g.   Emotional reactions

h.   Specific counseling techniques

        1.   A battered woman needs to know that she can talk freely and what she says will have meaning

        2.   Help her sort through her various issues by using problem solving skills

        3.   Help her establish a safety plan

        4.   Help her strengthen her self-esteem and define more objectively the alternatives available to her

I.   Suggestions for Macro Practice on Behalf of Battered Women

      1.   Strengthen legislation and service provision for battered women

        a.   Violence Against Women Act (VAWA) (1994)

           1)   Increased funding for shelters and programs

           2)   Tougher treatment of offenders

           3)   Establishment of a national hotline

           4)   Education of judges and other court staff, and youth in general about domestic violence

           5)   A provision that makes crossing state lines in pursuit of a fleeing partner a federal offense

        b.   *Highlight 13.5: An International Perspective on Domestic Violence*

           1)   Canada has similar programs to that of VAWA for helping battered women

           2)   The first study in Japan to use face-to-face interviews with a community-based sample of battered women

           3)   Domestic violence began to be recognized as a significant social problem in Japan only since the early 1990s

      2.   Continue lobbying actively for stronger legislation at the state and national levels

      3.   Advocate for the establishment of services within your community

X.   **The Feminization of Poverty**

    A.   Feminization of poverty—The fact that women as a group are more likely to be poor than are men

        1.   Women earn less than 75 percent of what men earn

        2.   Women are significantly more likely than men to be poor within their lifetimes

        3.   The two poorest groups in the United States are women raising children alone and women over sixty-five living alone

        4.   Families with children under age 18 that are maintained by women comprise over 18 percent of all white families, almost 52 percent of all African American families, and over 24 percent of all Hispanic families

        5.   Female-headed families are especially at risk of falling below the poverty line

        6.   Thirty-nine percent of African American and Hispanic female-headed families are poor

        7.   With the exception of Hispanics, people living in families headed by a single male are somewhat more likely to be poor than those living in families headed by a married couple

        8.   The risk of poverty for people living in female-headed families is almost double or more that of their male-headed family counterparts

        9.   Women are generally clustered in low-paying, supportive occupations

       10.   Women earn significantly less than men in every major occupation category except for service occupations when comparing their median incomes

    B.   *Figure 13.1: Percent of People in Families Living in Poverty: Comparisons by Family Structure and Race*

        1.   With the exception of Asian women, women of color suffer even greater risks of living in poverty than do white women

        2.   The average median weekly earnings of African American women are 92.6 percent of what non-Hispanic white women earn and Hispanic women only 78.5 percent

    C.   *Table 13.1: Comparison of Women's and Men's Median Earnings in Major Occupation Categories*

    D.   *Critical Thinking Question 13.5*

    E.   *Highlight 13.6: Women's Salaries in Social Work*

F.   Micro and Mezzo Perspectives on Women and Poverty

    1.   Five things you can do to enhance your client's strengths

        a.   Work to increase your client's self-confidence

        b.   Help your client to define and evaluate the realistic opportunities available to her

        c.   Educate her regarding the resources that are available and help her get involved with them

        d.   Do outreach to clients yourself

        e.   Teach and encourage each client to work with the system to her advantage

G.   Macro Perspectives on Women and Poverty

    1.   Reforming society's perspective

        a.   Only about 50 percent of fathers pay child support after a divorce

        b.   Men are less likely than women to be economically disadvantaged after divorce

        c.   The new Temporary Assistance to Needy Families (TANF) weakens the principle of entitlement, and threatens to bring much harm to poor and working class people

        d.   Problems in society's philosophy regarding women, work, and public assistance

            1)   The obsession with "put them to work" results in women taking jobs with income or benefits that are insufficient for their families' needs

            2)   Training available has too often been for traditionally female jobs that pay poverty-level wages and reinforce the ghettoization of women and the poverty that results

            3)   Even in training programs, often no provision is made for child care

2. Improving conditions in the workplace

    a. Numerous family responsibilities and the many roles women are expected to perform in their work and personal worlds

        1) In recent years although women have reduced and men slightly increased their hourly contributions to routine household tasks, women still do at least twice as much housework as men. Women are much more likely to multitask or perform a series of tasks simultaneously

        2) Women and men tend to do different kinds of tasks in the home. Women usually perform necessary, daily, repetitive tasks, while men do occasional tasks such as household repairs and outdoor maintenance

        3) Most women assume most of the responsibility for the care of their children

        4) Women who work outside of the home spend nearly as many hours with their children as women who are not employed, whereas fathers only spend slightly more time with their children when mothers are employed

    b. Jobs are segregated by gender

    c. Lack of female leadership in powerful positions

    d. Discrimination

        1) Glass ceiling—The phenomenon where women proceed smoothly in organizational advancement until they reach some barrier that prevents them from rising any further in the power structure

        2) Only 9 Fortune 500 companies have women CEOs or presidents (just under 2 percent) and another 10 women CEOS are in the Fortune 1000

        3) Although women make up more than 60 percent of the nonprofit workplace, they still lack access to top management positions, share of foundation dollars, and board positions

    e. Sexual harassment

        1) *Highlight 13.7: Confronting Sexual Harassment*

            a) Confront your harasser

            b) Be assertive

         c)   Document your situation

         d)   Talk to other people about the problem

         e)   Get witnesses

3.   Improving legislation for equality

    a.   Antidiscrimination legislation

        1)   Equal Pay Act of 1963

        2)   Civil Rights Act of 1964

        3)   Family and Medical Leave Act of 1993

    b.   Affirmative action

        1)   Can be used to monitor the proportion of women in any particular job category

        2)   Can be used to identify areas in which women are poorly represented, setting goals for improvement, and monitoring those goals

        3)   Can be helpful in wiping out discriminatory policies and practices

    c.   Comparable worth

        1)   Comparable worth (pay equity)—Calling for equal pay for males and females doing work requiring comparable skill, effort, and responsibility under similar working conditions

        2)   There is currently no federal legislation

        3)   Australia, Great Britain, and Canada have made greater strides in implementing comparable worth principles than has the United States

EXPERIENTIAL EXERCISES AND SIMULATIONS[1]

Five exercises focus on gender-sensitive social work practice. Exercise 1 concerns the exploration of personal values about a range of gender-related issues. Exercise 2 incorporates a macro perspective on micro practice situations by addressing the distribution of scarce resources. Building on the second

---

[1] Exercises 1 through 4 are published with permission of *Arête*, University of South Carolina, College of Social Work, Columbia, SC 29208. The exercises are variations of those published in "Feminist Values and Social Work: A Model for Educating Non-Feminists," by Karen K. Kirst-Ashman, in *Arete*, 17 (Summer 1992), pp. 13-25.

exercise, Exercise 3 concerns establishing intervention strategies on behalf of women in need. Exercise 4 addresses the issue of sexual harassment. Finally, Exercise 5 concludes with a values-oriented questionnaire regarding feminism. The exercises are designed to urge students to evaluate their personal values, biases, and opinions regarding the impacts of gender-related oppression. They then aim to help students establish relationships between values (both personal and professional) and actual practice.

Exercise 13.1: Gender Relations Quiz

A.   Brief description:
        You will be given a variety of provocative statements concerning male and female gender roles and asked to discuss your own opinions.
B.   Objectives:
        You will be able to:
        1.   Recognize your own personal opinions and biases on a number of gender issues which focus on work, leadership, pregnancy, and personal relationships.
        2.   Examine the distribution of power and opportunity between genders on these issues and assess the extent to which the situations are fair.
        3.   Formulate suggestions for addressing these issues.
        4.   Begin to recognize your attempts to deny that attitudinal problems do exist.
C.   Procedure:
        1.   Complete the "Gender Relations Quiz" below. For each statement, check whether you agree or disagree. You must commit yourself to one answer or the other. Additionally, note briefly the reasons for your answers.

Gender Relations Quiz

a.   Employers should treat men and women equally in work settings.
                ☐ Agree   ☐ Disagree
        Reason: _____
        _____

b.   Men make better supervisors than women.
                ☐ Agree   ☐ Disagree
        Reason: _____
        _____

c.   Men make better leaders than women.
                ☐ Agree   ☐ Disagree
        Reason: _____
        _____

d.   A woman would probably not be elected president.
                ☐ Agree   ☐ Disagree
        Reason: _____
        _____

e.   Mothers of small children should remain at home to care for them.
                ☐ Agree   ☐ Disagree
        Reason: _____
        _____

---

f.   Women should automatically be granted several months leave of absence from paid employment when having a baby.
☐ Agree   ☐ Disagree

Reason: _____
_____

g.   Employers should continue paying such women full salary during their absences.
☐ Agree   ☐ Disagree

Reason: _____
_____

h.   In a heterosexual couple, a man should be the "head of the house."
☐ Agree   ☐ Disagree

Reason: _____
_____

i.   Among heterosexual couples, men generally are the "heads of the house."
☐ Agree   ☐ Disagree

Reason: _____
_____

j.   Women and men living together should share housework (for example, taking out the garbage, cleaning the bathroom, doing the laundry, washing dishes, cooking, grocery shopping, taking care of the children) equally.
☐ Agree   ☐ Disagree

Reason: _____
_____

k.   Women and men living together really do share housework equally.
☐ Agree   ☐ Disagree

Reason: _____
_____

l.   If you marry (or are married), you will share (or do share) housework equally with your spouse.
☐ Agree   ☐ Disagree

Reason: _____
_____

2.   Divide into groups of four to six persons. Discuss the Gender Quiz statements, your respective answers, and your rationales for each. After your discussion, a volunteer from each group will be asked to summarize the group's findings and ideas for the entire class.

3.   After approximately twenty minutes, each group's volunteer should present her or his summary. Then address with the entire class the following questions:
   a.   Is power and opportunity distributed equally between genders? Why or why not?
   b.   What are your own opinions and biases about these issues?
   c.   How do these coincide with professional social work values?
   d.   In those instances where you perceive inequities, what suggestions do you have to make changes?
   e.   What can you *personally* do to bring about positive change?

Exercise 13.2: Allocation of Scarce Resources

A. Brief description:

In small groups you will be directed to allocate a significantly inadequate amount of resources among a variety of women needing services.

B. Objectives:

You will be able to:
1. Recognize the critical significance of scarce resources.
2. Identify some of the gender-related social and legal aspects of oppression.
3. Begin to negotiate a troublesome reality.
4. Evaluate the potential success of such negotiation.

C. Procedure:
1. Divide into small groups of four to six persons.
2. Each group will theoretically have a total of $35,000 that it may allocate to any one of the client situations described below. You may only allocate the total amount to address one situation. Assume that any lesser (or divided) amount would be inadequate to meet the need and, therefore, would be useless.

Situation 1

Julia, age twenty-three, and her four young children are homeless. All the shelters are filled. She married at age seventeen and never worked outside of the home. She and her children had always been poor, her husband jumping from one low-paying, blue-collar job to another. Last month her husband told her he was sick of her and all of his responsibility. He abruptly left without telling her where he was going. Julia has no money at all. She also desperately needs food and clothing for her family. She has no access to relatives or other personal support systems who could help her. Additionally, to remove herself from her homeless situation permanently, she needs job training along with concurrent daycare.

Situation 2

Jeannette, age twenty-nine, was raped fourteen months ago and now has discovered she has AIDS. Her assailant has been apprehended and she has learned he is HIV-positive. Thus, she thinks he was the one who contaminated her. Her health has deteriorated rapidly. She desperately needs expensive health care including the new "cocktail drugs" which could help her keep at least some of the more severe diseases at bay. She had been a secretary. Her health problems no longer allow her to work. Nor does she have any health insurance. Her savings are completely depleted.

Situation 3

Danielle, age fifteen, has been on the streets for two years. She thinks she is cocaine and alcohol addicted. She ran away from home because her stepfather had been sexually abusing her since she was eleven. She couldn't stand it anymore. She needs both a home and an expensive rehabilitation program to survive.

---

3. Take approximately fifteen minutes for discussion. A volunteer from each group should be prepared to share with the entire class the group's decision regarding how to spend the money.
4. Rejoin the entire class for a discussion which addresses the following questions:
    a. What were your reasons for choosing the situation you did to allocate the resources?
    b. To what extent did you find the experience frustrating and why?
    c. Whose fault was it that each situation occurred?
    d. Did you feel our society failed these people, and, if so, how?
    e. What aspects of policies, social programs, and laws contributed to these people's problems?
    f. Do you see aspects of sexism and oppression based on gender, and, if so, what are they?
    g. How do you think you'd feel if you were in a situation similar to each one described above?

Exercise 13.3: Proposing Intervention Strategies for Women in Need

A. Brief description:
    A series of vignettes illustrating gender-related problems will be presented. You will then be asked to propose alternative intervention strategies for each.
B. Objectives:
    You will be able to:
    1. Recognize and examine feminist issues more objectively and accurately.
    2. Formulate appropriate alternatives for change.
    3. Articulate the relationship between feminism and social work.

C.   Procedure:
    1.   Review once more the vignettes presented above in Exercise 2.
    2.   Break up into small groups of four to six persons.
    3.   For each vignette, the groups should establish an intervention alternative. Allow thirty minutes for this process.
    4.   A volunteer from each group should explain the group's recommendation to the entire class. Vignettes should be addressed one at a time. Discussion should focus on which intervention alternatives are most doable and have the greatest potential for effectiveness.
    5.   Review the definition of feminism. Discuss with the group the extent to which each alternative reflects feminist perspectives.

Exercise 13.4: Confronting Sexual Harassment

A.   Brief description:
    You will be asked to respond to a variety of vignettes illustrating incidents of sexual harassment.
B.   Objectives:
    You will be able to:
    1.   Define and recognize some aspects of sexual harassment.
    2.   Explore some of the interpersonal dynamics involved in such incidents.
    3.   Assess your own feelings and reactions to such treatment.
C.   Procedure:
    1.   Review the material in the text concerning improving conditions in the workplace, especially that about sexual harassment.
    2.   Read the following vignettes one at a time.

> **Vignette #1**
> *Ann*'s boss states that if she doesn't go to bed with him, she won't make it through her six-month probationary period. She really needs the job. She knows she has the right to complain, but knows she would be labeled a troublemaker. The management would probably find a way to "let her go." They had done so with others before. She doesn't know what to do.
>
> **Vignette #2**
> *Barbara*'s male supervisor likes to sneak up behind her and surprise her by putting his arms around her. This makes her feel very uncomfortable. However, he's responsible for scheduling her hours, evaluating her work performance, and giving her salary increases. She is terrified of confronting him.
>
> **Vignette #3**
> *Lavinia* really needs to get a good grade in a course she's taking with a male professor, Dr. Driven, in order to keep her scholarship and stay in school. So far, she has only achieved a grade of D+. When Lavinia goes to see Dr. Driven, he frequently touches her arm and pats her knee. He acts exceptionally friendly with her. Last Thursday Dr. Driven said he would "see what could be done about improving the grade" if Lavinia would start dating him. Lavinia feels trapped. She doesn't know what to do.

3. After presenting a vignette, take about ten minutes for each to discuss the following questions:
   a. How does this situation fit the definition of sexual harassment?
   b. To what extent are the victim's feelings valid?
   c. How do you feel about this situation?
   d. What do you think the victim should do?
   e. What do you think you would do in this same situation?

Exercise 13.5: Are You a Feminist?

A. Brief description:
   You will answer a questionnaire regarding feminism and discuss your own values concerning the issue.
B. Objectives:
   You will be able to:
   1. Explore your feelings about feminism.
   2. Identify the definition of feminism.
C. Procedure
   1. Review chapter 13, "Gender Sensitive Social Work Practice."
   2. Individually, read the questionnaire cited below and check "yes" or "no" for each question.

> **Questionnaire:**
> **Are You a Feminist?**
>
> a. Do you believe that women should have the same rights as men?
>   ☐ Yes   ☐ No
> b. Do you believe that women should have the same access to jobs and social status as men?
>   ☐ Yes   ☐ No
> c. Do you believe that women should *not* be discriminated against or *denied* opportunities and choices on the basis of their gender?
>   ☐ Yes   ☐ No
> d. Do you believe that, ideally, both people's attitudes and behavior should reflect the equal treatment of women?
>   ☐ Yes   ☐ No
> e. Do you think that many people need to become more educated about women's issues?
>   ☐ Yes   ☐ No
> f. Would you be willing to advocate on behalf of women (for instance, for poor women or women who have been raped)?
>   ☐ Yes   ☐ No

g.   Do you believe that both men and women have the right to their own individual differences (that is, of course, differences which don't harm other people)?

☐ Yes   ☐ No

h.   Do you think that our society is generally structured legally, socially, and economically by and for men instead of women? (This last question is probably the most difficult, and, perhaps, the most painful, to answer.)

☐ Yes   ☐ No

3.   Count the number of times you answered "yes" to the eight questions.

4.   Focus specifically on the definition of feminism which includes the following concepts:

a.   Philosophy of equality.

b.   Involvement of both attitudes and actions.

c.   Involvement of all aspects of life.

d.   Necessity of providing education and advocacy.

e.   Appreciation of individual differences.

5.   With the entire class, take about fifteen minutes to discuss the following questions and issues:

a.   Are you or are you not a feminist? Explain why or why not.

b.   How would you define feminism?

c.   What negative images does feminism conjure up for many people?

d.   To what extent do feminist principles contradict or coincide with professional social work values?

I. **Introduction**

II. **Defining Advocacy**

    A.   Advocacy and the Generalist Intervention Model

    B.   Case Advocacy—Activity on behalf of a single case

    C.   Cause Advocacy—Addresses an issue of overriding importance to some client group (also called class advocacy)

        1.   The need for class advocacy may become more obvious after repeated cases arise having similar characteristics

        2.   Beyond the agency level, advocates are much more likely to involve themselves in coalitions with other workers and agencies

        3.   Cause advocacy often involves resistance because it requires significant change in the status quo

        4.   Some cause advocacy has resulted in lawsuits challenging official regulations and governmental inaction

        5.   *Critical Thinking Question 14.1*

    D.   Useful skills in advocacy

        1.   Government documents

        2.   Political process

        3.   Public speaking

        4.   Tolerance for conflict

III. **The Goals of Advocacy**

    A.   Access to Existing Rights

    B.   Social Action to Secure New Rights and Entitlements

    C.   Advocacy and Empowerment

IV.   **Targets of Advocacy**

    A.   Increase Accessibility of Social Services to Clients

    B.   Promote Service Delivery that Does Not Detract from Clients' Dignity

    C.   Assure Equal Access to All Who Are Eligible

    D.   *Highlight 14.1: Indications for Advocacy*

        1.   When organizational barriers to services are created by agency policies or procedures

        2.   When clients are refused legally entitled benefits or services

        3.   When existing services are inadequate

        4.   When services provided are inhumane or dehumanizing

        5.   When agencies or staff discriminate against clients

        6.   When services or benefits are not provided to clients in a manner consistent with the immediacy of their need

        7.   When multiple clients clearly have the same need for which no services or benefits yet exist

        8.   When clients cannot adequately protect their own interests or act on their own behalf

        9.   When existing services or benefits make the situation worse

        10.   When clients are denied civil rights or other legal protections

        11.   When clients are denied a voice in the planning for or creation of services

        12.   When social workers can help clients mobilize in their own interest to obtain services or benefits routinely available to those with more resources

        13.   When social workers can help achieve social and economic justice for individuals or groups of clients

V.   **History of Advocacy in Social Work**

    A.   Chronology

        1.   1895 to 1915 considered a progressive era in social work. Social workers were more likely to act as brokers or facilitators than advocates

            a.   Charity Organization Society movement saw individual clients as dysfunctional and tried to change the clients

            b.   Social settlement house workers tried to reform the social environment that made people losers

2. After progressive era more attention was paid to psychological treatment

3. Resurgence of advocacy occurred during the Great Depression

4. 1960s marked another resurgence

5. 1970 and 1980s showed less advocacy for oppressed groups as the nation experienced a period of conservative political leadership

6. 1990s saw the growth of advocacy-oriented, self-help groups

7. Today advocacy is an important role in social work

VI. Observations About Advocacy

A. Observations About Power

1. Those who hold power are generally reluctant to give it up

2. Those who hold power generally have greater access to resources

3. Resources in general are not distributed equally

4. Conflict is inevitable when those in power treat those with less power unfairly

5. You must have power to change existing organizations and institutions

B. Observations About Organizations

1. There are many reasons why organizations and institutions fail to meet client needs

2. Agencies and organizations *do* have potential to change

3. Many agency leaders prefer that workers not advocate for changes in their organization

4. Agencies may subvert the rules or try to be secretive

C. Observations About Clients

1. Clients influence and are influenced by their environment

2. Clients should be helped to help themselves

3. Clients should always have prior knowledge and consent of advocacy

VII.   Knowledge Required by Advocates

    A.   Knowing the Rights of Clients

            1.   Rights—Those things to which individuals and society at large have a just claim

            2.   Two types of rights

                      a.   Individual—Those rights that you as an individual are guaranteed

                      b.   Societal—The collective rights of the people as a whole that are considered more important than individual rights

            3.   Sometimes individual and societal rights are in conflict

    B.   Avenues of Appeal

            1.   Challenging the actions of agency administrators or employees requires a thorough knowledge of the avenues of redress or appeal open to the client

            2.   Entitlements—Services, goods, or money due to an individual by virtue of a specific status

            3.   Appeal procedures frequently appear in agency handbooks or regulations

    C.   Available Resources

            1.   Attorneys

            2.   American Civil Liberties Union

            3.   Legal Aid

            4.   Alliance for the Mentally Ill

            5.   Federal Office of Civil Rights

            6.   *Critical Thinking Question 14.2*

    D.   Tactics and Strategies of Intervention

            1.   General intervention skills

            2.   Skills for particular situations

VIII. Assessment in Advocacy Situations

A. Self-Assessment

B. What Are Your Sources of Power?

1. Legitimate power—When person A believes person B has the "right" to influence her

2. Reward power—Ability to provide positive reinforcement to another person

3. Coercive power—Ability of someone to punish or use negative reinforcement on another individual

4. Referent power—One person is influenced by another person because of admiration for that individual

5. Expert power—Those we consider an authority or especially proficient in some area

C. Other Assessment Considerations

1. The Nature of the Problem Situation

   a. Target system—The individual, group, or community to be changed in order to accomplish our goals

   b. *Highlight 14.2: When the System Is Not Working*

2. Assessing the client

   a. Acting on behalf of a client without their full awareness of the potential consequences is unethical

   b. Attempts to bring about change on behalf of others without their complete investment in the process is dangerous on both the local and global level

3. Assessing the adversary

   a. How open to change is the adversary?

   b. What is the degree of vulnerability of the adversary?

   c. How has this adversary handled complaints or challenges in the past?

   d. What are the values of the adversary?

IX.   Planning in Advocacy Situations

    A.   Resources—May include money, power, prestige, authority, commitment, and any other means you can muster to help reach your goal

    B.   Strategy—Broad issues and your plan for approaching advocacy

    C.   Tactics—The specifics of your plan such as how conflict is used and when

    D.   The Ultimate Decision—The social worker must make a decision about when and when not to advocate

X.   Intervention: Advocacy Strategies and Tactics

    A.   *Highlight 14.3: Guidelines for Advocacy*

        1.   Serve only with clear permission of your client

        2.   Acknowledge that acting as an advocate can impact your relationships with other people and organizations

        3.   Advocacy is appropriate only to help the client, not to pursue your personal agenda

        4.   Get the facts first

        5.   Always enter an advocacy situation with a clear list of concerns and questions

        6.   Look at issues from both sides

        7.   Keep a record of things that are said in meetings that relate to your goal

        8.   Always find out who makes decisions at the next-higher level

        9.   Record all steps you take to resolve an issue

    B.   Persuasion

        1.   Steps to approaching persuasion

            a.   Clearly state the issue of concern

            b.   Allow adequate time for discussion and questions

            c.   Identify exactly what you want done

            d.   Summarize areas of agreement

            e.   Find common ground whenever possible

            f.   Avoid vague statements

g. Be candid about what you'll do if the problem is not remedied

h. Convey your sincerity and determination to resolve the matter

i. Maintain eye contact and avoid any gestures that might undercut your firmness

j. Approach an adversary as if you both have a desire to resolve things

k. Do not filibuster or monopolize the conversation

l. Do not lose your cool

2. When persuasion does not work

C. Fair Hearings and Legal Appeals

1. Fair hearings and grievances—Administrative procedures designed to ensure that clients or client groups who have been denied benefits or rights to which they are entitled get equitable treatment

2. An attorney's letter presenting the possibility of legal action is frequently sufficient to cause adversaries to change their position

D. Political and Community Pressure

E. Using the Media

F. Petitioning

XI. Selecting a Strategy for Advocacy

A. Three conditions before deciding to exert pressure and cause a confrontation

1. You have already tried less confrontational ways of instituting change

2. You have enough proof that clients have been treated unfairly and are absolutely certain that your grievance is consequential

3. You determine that you have a good chance at succeeding by exerting pressure and initiating a confrontation

XII. Whistle Blowing

A. Whistle-blowing—Informing those people in positions of influence or authority outside an organization about the existence of an organization's practices that are illegal, wasteful, dangerous, or otherwise contrary to its stated policies

B. Whistle-blowing carries a degree of risk that varies in direct proportion to the seriousness of the allegations

XIII.   Legislative Advocacy

A.   Legislative Advocacy—Specifically entails efforts to change legislation to benefit some category of clients

B.   *Highlight 14.4: Writing Elected Officials*

   1.   Letters to the President

   2.   Letters to U.S. Senators

   3.   Letters to members of the House of Representatives

   4.   Letters to Cabinet Secretaries

   5.   Additional guidelines for writing to elected officials

C.   Factors Affecting Legislative Advocacy

   1.   The fiscal consequences of a bill

   2.   The popularity of a bill

D.   Steps in Legislative Advocacy

   1.   Step 1: Developing and revising the draft bill

   2.   Step 2: Identifying, obtaining, and maintaining the bill's supporters

   3.   Step 3: Arranging for sponsorship of the bill

   4.   Step 4: Introducing the bill

   5.   Step 5: Working with interest groups to broaden support for the bill

   6.   Step 6: Educating the public

   7.   Step 7: Influencing legislative committee consideration

   8.   Step 8: Influencing action on the floor

E.   NASW's Political Action for Candidate Election (PACE)—To help elect candidates favorable to social work positions on issues

There are four exercises in this chapter focusing on the topic of advocacy. The first exercise requires the student to assume the role of an advocate in a dispute between tenants and their landlord. The second exercise confronts the worker with a possible whistle-blowing situation which requires careful thought. Exercise 3 provides a flawed example of persuasion and asks the student to identify the mistakes which were made. The last exercise is a letter writing activity based on the premise that social workers will want to (and have to) influence their elected representatives.

Exercise 14.1: Advocating for Renters

A. Brief description:
    You will be deciding appropriate strategies for engaging in advocacy for a specific group of clients. This will give you practice in the role of an advocate.
B. Objectives:
    You will be able to:
    1. Identify appropriate strategies for advocacy.
    2. Determine the logical steps to take to carry out your advocacy.
C. Procedure:
    1. The instructor will divide the class into groups of four to six students. Each group will be responsible for reading the case situation and answering the questions. Appoint one person to record each group's decisions.
    2. Read the case situation and answer the questions.

Case Situation

The student residents of the Littlejake House were angry. The owner, Dwight Cackle, had taken advantage of Christmas break and began to remodel their apartments without informing them of his intentions. Cackle, hoping to increase his income, was combining an entry hall with portions of the original apartments to create another two apartments. His plan called for shaving three feet off the rooms on either side of the hallway and adding it to the hallway space. The diagram below shows his plan.

     The new apartments affect all the residents, who will each lose three feet from the end of their apartments. They will also lose the second exit since all apartments had two exits, one to the hallway and one to the outside. To make matters worse, he has turned off the water in the building since he says he has to do this to work on the new apartments. As a consequence, residents have no water, cannot use the bathrooms, and must listen to the pounding as work on the apartments continues. They have complained to Mr. Cackle, who has told them they're just complainers and he has no intention of stopping work on his project.

     As the ombudsman for the student housing office, you have often heard complaints about Mr. Cackle's actions toward tenants, including refusing to return security deposits, not following terms of the lease, and generally abusing residents of his apartments. Now the tenants have come to you for help. You must decide what you can do to assist them.

```
 _____|___   _____
|        _____    | |  | |    _____      |
|       | Apartment    | | | Proposed | |  Apartment  _  |
|  _    |   # 1        | | | Apartment | |   # 2       |
| |     |_____|_| |  #7      |_|_____   |
| |     |        _____   | |    | |   _     _____   |
| |     | Apartment  |_ |_____|  |_|  | Apartment  _  |
| |     |   # 3      | |          | |  |   # 4       |
|  _    |_____|_| | Proposed |_|_____   |
| |     |        _____   | | Apartment | |            |
| |     | Apartment  | |  |    #8     | |  Apartment  _  |
|  _    |   # 5      | |  |           | |    #6       |
| |     |_____|_|_|___   ___|_|_____   |
|_____|_____|
```

a.   Which of the problems appear most serious to you? Why?
b.   What information about the tenants would you like to have before attempting to help them?
c.   List all possible sources of power available to you and the tenants.
d.   What information about Mr. Cackle would help you assess his willingness to respond to your advocacy efforts?
e.   What steps would you take to bring about change in this situation?

3.   Each group should report its findings to the entire class.

Exercise 14.2: Whistle Blowing

A.   Brief description:
You will confront the situation of an agency worker who learns about unethical behavior on the part of his supervisor.

B.   Objectives:
You will be able to:
1.   List alternative courses of action.
2.   Weight the risks of each course of action.
3.   Select a course of action acceptable to you.

C.   Procedure:
1.   Read the case situation below, placing yourself in the position of Ned. Follow the steps listed after the case situation.

> **Case Situation**
> Ned is the chief social worker in a residential treatment center for disturbed adolescent males. He has worked there for eighteen months and likes his job, which consists of planning and leading treatment groups for residents of the center, designing entertainment such as sporting events, dances, and extracurricular activities, and supervising cottage parents who provide day-to-day supervision for the adolescents. In a conversation with a cottage parent, Ned hears an allegation that the treatment center director is pocketing financial donations to the center and diverting other resources to his own use. The cottage parent says this has been going on for a long time and he thought everybody knew about it. You indicate you knew nothing about this.

a. If you were Ned, what would you say to the cottage parent who is your subordinate?

b. Would you take any steps to determine whether this allegation is true? If so, what steps would you take?

c. If you determined that the allegations were true, what possible steps (if any) might you take?

d. For each possible step, list the advantages and risks involved.

e. Which of the options would you be most likely to pursue? Why?

Exercise 14.3: Persuasion

A. Brief description:

This case provides an example of a social worker who has not followed the guidelines for persuasion described in the chapter. Your task will be to identify the mistakes made by the worker.

B. Objectives:

You will be able to:

1. Recall the guidelines for persuasion.

2. Identify guidelines which have been misused or otherwise not followed.

C. Procedure:

1. Review the section of the chapter describing the guidelines for persuasion.

2. Read the case illustration and answer the questions.

> **Case Situation**
>
> Naomi Grunge was livid. "You don't care why I'm here or whether my client is in need or not. You have no right!" she shouted at Don Nedlin, Income Maintenance worker for Ashford County Human Services. "My client is entitled to lots of things and you have no basis for denying her," she continued. "What exactly are you asking for?" he said. "I want all my client is entitled to," said Naomi. Don started to respond by reciting the regulations he had to work with. "No! I want none of that crap about regulations. You give my client everything she's supposed to get or else." At that point Don escorted Naomi to the front door of the agency, abruptly turned, and walked back to his office, locking the door behind him as he entered.

a. Which of the eight guidelines on persuading others did Naomi violate?

b. What effect did Naomi's shouting likely have on the person she was trying to persuade?

c. Was the "or else" threat a credible one? Why or why not?

d. Assume that you are a friend of Naomi's and that she would listen to you. What advice would you give her about how to handle this situation?

Exercise 14.4: Letter Writing

A. Brief description:

Writing letters to elected officials is a common component of the social worker's job. This exercise will give you experience drafting such a letter.

B. Objectives:

You will be able to:

1. Prepare a professional letter having the correct format.

2. Clearly communicate your position on a pending piece of legislation.

C.   Procedure:
    1.   Review the information on writing to elected officials contained in the text.
    2.   Read the scenario below and draft a letter to Representative Hosea Williamson, your state representative. Give the correct address and salutation and clearly specify your position on the pending legislation. Support your position with several reasons.

> **Case Situation**
> You are a member of the Political Action Committee for the state National Association of Social Workers chapter. A bill is pending in your state legislature which will provide funds enabling welfare recipients to receive a college education. Representative Williamson is not yet committed to supporting this bill but may be persuaded if enough of his constituents indicate their interest.

    3.   Describe three steps you could take (alone, or with the help of colleagues) to convince Representative Williamson.

    4.   Be prepared to read your letter aloud and to share your steps when the instructor calls upon you.

Chapter 15
Brokering and Case Management

I. **Introduction**

    A.   A Definition of Brokering

        1.   Brokering—The linking of client systems to needed resources, assuming that client needs can be met through existing services and resources

        2.   The role of broker in social work has appeared in social work literature for over 65 years

    B.   Importance of the Brokering Role in Generalist Practice

II. **The Effective Broker**

    A.   The Importance of Knowing Resources

        1.   Eligibility criteria of resource agencies

        2.   Characteristics of resource agencies

        3.   Contact persons in resource agencies

    B.   Types of Resources

        1.   Community resource directories

            a.   *Highlight 15.1: Community Resource Directory Index*

            b.   *Highlight 15.2: Resource Directory Listing*

        2.   Telephone books

        3.   Information and referral services

        4.   Service organizations and clubs

        5.   Internet resources

            a.   *Table 15.1: On-Line Resources for People with Disabilities*

        6.   Other informal natural resource systems

        7.   *Critical Thinking Question 15.1*

C.   The Planned Change Process in Brokering

1.   Identifying and assessing client needs

2.   Identifying and assessing potential resource systems

3.   Helping the client select the best resource system

4.   Making the referral

    a.   Actions you can take that will enhance the success of the referral

        1)   Write out the necessary information about the agency and give it to the client

        2)   Send the new agency a written description or referral outlining the client's needs

        3)   Set the actual appointment time for the client before he or she leaves your office

        4)   Accompany the client to the new agency

5.   Helping the client use resource systems

6.   Follow-up and evaluation of resource systems

III.   Case Management

A.   Case management has existed since the nineteenth century but has recently received more attention

B.   In 1984, the National Association of Social Workers published standards for case management services to functionally impaired client populations, and in 1992 a set of ten standards were adopted

C.   What Is Case Management?

1.   Case management—A method of providing services whereby a professional social worker assesses the needs of the client and the client's family, when appropriate, and arranges, coordinates, monitors, evaluates, and advocates for a package of multiple services to meet the specific client's complex needs

2.   Principles of case management

    a.   Individualization of services—Services are developed or designed specifically to meet the identified needs of the client

    b.   Comprehensiveness of services—Encompass all areas of the client's life and help ensure that no need will go unfulfilled

        c.   Parsimonious services—Duplication of services will be discouraged and costs for services will be controlled

        d.   Fostering autonomy—Helping clients become as self-sufficient as possible

        e.   Continuity of care—As the client moves through life, requiring in-patient services and help in the community, case management services will ensure continued monitoring of needs

    3.   The role of case manager goes well beyond that of broker; the case manager has the broader task of ensuring that a wide spectrum of clients' needs are met in an efficient and effective manner

    4.   Some authors argue that case management is what most social workers do in most fields of practice most of the time

D.   *Highlight 15.3: An Overview of Case Management*

    1.   Definition—Providing multiple services to meet specific client's complex needs

    2.   Purpose

        a.   Promoting the skills and capability of the client in using social services and social supports

        b.   Developing the abilities of social networks and relevant service providers to further the functioning of the client

        c.   Promoting effective and efficient service delivery

    3.   Focus

        a.   Formulating client support network that integrates client skill development; involvement of social networks, and involvement of multiple providers

    4.   Tasks

        a.   Assessing of client needs, social network capacities, and abilities of social service providers

        b.   Developing a comprehensive service plan

        c.   Intervention directly with client to strengthen skills and capacities for self care and/or indirectly with systems impinging on client

        d.   Monitoring of service plan implementation and tracking of client status

        e.   Evaluation of service plan effectiveness and its impact on client functioning

E.   *Figure 15.1: Worker Responsibilities in Case Management*

F.   Importance of Case Management for Generalist Practice

      1.   Increased emphasis on maintaining clients in the least restrictive environment

      2.   The goal of keeping people out of institutions

      3.   The objective of maintaining the elderly in their homes as long as possible

      4.   Efforts to reduce or contain costs of providing health and other forms of care to clients

      5.   Increased attention to rights of clients who often lack awareness of available resources

      6.   Awareness that some clients cannot follow through on the ordinary referral because of their limited capacities

      7.   Increased focus on how the environment contributes to client problems

      8.   Decreased focus on the medical model of practice

      9.   Expansion of human service programs and increased complexity and fragmentation of services

      10.   Inclusion of case management services in federal legislation

G.   Assessment

      1.   Assessing the client's ability to meet environmental challenges

      2.   Assessing the caretaking ability of the client's informal support group

      3.   Assessing the resources of formal support systems

            a.   Availability

            b.   Adequacy and appropriateness

            c.   Acceptability

            d.   Accessibility

      4.   Assessment process

            a.   Need-based—Focus specifically on client needs

            b.   Holistic/comprehensive—Assess clients' needs in all areas, instead of just a few

  c. Interdisciplinary—Use the expertise of various disciplines to understand clients' needs

  d. Participatory—The client is fully involved in assessing his or her own needs and maintains maximum self-determination

  e. A process—Simple recognition that assessment is an ongoing, changing, progressive type of interaction

  f. Systematic—Ensure that each area of potential need is explored in sufficient depth and breadth

  g. A product—When completed, the assessment should be in written form that guides planning and intervention

 5. *Table 15.2: The Structure of Case Management*

H. Planning

 1. Service plans—six dimensions

  a. Client needs are prioritized

  b. Goals and objectives of service are established

  c. Resource systems that will be involved are identified

  d. Time frames are identified within which services will be delivered and goals achieved

  e. Outcome measures are formulated that will be used to evaluate achievement of case plans

  f. Specific tasks are assigned to individuals and groups so that it's clear who is responsible for what

 2. Impact goals—Goals that result in changing some major aspects of the client's life and are the expected results of our intervention

 3. Service objectives—Describe steps that must be undertaken to achieve an impact goal

  a. *Figure 15.2: Case Management Plan*

  b. *Table 15.3: A Completed Service Plan*

I.   Intervention Implementation

    1.   Direct services—May include crisis intervention, supporting clients making difficult decisions, helping to modify clients' environments, and helping clients overcome emotional reactions to their crisis situations

    2.   *Highlight 15.4: Motivating Techniques*

        a.   Begin by asking about the plans a client has for her- or himself

        b.   Contribute realistic suggestions aimed at enhancing the client's life and forestalling relapses

        c.   Discuss points of disagreement between worker and client and work out realistic compromises

        d.   Develop a contract with the client specifying mutual goals

        e.   Identify the steps that must be taken and the service providers that can help the client to reach agreed goals

        f.   Provide the client with data about service providers

        g.   Discuss any of the obstacles the client can foresee in using the proposed services

        h.   Review what the responsibilities of each party will be in completing the linkage with a particular service provider

    3.   Indirect services

        a.   Linking clients with needed resource systems

        b.   Advocating with various systems on behalf of clients

    4.   Monitoring—One of the primary tasks in which the case manager continues to communicate with service providers

    5.   Additional roles

J.   Evaluation in Case Management

K.   Termination in Case Management

L.   Follow-Up in Case Management

M.   *Highlight 15.5: Case Management for a Client Who Has Mental Disabilities*

N.   Factors Influencing Case Management Service Delivery

     1.   Level of caseloads—Caseloads over about 30 begin to reduce the effectiveness and quality of services provided by case managers, in large rural areas this may be much too great

     2.   Extent to which the case manager's responsibilities are clearly delineated

     3.   The quality of supervision that supervisors provide to case managers

     4.   Stress and burnout of case managers

O.   *Critical Thinking Question 15.2*

EXPERIENTIAL EXERCISES AND SIMULATIONS

The four exercises in this chapter are designed to illustrate the work of the broker and case manager. The first three give experience in thinking about and locating resources, perhaps the most important task of the social worker in the broker role. The last exercise is focused on helping familiarize you with key concepts used in case management.

Exercise 15.1: Mrs. Darwin

A.   Brief Description:
     As a task group member in this case, you will be asked to prioritize the problems experienced by the client and identify potential resources that may be accessed.

B.   Objectives:
     You will be able to:
     1.   Identify tasks that must be completed in order to assist the client.
     2.   Prioritize the tasks in order of importance.
     3.   Identify possible community resources to which the client can be referred.

C.   Procedure:
     1.   The instructor will divide the class into several groups of four to six members. A group recorder will be selected by members of each group.
     2.   Read the case situation below.

Case Situation

Mr. B. Darwin arrived at the trauma center after suffering a heart attack on the interstate highway. Attempts to revive him failed and the emergency room physician was about to talk to his wife. The Darwins, both in their late sixties, had apparently been traveling through the state on the way to visit relatives.

     Mary Ann accompanied the doctor to the trauma center waiting room where they met Mrs. Darwin. A petite woman not even five feet tall, Mrs. Darwin looked very weary. The crumpled handkerchief in her hand was damp from tears. The doctor first introduced herself and Mary Ann. Mary Ann then sat next to Mrs. Darwin.

     "Is he dead?" Mrs. Darwin asked quietly. The doctor slowly nodded his head and responded, "Yes, he is."

     Mrs. Darwin put her head in her hands and cried softly for a minute. She raised her head and asked, "What am I going to do now?"

Mary Ann said that she knew this must be a terrible time for Mrs. Darwin and she offered to do everything she could to help her. She invited Mrs. Darwin to come to the social work office. As the doctor departed, Mary Ann reached out her hand and helped Mrs. Darwin to her feet. Together they took the elevator to Mary Ann's office.

Mary Ann again expressed her sensitivity to Mrs. Darwin's situation and asked her if there was anything that she (Mary Ann) could do. Slowly, Mrs. Darwin described the events of the day that preceded the death of her husband. In a few minutes, Mary Ann discovered the following information.

The Darwins were residents of Wisconsin traveling through Minnesota to visit relatives in Iowa. They had car trouble about fifteen miles from the hospital. When Mr. Darwin got out to check on the car, he fell to the ground. A passing trucker radioed a nearby highway patrol officer, and together they attempted cardiopulmonary resuscitation. Shortly, an ambulance arrived and transported Mr. Darwin to the hospital. The highway patrol officer brought Mrs. Darwin to the hospital with their pet, a small dog. Mrs. Darwin said the car was still on the side of the highway and contained a large load of frozen meat in the trunk. It was to be a gift to her daughter in Iowa, she explained. As they talked, Mary Ann began to make mental notes of the tasks ahead. She also learned a little about Mrs. Darwin. This would prove helpful as they worked together to resolve the woman's concerns.

3. Prepare a list of tasks that must be completed in order to assist this client.
4. Prioritize the tasks from most important to least important.
5. Identify possible community resources to which the client might be referred.
6. A volunteer from each group will be asked to report back to the class on responses to questions 3 through 5.

Exercise 15.2: Knowing Your Own Resources

A. Brief description:
This activity requires you to assess your own resources. The purpose is to assist you in recognizing the many resources the average person can call upon in times of need.

B. Objectives:
You will be able to:
1. Identify personal resources which might assist you in times of need.
2. Categorize resources according to a predetermined system.

C. Procedure:
1. Read each of the "Need statements" below and list three resources that you could reasonably count on to assist you.

Needs Statements

a. Your car just quit working and you have a doctor's appointment in one hour.
Resource: _____

_____

b. You are sick and need a prescription picked up at the pharmacy.
Resource: _____

_____

_____

---

c.   You must pay your tuition of $1,000 by tomorrow morning or your enrollment in classes for this semester will be cancelled.
Resource: _____
_____
_____

d.   You need a pair of dress slacks for a job interview and don't want to have to buy one.
Resource: _____
_____
_____

e.   You need a special book for your social work class tomorrow. The book costs $50. You have only $5 but your part-time job will pay you $75 in one week.
Resource: _____
_____
_____

f.   You have a job interview and need three letters of reference by tomorrow evening.
Resource: _____
_____
_____

g.   You need a haircut or perm by 5:00 p.m. today but have no money.
Resource: _____
_____
_____

h.   You have a date tomorrow night and no transportation. You definitely need a car to drive.
Resource: _____
_____
_____

i.   You have a chance for a part-time job that pays rather well, but you need to borrow a rake, hoe, and lawnmower.
Resource: _____
_____
_____

j.   You have nothing to eat in the house and have no money.
Resource: _____
_____
_____

k.   Your computer printer just quit in the middle of your final social work paper, which is due by noon tomorrow.
Resource: _____
_____
_____

l.   You are very sick, don't have a local physician, and don't know what to do.
       Resource: _____

       _____

m.   Your favorite friend of the opposite sex just broke up with you and you need to talk to someone.
       Resource: _____

       _____

       _____

Exercise 15.3: Community Resources

A.   Brief description:
       In this out-of-class exercise you will be required to identify at least one resource for each of several client needs.
B.   Objectives:
       You will be able to:
       1.   Locate resources that might assist clients in meeting specified needs.
       2.   Learn to use a variety of data sources in your search for client resources.
C.   Procedure:
       1.   Select two of the client situations listed below.

Client Situations

a.   Twenty-two-year-old single mother of two children (ages one and three) has just lost her job and has no savings, no family, and no income.
       Resource: _____

b.   Sixty-eight-year-old man being discharged from hospital to his own home needs a hospital-type bed provided at no charge.
       Resource: _____

c.   Child has a serious vision disorder and needs corrective surgery. His parents are poor but not on welfare.
       Resource: _____

d.   Father of six children has just lost his job and needs help locating another.
       Resource: _____

e.   Homeless family just arrived in town and needs shelter for tonight and tomorrow night.
       Resource: _____

f.   Child dying of cancer wants to go to Disney World before he dies.
       Resource: _____

g.   Tenant needs legal advice on whether her landlord can evict her for reporting him to the health department for bug infestation.
       Resource: _____

h.   Woman battered by her husband needs emergency shelter for herself and her five children.
       Resource: _____

i.   Alcoholic client needs to know meeting place and time of nearest Alcoholic Anonymous group.
       Resource: _____

j.	Child burn victim needs reconstructive surgery and parents have no money. Resource: _____		
k.	Suicidal client needs to talk with someone immediately. Resource: _____		

2. Using any existing community resource directories, services, or telephone books, locate at least one resource for each of the client situations.
3. List the resource under the problem situation.
4. The instructor will poll the class to determine the resource array which has been located for each problem.

Exercise 15.4: Matching Concepts

A. Brief description:
A matching exercise using various case management concepts described in the text.
B. Objective:
You will be able to:
1. Correctly match major concepts and their meanings.
C. Procedure:
1. Match the concepts in the left column with the meanings in the right column.
2. The instructor will go through each answer orally after all members of the class are through.

1)	Individuation of services	A.	Person or team who organizes, coordinates, and sustains a network of formal and informal supports and activities to maximize the functioning of people with multiple needs.
2)	Parsimonious services	B.	Discouragement of duplication of service and controlling of costs.
3)	Fostering autonomy	C.	Helping clients become as self-sufficient as possible.
4)	Continuity of care	D.	Developing or designing services specifically to meet client needs.
5)	Comprehensiveness of services	E.	Focus on services meeting client needs in all areas of life including housing, financial, and medical.
6)	Case manager	F.	Assures regular monitoring of clients' needs throughout their lives.

Chapter 16
Recording in Generalist Social Work Practice

I. **Introduction**

II. **The Importance of Writing in Social Work**

    A.   Identifying the Client and the Need

    B.   Documenting Services

    C.   Maintaining Case Continuity

    D.   Interprofessional Communication

    E.   Sharing Information with the Client

    F.   Facilitating Supervision, Consultation, and Peer Review

    G.   Monitoring the Process and Impact of Service

    H.   Educate Students and Other Professionals

    I.   Providing Data for Administrative Tasks

    J.   Providing Data for Research

III. **What Is in the Record?**

    A.   Seven major types of information

        1.   The date of your interaction with the client

        2.   Basic information about the client

            a.   Face sheet—A page of information, usually placed at the front of a client's file or in the beginning of a record that provides basic identifying information about the client

            b.   *Figure 16.1: An Example of a Face Sheet*

            c.   Licensing—A designated government agency grants agencies that abide by specified standards the right to operate legally

        3.   Reasons for client contact

4. More detailed information about the client's problem and situation

    a. Intake—Involves the established procedures for an agency's initial contact with a client

    b. *Figure 16.2: An Example of an Intake Form*

    c. Social history—A comprehensive portrayal of a client's current situation and past, developed by gathering information about the client's development, family, interpersonal relationships, education, and socioeconomic status

        1) Social histories oriented toward children age 0 to 5 years would stress detail about achievement of developmental milestones

        2) A social history of a child age 6 through 11 would also focus on specific academic strengths and weaknesses, peer relationships, skills, achievement, extracurricular activities, and education about sexuality

        3) A social history of a 12 to 17-year-old would stress aspects such as educational participation and performance, peer relationships, after school activities, employment history, romantic relationships, and development of sexual identity

        4) Social histories of adults would place greater emphasis on variables like social relations, intimate relationships, family relations and dynamics, employment/education, military service, contributions to community, daily living habits and activities, spirituality and religion, alcohol or other drug abuse, mental health, health condition and issues, criminal activity, and self-perceptions

        5) Social history content for an older adult anticipating residential care placement would minimize or omit the early developmental history of childhood and focus on such dimensions as current social and emotional functioning, health issues, ability level, self care skills, financial situation, in addition to family and social support systems

    d. *Figure 16.3: An Example of a Social History Format*

    e. *Critical Thinking Question 16.1*

5. Aspects of the implementation process

    a. Your impressions concerning assessment of the client-in-situation, your specific plans for intervention, contacts you have had with clients and others involved in the case, progress made, and information about how the case was terminated

    b. *Figure 16.4: An Example of a Progress Note Format*

6. Follow-up information

7. Comments and questions to discuss with a supervisor or another worker

IV. Recording Formats

A. Process Recording

   1. Progress recording—A specialized and highly detailed form of recording. Everything that takes place in an interview is recorded. Most progress recording uses direct quotes

   2. *Figure 16.5: Portion of a Process Recording with a Client Who Has Just Entered a Nursing Home*

   3. Process recording is time consuming; therefore, this type of recording is used primarily for students in their internship

B. Using Digital Recording, Videotapes and Audiotapes

   1. Recording can supply you with general feedback about yourself and your interviewing and problem-solving style

   2. Six steps for using recording technology

      a. You must get the client's explicit permission to conduct the recording

      b. The actual recording process

      c. Writing out what transpired during the recording word by word

      d. Writing a summary of the recording session

         1) Briefly summarize chronologically the most significant critical points that occurred during the interview

         2) What specific problems, needs, and strengths surfaced during your meeting?

         3) What specific methods did you use during the interview? For each method, describe the extent to which you felt it was effective or not effective

         4) Where during the interview do you feel you could have used more effective techniques? Describe your recommended techniques

         5) What are your recommendations for your next meeting with the client?

    e.   Review your recording, the summary, and perhaps, the verbatim record with your supervisor

    f.   Adapt what you have learned during this discussion and write a report that complies with the conventional format your agency uses

   3.   *Critical Thinking Question 16.2*

C.   Progress Notes

   1.   Progress notes (interim notes)—Describe and assess the client-situation and the service transaction at regular intervals

   2.   SOAP—Subjective information, Objective information, Assessments, and Plans

   3.   Taking Notes During the Interview

   4.   *Critical Thinking Question 16.3*

D.   Narrative Recording

   1.   Narrative recordings—Reports that summarize the main issues addressed, plans developed, and results achieved with a client during the intervention process. They are written in a narrative format

   2.   Summary Narrative Recordings—The culmination of progress notes recorded over weeks or even months, organized chronologically, and kept in one place

   3.   Focusing on strengths is important whenever possible with any type of record

E.   Summaries of Treatment Conferences

   1.   Treatment conference—A meeting where various professionals, often from various disciplines, come together to discuss clients' problems, progress, and plans (also called case conferences)

   2.   Clearly specify plans and goals

F.   Problem-Oriented Recording (POR)

   1.   Database—A collection of information stored electronically so that it is accessible by computer and digitally searchable

   2.   Problem list—A numbered list of problems identified by client and worker during the assessment process

    a.   Listing strengths often provide the basis for determining solutions

    b.   *Figure 16.6: An Example of a Format for Prioritizing Problems*

   3.   Initial implementation plans

4. Progress in Plan Implementation (SOAP)

    a. *S*ubjective information

    b. *O*bjective information

    c. *A*ssessments

    d. *P*lans

    e. *Figure 16.7: An Example of a Format for SOAP Progress Notes*

5. *Highlight 16.1: An Amended Case Example of Problem-Oriented Recording: A Focus on Strengths*

6. Advantages of Problem-Oriented Recording

7. Disadvantages of Problem-Oriented Recording

G. Standardized Forms

1. *Figure 16.8: An Example of a Standardized Form*

2. Purposes of standardized forms

    a. Direct the worker to the specific type of information needed and encourage gathering data quickly

    b. Provide means for evaluating data involving a large number of clients

    c. Easy documentation of which services have been provided to which clients

    d. Clear compatibility with computerized analyses

    e. Sometimes you can give standardized forms to the clients themselves for completion

    f. Standardized forms involve brevity and easy collection of large amounts of specific information

3. Well-written standardized forms

    a. Should have a clearly identified purpose

    b. Questions and other calls for information should be clearly articulated

    c. Appropriate, clearly stated categories of information from which to choose

        d.   Questions should be organized in a logical order and there should be enough space to write answers

    4.   *Critical Thinking Question 16.4*

H.   Recording Progress in Groups

    1.   Reasons for recording in mezzo practice

        a.   Initially assessing a group's functioning

        b.   Evaluating the effectiveness of specific intervention approaches

        c.   Assessing the progress of individual members and the entire group toward achieving goals

        d.   Rendering accountability to funding sources concerning a group's usefulness and effectiveness

        e.   Providing feedback to group leaders so that they might improve their skills

        f.   Providing a means for group members to express satisfaction or dissatisfaction with the group and its process

    2.   Suggestions where recording might be helpful in mezzo practice

        a.   A group leader might want to monitor a group to determine if its goals are being met

        b.   Sociograms—Diagrams reflecting how people relate to each other in a group at a particular point in time

    3.   *Figure 16.9: An Example of a Recording Form for Group Process*

I.   Writing Letters

    1.   Points to remember when writing letters

        a.   Think carefully about and plan what you want to say in a letter, even if the letter is brief

        b.   Reread letters to modify them and make improvements. Always proofread a letter before sending it out

        c.   Create model letters or portions of letters that concern issues frequently addressed in your work setting

d.   Remember that a professional letter will have at least the following parts

    1)   Letterhead

    2)   Date

    3)   Inside address

    4)   Reference line or subject line

    5)   Salutation

    6)   Body

    7)   Complimentary close

    8)   Typed signature

    9)   Written signature

    10)   An enclosure notation (Enc.) or attachment (Att.) when appropriate

    11)   A copy notation (c. or cc.) listing names of others receiving the letter

    12)   Blind copies—sending copies of the letter to people other than the identified recipient without indicting on the letter that you are doing so (only for some clearly identified reason or purpose)

e.   When writing letters in which you are complaining, criticizing, making objections, challenging, or insisting, be assertive by striking an appropriate balance between being overly pushy or aggressive and ineffectively timid and apologetic

f.   Think of the person to whom you are writing as a real person

g.   Do not be overly friendly, especially when writing formal letters to people in prominent, influential positions

h.   Be cautious about using the word "I" too often

i.   Address people by using appropriate titles (Mr., Ms., or Dr.)

j.   Be conscious of who might read the letter after it is sent

k.   When writing to clients, use words that they can clearly understand

l.   Beneath your typed signature, use your appropriate formal title, which conveys to people how to refer to you in their responses

m.   *Never* send out a letter without keeping a copy

2.   Formatting letters

3.   *Figure 16.10: An Example of a Letter*

J.   Memos

    1.   Suggestions for writing memos

        a.   Make the memo as short and to the point as possible

        b.   Memos should be clear

        c.   Memos should be sent out early enough to allow plenty of time for the recipient to respond or comply with your wishes

        d.   Clearly state the purpose of your memo right at the beginning

        e.   Address only one topic per memo

        f.   Do not write memo when you are angry

        g.   Memos can be used to clarify and document proposed plans

        h.   Memos can be used to document for the record your own performance

    2.   *Figure 16.11: An Example of a Memo*

K.   Recording in Meetings

    1.   Agenda—A list of topics to be addressed at a meeting in a prioritized order

    2.   *Figure 16.12: An Example of an Agenda*

    3.   Minutes—Provide a written record of announcements, reports, significant discussions, and decisions that have taken place during a meeting

        a.   Name of group and meeting

        b.   Date, place, and time meeting was called to order; time of adjournment

        c.   Names of persons present (if applicable, names of persons absent)

        d.   Approval of (or additions to) the agenda

        e.   Disposition of any previous minutes

        f.   Announcements

        g.   Summaries of reports

        h.   Motions presented and actions taken on motions

i. Summaries of significant discussions

j. Name and signature of person compiling minutes

4. *Figure 16.13: An Example of a Meeting's Formal Minutes*

5. *Figure 16.14: An Example of Minutes for a Meeting*

L. Other Types of Recording Formats

V. Technological Advances

A. Computers

1. Recommended proficiency

a. Installing and maintaining software

b. Virus protection

c. File protection

d. Negotiating the Web

e. Learning to use graphics and presentation software

f. Developing and using web pages

g. Client confidentiality

2. *Highlight 16.2: Confidentiality and Electronic Record-Keeping*

a. Suggestions to minimize the potential for breaches in confidentiality

1) Be aware of current legislation concerning confidentiality in addition to recent court determinations

2) Look to the NASW Code of Ethics when possible

3) Assess the level of confidentiality that is needed

4) Find out what protections for confidentiality are offered by your agency and other agencies with which your clients are involved

5) Clarify to the client the limits of confidentiality

6) Develop collaborative plans that maximize confidentiality

7) Educate professionals, providers, and students about confidentiality with advanced technology

8)   Carefully evaluate how a computer system is used in your agency and search for possible ways that confidentiality may be breached

9)   Use safeguards such as passwords whenever possible to keep information out of unauthorized hands

10)   Establish clearly defined procedures for how data should be processed and records kept

B.   E-Mail

1.   E-mail—An electronic mailbox to which messages can be sent via phone, computer, and Internet connection on an immediate basis

2.   Reasons for using e-mail (questions to ask yourself)

      a.   Do I really need to write this e-mail or memo?

      b.   Should I send an e-mail or a hard-copy memo?

      c.   Why am I writing?

      d.   How will the reader react?

      e.   How can I save my reader's time?

3.   Composing an e-mail message

      a.   Make an outline of the points you wish to cover

      b.   Each paragraph should begin with the main point and backed up by details

      c.   A strong introduction is important

      d.   The body of the e-mail provides more information about the reason for writing

      e.   The closing should be purposeful and generally one of these three things

            1)   It can indicate what action is needed

            2)   It can summarize the communication to help the reader clarify it

            3)   It might end with a concluding reflection and some closing thought to prevent a feeling of abruptness

4. The importance of proofreading

    1) Revise for clarity

    2) Proofread for correctness

    3) Plan for feedback

5. Responses to e-mail

    1) Answer promptly

    2) Read the entire message first

    3) Answer all questions completely

    4) Comment directly in the sender's message

6. Additional suggestions for using e-mail: Netiquette—The term for polite online interaction

    1) Avoid using a series of all capital letters in the body of your message

    2) Be cautious about using both humor and sarcasm in e-mail

    3) If you send an e-mail to a mailing list, be brief and to the point

    4) If you mistakenly receive an e-mail meant for someone else, inform the sender about the mistake or forward the e-mail to the intended recipient

    5) Always remember that any e-mail you send to one person may be forwarded to other people

    6) Never respond to an e-mail when you're angry

7. *Critical Thinking Question 16.5*

C. Faxes

VI. Writing Skills and Recording

A. *Highlight 16.3: Some Basic Good Writing Suggestions*

    1. Choose your words carefully

    2. Avoid slang

    3. Avoid words such as always, average, perfect, or all

    4. Avoid sexist language

    5. Avoid labeling people with terms such as sleazy, strange, punks, slobs, or low class

6.   Avoid using abbreviations

7.   Be as concise as possible

8.   Use paragraphs to divide content into different topics

9.   Distinguish between verified facts and your impression of the facts

10.   Proofread your written products before they go out

VII.   Privacy Principles

A.   Confidentiality—The ethical principle that workers should not share information provided by a client or about a client unless the client has given explicit permission to do so

B.   Abridgment—Restricting the type of information that is put into the record and the period of time over which the record can be retained

C.   Access—The client's right to see what and how information is being recorded

D.   Anonymity—Using recorded information about clients but omitting identifying data

E.   *Figure 16.15: An Example of a Release of Information Form*

EXPERIENTIAL EXERCISES AND SIMULATIONS

Four exercises for this chapter provide different types of writing experiences. They include filling out a standardized face sheet form, recording a social history, writing a memo, and composing a professional letter.

Exercise 16.1: Filling Out a Face Sheet

A.   Brief description:
You will break up into pairs and role-play a client and worker. The worker then interviews the client to get information needed to fill out a form. Class discussion will follow.

B.   Objectives:
You will be able to:
1.   Recognize the types of information required on a face sheet.
2.   Demonstrate how information is gathered to fill out a form.

C.   Procedure:
1.   Review chapter 16 in the text prior to beginning this exercise.
2.   Break up into pairs. Arbitrarily decide who will role-play the worker and who will role-play the client. The worker should interview the client to get the information necessary to fill out the face sheet displayed below. The face sheet is a type of standardized form which provides basic identifying information and is generally placed at the beginning of a client's file. This particular face sheet is for families applying to be foster families. In the role-play, the client should make up answers to the worker's questions.

Foster Home Licensing and Face Sheet[1]

_____ _____ _____
Last Name   Address   Telephone

                           _____ _____
                           City   County

Husband or Single Person   Wife

_____   _____
First Name   Birthdate   First Name   Birthdate

_____   _____
Race   Religion   Race   Religion

_____   _____
Occupation   Occupation

_____   _____
Work hours and phone   Work hours and phone

Ages of own children in home:
                                            _____
                                            Boys

                                            _____
                                            Girls

List names and ages of foster children now in home _____

_____

Schools foster child might attend _____

_____

Special child care skills _____

_____
License Information: # of children _____   Sex of children _____
Age of children _____ Other limitations _____
Description of Home: total # of rooms _____ Number of bedrooms _____
Occupants in Home: Number of adults _____ Number of own children ____
      Number of other persons (excluding foster children) _____
Agency responsible for licensing _____
Agency responsible for supervision _____
      Date of License: From _____ To _____
Submitted by _____ _____
                 Worker   Date
Approved by _____

---

[1] This form is adapted from one used by the State of Wisconsin Department of Health and Social Services (DHSS). Printed with permission of the Wisconsin DHSS, 1 West Wilson, Madison, WI.

3.   After about fifteen minutes, your instructor will end the role play and begin a class discussion focusing on the following questions and issues:

       a.   How easy or difficult did the workers find filling out the form?

       b.   Were there any areas on the form which you found difficult to fill in? If so, what were they and why were they difficult?

       c.   What other types of standardized forms might you have to use in real practice?

Exercise 16.2: Writing a Social History

A.   Brief description:

This is a take-home assignment in which you will be asked to interview a person for information to fill out the social history form provided below.

B.   Objectives:

You will be able to:

1.   Describe the types of information typically gathered in a social history.

2.   Demonstrate how such information is recorded on a standardized social history form.

C.   Procedure:

1.   Review chapter 16 in the text prior to beginning this exercise.

2.   Choose a person you would like to interview. This could be a friend, a relative, or an acquaintance. Explain to the person that social histories reflect the important aspects of an individual's development and help social workers assess the nature of client's problems. Feel free to show the person the social history form. The person needs to know exactly what to expect, especially since you will be asking some personal questions about his or her life.

3.   As you interview, fill out the social history form provided below. Remember that the purpose is not to investigate every minute detail of a person's life, but rather to gain a generalized understanding of what's most significant. In a real practice situation, you would be especially attuned to information relating to and clarifying the individual's designated problem. You would also pay special attention to identifying and evaluating the client's strengths.

Social History Format[2]

Name _____   D.O.B. _____

Address: _____

Telephone: _____

School and Grade: _____

Place of Birth: _____

Religion: _____

Outline for Social History

I.   Family Composition:

       (Note if any parent or sibling is deceased and date)

---

[2] Adapted from the form "Outline for Social History." This material is printed with permission of the Community Human Services Department, Waukesha County, 500 Riverview Ave., Waukesha, WI 53188.

Natural Father: D.O.B. _____
Address:
Occupation:
Religion:

Stepfather: (if appropriate)   D.O.B. _____
Address:
Occupation:
Religion:

Natural Mother: D.O.B. _____
Address:
Occupation:
Religion:

Stepmother: D.O.B. _____
Address:
Occupation:
Religion:

Siblings:
Name, d.o.b., school, and grade. List all siblings, including those out of home, and current situation. If client or siblings are living with others, state names, addresses, and relationship.

II.   Child Under Consideration
Describe personality and physical characteristics.

III.   Reason for Referral:
Short statement about immediate concern, current situation, and by whom referred. Parent's and child's attitudes about possible placement outside the home.

IV.   Family Background:

A.   Mother:
1.   Relationship to each of her parents; relationship between her parents; evidence of emotional disturbance in family.

2.   Mother's educational and vocational history.

3.   Medical history if pertinent.

4.   Previous marriages, with significant details.

5.   History of her courting and marriage, including feelings about marriage and children.

B.   <u>Father:</u>

1.   Relationship to each of his parents; relationship between his parents; evidence of emotional disturbance in family.

2.   Father's educational and vocational history.

3.   Medical history if pertinent.

4.   Previous marriages, with significant details.

5.   History of his courting and marriage, including feelings about marriage and children.

C.   Family Development:

1.   Describe parental relationships, who disciplines whom and how, nature of and reasons for conflicts, family attitude toward current situation, family's financial situation and community involvement, family involvement with law enforcement and mental health agencies. What do you see happening in the family and why? This section should contain a historical perspective and comment on the past as well as the present.

2. Sibling Relationships:
Describe child's relationship with each sibling; to whom child is closest and from whom most alienated; and reaction to birth of next youngest sibling. Describe any specific problems or emotional difficulties siblings in family have or have had in the past and how handled by parents.

3. Other Significant Adults:
Ex-grandparents, aunts, uncles, neighbors, teachers. Indicate who and type of relationship and when it began.

4. Environment:
Significance of neighborhoods family has lived in and their dwellings.

V. Personal History of Child:

A. Developmental Data:
Parental relationship during pregnancy, reaction to pregnancy, preferred sex, mother's health (signs of miscarriage, emotional state, significant use or abuse of drugs or alcohol).

Birth:
Delivery: premature or full term spontaneous? Physical condition of mother and child, length of hospital stay.

<u>Early Months:</u>
Note any changes in mother's physical or emotional health. Any difficulties in adjusting to the home—was it stable at this time? Did child have colic or other problems? Was child breast or bottle fed? Any feeding difficulties? Note changes in any caretakers and significant losses.

<u>Later Months and Toddler Stage:</u>
Note ages at which child walked, talked, and was toilet trained. Note any difficulties re: sleep and eating patterns.

<u>Coordination and Motor Pattern:</u>
A general statement as well as noting any hyperactivity, sluggishness, head or body rocking, random or unorganized activity.

Parents' feelings regarding above and how they attempted to handle any difficulties.

B.   <u>Personality and Social Growth:</u>
Responsiveness: Did child like to be held or did he or she withdraw from people? Did the child play with adults and/or children? Did he or she play in group or prefer to play alone?

Relationships: Describe relationship with each parent as related by both parents and child. Explore any differences. What about relationships with siblings?

Separations from either or both parents: When, why, how long? Note also parental and child response toward separating to attend school.

Describe child's outstanding traits and fears if any, e.g., is the child happy, sullen, stubborn, dependent, independent? Does she or he have any persistent fears, phobias, or compulsions?

Discipline: How and by whom? How have parents and child reacted to it?

Sexual development: Amount of sex education. Who provided? Unusual behavior or preoccupations; kind of questions or curiosity displayed; masturbation; parental response.

C.   <u>Medical History:</u>
Any illness or disease suffered; injuries, falls, high fevers, convulsions, fainting or other spells, allergies or other somatic disturbances; child and parent reactions. Also any hospitalization history. Touch on any previous treatment for current problems, previous psychiatric treatment. Type and extent of drug usage, if any.

Birth disfigurements, speech defects, enuresis, handicaps.

Present health.

D.   <u>Educational Experiences:</u>
Schools and years attended, achievement, testing dates done by schools, M-Team reports, interpersonal relationships of child; parents' relationship with school systems, extra-curricular activities.

Psychological and psychiatric evaluations—previous referrals, contacts, treatment, and progress.

E.   <u>Employment Experience:</u>

VI.   <u>Previous Treatment</u>:
Prior placements and services, successful completion or failure of services and/or placements.

Substantiate that care and services that would permit the child to remain at home have been investigated and considered and are not available or likely to become available within a reasonable time to meet the needs of the child.

A.   What alternatives to the plan are available?

B.   What alternatives have been explored?

C.   Why are explored alternatives not appropriate?

D.   Discuss objectives of rehabilitation, treatment, and care.

4.   Turn your completed social history in to your instructor for feedback and grading.

Exercise 16.3: Writing a Memo

A.   Brief description:
You will be asked to write a memo concerning a specific issue. You will then break up into pairs and critique each other's work. Class discussion will follow.

B.   Objectives:
You will be able to:
    1.   Recognize the important facets of writing a memo.
    2.   Compose a memo concerning a specific issue.
    3.   Evaluate memos.

C.   Procedure:
    1.   Prior to beginning this exercise, review chapter 16, especially the material on memos.
    2.   In class, read the following situation:

Case Situation

You are a social worker for Oconomowoc County Social Services. You've been with the agency for a little over a year. All employees are supposed to have an annual performance review. Only workers whose supervisors submit a positive review of the workers' performance will receive a raise in salary for the next year.

You have what you consider an adequate relationship with your supervisor, Chuck Norris. You feel he's neither especially helpful nor knowledgeable. However, he's relatively easy going and lets you do your job "in peace." You get the help and consultation you need from your colleagues and other supervisors in the agency.

The problem is that you've asked Chuck three times, the last in writing, when he has time to sit down with you and do your review. Each time he passed off your request casually and said he didn't have time. The last time you approached him you even subtly reminded him that performance reviews are due within the next week or two. You know that if he doesn't do your review, you won't get a raise next year. You feel you really

---

worked hard this year and really need that raise. Your '97 Dodge Neon is on its last legs and you can't handle the monthly payments for a new car without a raise.

You don't think Chuck really likes to do performance reviews. In fact, you question his overall professional competence. You also don't think he's going to get around to doing your review. You feel that reminding him again would be useless.

You decide that the only way to handle the situation is to contact Chuck's supervisor, Ethyl Metttelschmerz, who is the agency's assistant director. She's very busy with her own responsibilities. You feel the only way to get her attention is to send her a memo about the situation.

You know you must choose your words carefully. You must get your point across without crucifying Chuck. You also don't want to sound angry. You want to state the facts as calmly and nonjudgmentally as possible. You realize that you will have to live with Chuck as your supervisor next year, too.

You write the memo . . .

3. Take fifteen minutes and write a memo to Ethyl about the situation.
4. Your instructor will tell you when the time is up. Break up into pairs and exchange memos. Take about five minutes to write constructive criticisms on your partner's memo.
5. Spend another ten minutes giving each other verbal feedback about the memos. Afterwards, exchange memos again so that you have your own back.
6. Your instructor will call you back to join a full class discussion in which you will address the following questions and issues:
   a. What did you write in your memo?
   b. What was most difficult about writing the memo?
   c. What constructive feedback did your partner give you?
   d. Did you follow the format provided in the text?
   e. What did you learn about writing memos from this exercise?

Exercise 16.4: Writing Professional Letters

A. Brief description:
   You will be asked to write a letter concerning a case situation. Class discussion will follow.
B. Objectives:
   You will be able to:
   1. Recognize the major components in good letter writing.
   2. Compose a letter responding to a case situation.
C. Procedure:
   1. Prior to beginning the exercise, review chapter 16, especially the part about writing letters.
   2. Read the following:

> **Case Situation**
>
> You are a Case Manager for a local family services agency. A major part of your job is to place young adults with cognitive disabilities in the community and coordinate the supportive services for them.
>
> One of the clients you've recently placed in her own apartment is Holly Wood, twenty-three. She is an attractive, well-dressed young woman who can read at a fifth-grade level. She is proud of her full-time job as a file clerk at a nearby hospital. Although many people with higher intellectual abilities might find this job dull, Holly performs the repetitive tasks involved responsibly and conscientiously. Holly's social life primarily involves a "social club" she belongs to, made up of other developmentally disabled people of similar ability. Group activities are supervised by the family services agency staff.
>
> The problem is that Holly's mother, Mrs. DeHavilland, calls you and screams irately that she will not allow Holly to date "those boys" in the social club. She feels strongly that Holly is not able to handle such activities and that she might get involved in "that sex thing."
>
> In fact, Holly has dated two men in the club. One date involved a movie and pizza, and the other a baseball game. Although Holly has not as yet gotten serious about any of the men in the club, the potential is certainly there.
>
> Your agency's philosophy is that clients have the right to make their own decisions and to develop relationships just as "normal" people do. Some of the supportive services you coordinate for clients include sex education and counseling to develop responsible decision-making skills. Clients are encouraged and helped to live "normal" lives. They participate in "normal" activities and make "normal" mistakes.
>
> You need to write a letter to Mrs. DeHavilland and tell her in a civil and supportive yet firm way that Holly has the right to make her own decisions. You can stress the help the agency is providing her. You can also emphasize your appreciation for Mrs. DeHavilland's concern about and love for Holly.

3. Using the suggestions for letter writing provided in the text, take fifteen minutes to write the letter mentioned in the vignette above.

4. Your instructor will tell you when it's time to participate in a full class discussion to address the following questions and issues:

    a. What did you write in your letter?
    b. What specific phrases did you choose to get your various points across?
    c. To what extent did you follow the format and suggestions provided in the text?
    d. What did you find most difficult about writing the letter?
    e. What did you learn about letter writing from this experience?